*The*

# FRANCO-RUSSIAN ALLIANCE

## 1891–1917

*By*

## GEORGES MICHON

*Docteur ès Lettres*

*Translated by*

### NORMAN THOMAS

LONDON

GEORGE ALLEN & UNWIN LTD

MUSEUM STREET

*The French original, "L'Alliance Franco-Russe", was first published in Paris*

FIRST PUBLISHED IN GREAT BRITAIN IN 1929

# INTRODUCTION

THE history of the Franco-Russian Alliance has never been written. It is curious—in fact, extraordinary—that no more or less semi-official historian has ever been tempted to narrate in detail this foremost diplomatic event in the history of France during the last half-century, an event of capital importance in the life of her people, availing himself of the archives of the Foreign Ministry, which are closed to the man in the street, and supplementing these with the comments and reminiscences and confidences of politicians, diplomats, and prominent soldiers.

Again, it is a strange thing that this Alliance, which for twenty-five years was incessantly lauded to the skies, regarded by successive Governments as the Ark of the Covenant, on which it would be sacrilege to lay hands, is now left without a single eulogist, and that those best in a position to sing its praises, those who have intoned the anthem almost to intimidation, seem with one accord to have thrown a veil over it, at all events to be enveloping it in silence. The fact is that the War revealed even to the blindest eyes the feet of clay of the Russian Colossus, and above all the perils to which the Alliance exposed France.

Let us, then, lift a corner of the veil cast over this Alliance, particularly since those clear-sighted Frenchmen who ventured to point out the extreme risks and perils which it involved were branded with infamy by the public authorities and the prosperous classes in France and delivered over to the execration of all patriots.

Let us try to throw a little light upon this pact, which nearly cost France her very life. Paléologue went so far as to write to Count Witte on September 12, 1914: "The world is in a welter of blood to-day for a cause which is primarily Russia's, a cause essentially Slav, a cause of no concern to France or to Britain."[1]

[1] Paléologue, *La Russie des Tsars pendant la grande guerre*, I, pp. 119–120.

In our narrative of the facts we want especially to throw into prominence the way in which the French Government and above all the French governing class conceived and applied this Alliance, the uses to which they put it, their real goal, and their handling of the whole episode in relation to the essential interests of the French and Russian peoples; and, finally, the way in which this handling of the Alliance reacted on the home policy of the two countries.

We hope that these elements in the story will be not without value to future historians or to our own compatriots, who will be able to realize how the interests of a great people have been dealt with—a people who, having made three revolutions in order to govern themselves, imagined that they were at last masters of their destiny.

# CONTENTS

|  |  | PAGE |
|---|---|---|
|  | INTRODUCTION | 5 |
|  | LIST OF AUTHORITIES | 9 |

CHAPTER

|  |  |  |
|---|---|---|
| I. | THE ORIGINS OF THE ALLIANCE | 11 |
| II. | THE FRANCO-RUSSIAN AGREEMENT OF 1891 | 24 |
| III. | THE MILITARY CONVENTION | 35 |
| IV. | HONEYMOON (1893–1898) | 71 |
| V. | DELCASSÉ'S VISIT TO ST. PETERSBURG | 101 |
| VI. | PRESAGES OF REVOLUTION | 108 |
| VII. | THE RUSSO-JAPANESE WAR | 110 |
| VIII. | THE 1905 REVOLUTION | 132 |
| IX. | RUSSIAN LOANS AND THE 1905 REVOLUTION | 146 |
| X. | RUSSIA'S FOREIGN POLICY, 1907–1911 | 175 |
| XI. | THE RESHAPING OF THE ALLIANCE | 191 |
| XII. | THE BALKAN WAR OF 1912 | 197 |
| XIII. | TOWARDS THE WORLD WAR | 262 |
| XIV. | PALÉOLOGUE'S VISIT TO PARIS (JUNE 1914) | 272 |
| XV. | RUSSIA AND THE WORLD WAR | 279 |
| XVI. | THE ALLIANCE AND THE RUSSIAN REVOLUTION | 300 |
| XVII. | THE CAUSES OF FRANCE'S BLINDNESS | 322 |
|  | CONCLUSION | 333 |
|  | INDEX | 337 |

# LIST OF AUTHORITIES

ALBIN: L'Allemagne et la France en Europe.

ANDRÉ: Cinq ans de ministère.

BOGITSHEVICH: Causes of the War.

BUCHANAN, SIR GEORGE: My Mission to Russia.

CAILLAUX: Agadir.

CYON, E. DE: Histoire de l'entente franco-russe.

DAUDET, E.; Histoire diplomatique de l'alliance franco-russe.

DEBIDOUR: Histoire diplomatique de l'Europe depuis le Congrès de Berlin jusqu'à nos jours.

DE FREYCINET: Souvenirs.

Die Grosse Politik der europäischen Kabinette, 1871–1914.

GAUVAIN: L'Europe avant la guerre.

GAUVAIN: L'Europe au jour le jour.

GREY, VISCOUNT: Twenty-five Years.

GUÉCHOFF: L'alliance balkanique.

HANSEN: L'Ambassade Mohrenheim à Paris.

ISVOLSKY: Mémoires.

JUDET: Georges Louis.

LALOY: Documents secrets des Archives du Ministère des Affaires Etrangères de Russie, publiés par les Bolchéviks.

LEROY-BEAULIEU: La France, la Russie, et l'Europe.

Livre jaune relatif à l'alliance franco-russe.

Livre noir, un: Diplomatie d'avant-guerre d'après les documents des Archives russes.

(LOUIS, GEORGES): Les carnets de Georges Louis.

MAURRAS: Kiel et Tanger.

MÉVIL, ANDRÉ: La Paix est malade.

NAUDEAU: Les dessous du chaos russe.

PALÉOLOGUE: La Russie des Tsars pendant la grande guerre.

POINCARÉ: Au service de la France.

RIBOT: Lettres à un ami.

RIVET, CH.: Le dernier Romanof.

ROSEN: Forty Years of Diplomacy.

TARDIEU: La France et les alliances.

TOURY, GOUTTENOIRE DE: Poincaré a-t-il voulu la guerre?

WITTE: Mémoires.

YURUSSOV, PRINCE: Mémoires.

# THE FRANCO-RUSSIAN ALLIANCE
## 1891–1917

### CHAPTER I

### THE ORIGINS OF THE ALLIANCE

ALTHOUGH the French "Yellow Book" dealing with the Franco-Russian Alliance contains no documents of earlier date than 1890, it is necessary to go somewhat further back to view in their true light the sources of the treaty entered into between France and Russia during the years 1891–1893.

The Congress of Berlin, by nullifying the results of the Treaty of San Stefano, had very seriously shaken the Three Emperors' League, founded in 1872. In the eyes of Russia, the settlement engineered by Bismarck, Andrássy, and, last not least, Disraeli, had cheated her of the fruits of victory in the Balkans, weakening, as it did, her influence there to the advantage of Austria, to whom she had already conceded, by the agreement of Reichstadt in 1876, the right of annexing Bosnia and Herzegovina. Not long afterwards, on October 7, 1879, a formal defensive Alliance against the risk of attack from Russia was concluded at Vienna between the German and Austrian Emperors. The Tsar Alexander II made no secret of his indignation, and it is not surprising that the profound resentment felt by the Russian Chancellor, Prince Gorchakov, should have led his mind from that time onwards in the direction of an understanding with France. There is justification for the assertion that the Franco-Russian Alliance was a product of the Near East question.

On the other hand, France's action in occupying Tunisia drove Italy into Germany's arms, with the result that on May 20, 1882, the Triple Alliance was established. Russia was now isolated, but the *rapprochement* with France still hung fire. After the death of Alexander II, Prince Gorchakov was succeeded by de Giers, whose sympathies lay rather with Germany, while the new Tsar had little love for the French Republic, regarding it as a standing menace to the principles of monarchism in Europe. Alexander III, at loggerheads with Great Britain over Afghanistan, preferred to enlist the good will of the Triple Alliance, fearing that he would otherwise incur their hostility in the Balkans. In these circumstances Bismarck had little difficulty in negotiating a secret agreement between the three Emperors, which was signed on March 21, 1884, and ratified at Skiernevice on September 14th of the same year. This made insurance doubly sure, binding each signatory to observe benevolent neutrality in the event of any one of them being attacked by another Power, and, furthermore, to join with the rest in pursuing a policy favourable to monarchism.[1]

The French Government could not regard this as exactly a friendly act. By the beginning of 1886, indeed, the tension had developed to the point of strained relations. The Tsar, already alienated by the expulsion from France of the members of the ex-reigning houses, protested against the release of Prince Kropotkin. The consequent withdrawal of the French ambassador, General Appert, in whom he placed entire confidence, aroused his anger, and he recalled his ambassador, Baron Mohrenheim, from Paris.[2]

After the union of Eastern Roumelia with Bulgaria, however —the outcome of the Philippopolis *coup d'état*—the need for a decision on the Balkan situation gradually began to develop a greater degree of mutual trust in the relations between the French and Russian Governments, and this tendency was facilitated by the hostility shown in the Russian Press towards Germany's policy in the Balkans as favouring Austria at

---

[1] Cf. P. Matter, *Bismarck et son temps*, III, pp. 434 sqq., and *Die Grosse Politik der europäischen Kabinette* (1871–1914), II.
[2] Cf. *Die Grosse Politik*, VI, pp. 104–116.

Russia's expense. Moreover, France, determined to break the isolation in which she found herself, took a more vigorous and direct initiative from 1886 onwards—an initiative which followed two distinct courses, one political, directed by the Foreign Minister, Flourens, and the other financial, inspired by a group of leading bankers. Flourens, who was strongly in favour of an Alliance with Russia, shaped all his diplomacy so as to manifest an unmistakable inclination towards an understanding with that country: for example, when a deputation from the Sobranye waited on him on January 9, 1887, to complain of Russian high-handedness, he enjoined the Bulgarians "in pretty vigorous language"[1] to come to terms with Russia. Again, on the occasion of the sacerdotal jubilee of Pope Leo XIII in 1887, French diplomacy acted as intermediary with Russia to secure a *rapprochement* between Tsarism and the Papacy. These various services found favour with the Russian Court, where the new French ambassador, de Laboulaye, speedily became *persona grata*.

At this same period, a Paris financier of Danish extraction, named Hoskier, together with several other prominent bankers, formed a syndicate, on which all the chief financial houses in Paris were represented, with the object of wresting from Berlin the control of the market in Russian bonds and bringing to an end the German tutelage over the financial affairs of Russia, for whom the floating of loans abroad was a constantly recurring necessity. The Russian Government of the day was, however, disinclined to seek an alliance with France and declined this assistance. The Foreign Minister, de Giers, remarked to the German *chargé d'affaires*, von Bülow:

There is a certain section in this country which holds that we should do well to take advantage of France's present attitude and let her pull the chestnuts out of the fire for us; but I am inclined to think, and the Emperor agrees with me, that any sort of effective intimacy with France would merely compromise us, both from the point of view of our

---

[1] E. Daudet, *Histoire diplomatique de l'Alliance franco-russe*, p. 205.

internal policy and with regard to our prospects in Near Eastern affairs.[1]

About this time, however, the Russian journalist Katkov, a man who had a great deal of influence with the Tsar, launched a violent campaign against the Triple Alliance in the columns of his newspaper, the *Moskovskaya Vyedomosti*. Katkov had a Paris correspondent named Elie de Cyon, whose letters he published regularly in the *Vyedomosti*, and the campaign in favour of an understanding with France was begun by three letters from de Cyon (May 3, 13, and 17, 1887) in which stress was laid on the great financial influence wielded by France. It was brought to a head by a leading article by Katkov himself (July 19th), which, bluntly suggesting that a change was necessary in the foreign policy of the Empire, caused a profound sensation throughout the educated classes in Russia. "We are anxious", wrote Katkov,

that Russia should maintain her present frank and friendly relations with Germany, but we are also anxious that relations of similar cordiality should be established with other Powers, and particularly with France, a nation which, for all that may be asserted to the contrary, does hold in Europe, and will hold in increasing measure, a position commensurate with her potentialities. What grounds of dispute have we with her, and why should we concern ourselves with her internal affairs?

De Cyon echoed: "There is no conflict between the legitimate interests of Russia and those of France in any quarter of the world. In many respects they are identical, while in the Far East they certainly run parallel."[2]

The urgent need of a journal in France which would champion this new cause soon became apparent, and de Cyon

[1] *Die Grosse Politik*, VI, p. 105: Bülow to Bismarck, December 23, 1886. De Giers added: "How can the French imagine for a moment that the Tsar would side with such people as Clemenceau against his own uncle! The very idea of such a grouping would be repugnant to the Emperor. He is not going to act as a cat's-paw for Communards." (Ibid., p. 108, January 1, 1887.) The Grand Duke Alexis expressed the same views (p. 106).
[2] E. de Cyon, *Histoire de l'Entente franco-russe*, pp. 153–4, 162–3.

opened up negotiations with Mme. Adam, founder and editress of the *Nouvelle Revue*, who at once offered to transfer to him the control of that organ.

Katkov, however, was by no means a Francophile. He was animated, indeed, neither by sympathy for France nor by hostility to Germany; he merely desired to see Russia throw off the influence of Germany and resume her full freedom of action, by means of which she might hold the balance in Europe instead of bartering her independence in tripartite alliances in which she ran the risk of being a cat's-paw. He emphasized the dangers of too close an intimacy with Germany if Austria were to be allowed to share it. Moreover, he spoke for the manufacturers and wholesale merchants of Moscow— possibly, too, indirectly for official circles—and was absolutist in sentiment, with a holy horror of republicanism. For this reason, amongst others, his campaign met, from the outset, with little more than a half-hearted reception in France. At his death, which occurred in the same year, the monarchist and Bonapartist press alone sang his praises; the *République Française* pointed out (August 26, 1887) that he was an Old Believer, filled with the idea of purging the Empire of all Western influences and re-establishing the traditional ideal of blind obedience to the Tsar, the representative on earth of the Almighty. The same paper reproduced one of Katkov's letters published in the *Secolo* of May 27th, in which he had said: "I detest France because she has always been, and still is, a hotbed of freethought and revolutionary propaganda, and I do not despair of one day seeing the armed forces of Law and Order in occupation there once again. But in present circumstances, in face of the threat to Russia from Germany and Austria, an Alliance with France is forced upon us as an unavoidable but disagreeable necessity." The *République Française* added: "What is the meaning of all these emotional obituaries, these laudatory telegrams, this pilgrimage by M. Déroulède to Katkov's grave? Let us, for Heaven's sake, try to retain in our political life some remnant of common sense, of proportion, of a sense of fitness."[1]

This criticism had its effect, and the idea of a Franco-Russian Alliance began to lose ground in Republican circles, who were also influenced by the fact that de Cyon, Katkov's Paris correspondent, had a somewhat peculiar record. Of Jewish race, he had been converted to Roman Catholicism, made no secret of his monarchist views, and had conducted in the *Gaulois*, of which he acquired control in 1881, a series of virulent campaigns against the progress of secular education and the measures adopted to consolidate the Republic. In 1886, in the *Russkoi Vyestnik*, he had published attacks on the alleged venality of the French Press, on the Parliamentary system, and on the ideal of political liberty, attacks which called forth a spirited rejoinder from the *Siècle* and provoked a controversy in which de Cyon came off decidedly the worse.

Flourens, however, continued to pursue whole-heartedly his aim of close co-operation with Russia, and even after discussion with the ambassador Mohrenheim, who fully agreed, determined to place before the Russian Government a definite proposal for a defensive Alliance. In February 1887 he had decided to send Count de Vogüé to St. Petersburg with the draft agreement, but before his emissary had started de Giers intimated that, while the Tsar was anxious to maintain the relations of friendly intimacy that existed between Russia and France, it was not considered that the time was ripe for the conclusion of a formal Alliance, which might have the effect of creating alarm amongst the other Powers.[2] Simultaneously there appeared in the semi-official *Syever* of February 19th an article in which a clear indication was given of the Russian Government's intentions:

Russia's chief aim in Europe is to maintain peace and a rightful Balance of Power. In pursuit of this twofold ideal her policy must

---

[1] Cf. the article on Katkov in the *Journal des Débats* of February 3, 1887.
[2] Hansen, *L'Ambassade Mohrenheim à Paris*, p. 36.

obviously be, first of all to avoid any and every source of discord, such as, for example, an Alliance with France would represent, and in the second place to act as guardian of that balance in the event of its being threatened by an outbreak such as a declaration of war between France and Germany, should that prove impossible to prevent. To enable Russia to throw her full weight into the scales in such circumstances, and to safeguard that necessary equipoise in European politics against such a menace, it is essential that she should maintain an unfettered liberty of action, neither raising false hopes nor inspiring unwarranted fears in any quarter, but remaining for all an object of respectful conjecture.[1]

The Russian Government's mouthpieces all suggested that, if France were given tangible proof, in the shape of a treaty of Alliance, that she was no longer friendless, she would be encouraged to make war. The Tsar, who was notoriously a lover of peace, was afraid that General Boulanger would involve him in some bellicose enterprise.[2] He wanted to avoid committing himself to either camp and dreamed of wielding the casting vote in all European disputes, as in fact he endeavoured to do in connection with the Schnaebelé incident. The conservative de Giers, for his part, was determined that nothing should mar the excellent relations that existed with Germany,[3] and was, moreover, mainly concerned with Near East politics. Thus France's first proposal met with a rebuff.

About this time, however, Alexander III, who had fallen under the influence of the Slavophil party, began to introduce drastic measures of russification in the Western provinces, thereby antagonizing agrarian interests in Germany, who were now debarred from acquiring land over the border. They retorted by organizing an attack on the Russian bond market, and the prices of Russian loan stock on the Berlin Bourse

---

[1] Quoted in Albin, *L'Allemagne et la France en Europe*, p. 253.
[2] Cf. Daudet, p. 319.
[3] *Die Grosse Politik*, VI, p. 109: von Schweinitz to Bismarck, March 9, 1887. De Giers stated to Bülow: "I am constantly telling them (the French) to keep quiet about Germany and to do nothing rash. . . . I would take my oath that the Tsar will never, never lift a finger in opposition to the Kaiser, nor to his son, nor to his grandson." (Bülow to Bismarck, December 24, 1886, and September 28, 1887. Ibid., pp. 107, 116.)

B

slumped. The London Stock Exchange was hostile, too, so
that it was not possible to float a new Russian loan there. In
these circumstances Russia had no alternative but to close with
the offer of the Hoskier group, French capital being the only
source open to her of the credit of which she stood in need.[1]

In the meantime de Cyon had not remained idle in Paris.
According to his own statements, he was commissioned by the
Russian Minister to negotiate with the leading Paris bankers
for the transfer from Berlin of the Russian bond market, since
"Russia was not in a position to cope unaided with the avalanche
of bonds which the German holders were throwing on the
market". If de Cyon is to be believed, he had suggested to
M. Vishnegradsky that action should be taken with all speed
along two separate lines: first, that financial syndicates should
be formed in France to take up part of the bonds in question
and thus check the fall in the quotations before they touched
bottom, and, secondly, that a systematic campaign should be
organized in the French press on behalf of Russian credit,
with a view to persuading French capitalists, big and small, to
buy the Russian securities now being jettisoned, seeing that
they could now acquire them at exceptionally favourable
prices. The Finance Minister had concurred, but on condition
that de Cyon not only took all the risks but bore the initial
expenses of the press campaign. The latter succeeded in forming
a syndicate on which all the chief financial houses of Paris were
represented, all being at one in their desire to find an opening
for French capital in the immense Russian market and at the
same time to come to the assistance of the Russian Treasury.
"Filled with patriotic ardour, the directors of the leading
Protestant banking establishments did not hesitate to combine
with those of the principal Jewish firms; monarchist bankers
united with Republican bankers, and the group thus welded
together formed a reservoir of financial power that I was proud

---

[1] Cf. Albin, pp. 255–256, and Debidour, *Histoire diplomatique de l'Europe
depuis le Congrès de Berlin jusqu'à nos jours*, I, p. 137.

to be able to place at the disposal of the Minister." (In point of fact, it would appear that the syndicate in question was conterminous with the Hoskier group.[1]) And soon, says de Cyon, almost the whole of the French press, beginning with the *Journal des Débats* and a large number of provincial papers, had begun to belaud Russia's credit.[2]

Not long afterwards the Russian Government decided to re-arm the infantry, and requested the permission of the French Government to place a large order with the National Small Arms Factory at Châtellerault. The Foreign Minister, de Freycinet, agreed with alacrity, merely adding: "We hope these rifles will never be used against our troops". Negotiations were conducted by Baron Frederics, who gave de Freycinet the fullest assurances on the point, and a number of Russian officers then came to France to inspect the manufacture of the arms. This led to close touch being maintained between the General Staffs of the two countries. The order amounted to a very large figure, and accommodation was not unnaturally sought in France. The Russian Government now looked upon the financial assistance offered by the Hoskier syndicate with a more favourable eye than in 1886, and towards the middle of 1888 the Russian Finance Minister caused an intimation to be conveyed to Hoskier and his associates that he would be glad to enter into negotiations with them, being desirous of sounding the French market by the issue of a loan to liquidate the debt contracted for the rifles.

Hoskier and his friends undertook to float this loan in France. An agreement was signed in November, and on December 10, 1888, a 4 per cent gold loan was issued with entirely satisfactory results. Within the next few years the French money market had established relations of entire confidence with Russia and enabled her to throw off the financial

---

[1] Albin, pp. 337–340.
[2] *M. Witte et les finances russes*, pp. 22–25. *Le bilan de la gestion financière de M. Wyschnegradski*, p. 28.

yoke of Germany. Russian credit had been preserved from catastrophe, and fresh loans now followed regularly, with seldom a greater interval than one year. Russia had been driven by dire necessity into the arms of France.

What was the attitude of French public opinion towards a *rapprochement* with Russia during this first period of preparation? The Conservatives, for purely party reasons, welcomed the prospect of an understanding with a sacrosanct autocrat, realizing that this could not fail to exercise some restraint upon the policy of the Republic. Opportunists accepted the idea as inevitable. The *République Française* recognized the gulf that existed between the French outlook and that of mystical, autocratic Tsarism, but opined that the two countries shared "one vast interest in common, the instinct of self-preservation". Germany was inspired with the spirit of domination, but neither Russia nor France intended to allow herself to be dominated. "What does it matter whether there is or is not any close sympathy between them? Politics in these critical days are not based on sympathy or antipathy" (July 26, 1887).

Delcassé, writing about the same time, asserted that:

To France and to Russia alike, a common peril calls imperatively for the closest co-operation. . . . They will both be obliged to bring pressure of the same sort upon Germany. Each acts as a counter-weight in Europe, one in the East, one in the West, to the Teutonic giant, just as they act as bulwarks in Asia, one in the North, one in the South, against the encroachments of China and Great Britain. Everywhere they confront the same enemies, share the same interests, cherish the same aspirations. The astonishing thing is that an Entente of such obvious mutual advantage should have taken so long to fructify.[1]

Thus, even at this early stage, Delcassé attached no importance to the fundamental discrepancies between the institutions and the customs of the two nations. Authoritative critics were, however, not lacking who opposed the idea of an Alliance. Anatole Leroy-Beaulieu devoted an article in the *Revue des*

[1] *Paris*, June 7, 1887.

*Deux Mondes* (February 15, 1888) to a careful examination of the risks it involved. He drew attention to all that tended to keep the two countries apart: their divergences in social structure, their differences in political outlook. France and Russia stood at opposite poles in the modern world, personifying in the eyes of the peoples of all nations two utterly incompatible principles. "There are some cases", he remarked, "in which it is difficult to combine friendship and sincerity." To reach Russia, France would have to step over the body of Poland.

Another point brought out by Leroy-Beaulieu was that the wooing was somewhat one-sided. On the French side it had been forgotten that one of the approved methods of attracting admirers was to let them pine. "No great nation sets about concluding an Alliance in this fashion", he said, in reproof of the over-enthusiastic behaviour of certain French publicists who seemed to be wanting to "push France prematurely into the arms of Russia". He went on to define the dangers which France might incur in such an alliance:

If, unhappily for Europe, a Russian *démarche* in Bulgaria were to bring about a conflict between Russia and Austria, imagine the situation for France, left face to face with Germany like two hostile seconds at a duel! Is not this consideration sufficient to suggest the desirability of extreme caution on the part of the French people? There is another consideration which should weigh equally; that is, Russia's internal condition, her political constitution, her financial status, her military system, her mobilization difficulties—in short, the very basis of the existence of this lumbering Russian giant. . . . For all the contrasts between the Russia of autocracy and republican France, there is this much of resemblance, that any political calculation must allow for the factor of the unexpected.

With astonishing far-sightedness, Leroy-Beaulieu, after analysing the Russian budget and describing the gangrenous state of corruption of every branch of her administration, expressed the opinion that, if a major war came, there was no guarantee that the imperial army would not suffer the same humiliations as in the last war in which it was engaged. The crux of the matter was the time Russia would take to mobilize, and the dangers of war would not be equally shared between the two Powers. "France would be putting heavier stakes into the game." She would sustain the brunt of the attack and, though the more vulnerable of the two, would be the more exposed. "Thus a Franco-Russian Alliance would bring Russia the lion's share of the advantages, but would saddle France with the bulk of the risks, both diplomatic and military."

The problem could not be more clearly stated. These lengthy extracts have been quoted in order to show that the French public, and in particular the governing class, was actually warned by a prominent public man, well versed in Russian affairs and under no possible suspicion as regards either impartiality or moderation of views. It is noteworthy that neither the industrial nor the political leaders, whose primary duty should have been to ascertain the precise facts, paid any attention to this authoritative counsel.

Shortly afterwards Leroy-Beaulieu republished his article, in somewhat elaborated form, as a book under the title of *La France, la Russie, et l'Europe.* "Here will be found un-diluted", he announced, "the same frankness and the same hostility to those illusions on which would-be patriots are so prone to feed." And in summing up he said:

Any agreement between Paris and St. Petersburg should be based on considerations of peace, not of war. For such purposes there is no need of either a treaty or a formal alliance.[1]

A similar view was held by Jules Grévy, who said:

We have no need to ally ourselves with anybody. If we stay quietly at home, no one will come and attack us.[2]

Jaurès, who had then just recently entered the political arena, pointed out that all alliances presuppose some definite object, and the definite object in this case could only be war:

[1] Pp. 120–121.      [2] Daudet, p. 207.

Apart from defensive alliances entered into on the spur of the moment, which, if real danger comes, we are not likely to lack, because our danger would be Europe's danger, any other alliance would merely open the door to military adventures. Is that what the diplomatists of monarchism are offering us?[1]

In actual fact, whenever Russia or Great Britain had intervened in favour of France, in 1887 as in 1875, their action had sprung from a recognition of where their immediate self-interest lay. But all these warnings were in vain.

[1] *Dépêche de Toulouse*, February 26, 1887.

# CHAPTER II

## THE FRANCO-RUSSIAN AGREEMENT OF 1891

DE FREYCINET was determined that the financial support rendered by the French should be requited by the Russian Government with something more than compliments and congratulatory speeches.

To get into touch with the Tsar, who was not always readily accessible to the French ambassador, the Foreign Minister had recourse to the offices of a go-between named Hansen, a man of Danish extraction, who was in a position to submit reports to Alexander III through his association with Rachkovsky, a friend of Prince Obolensky, who was in the Tsar's confidence. It was through this channel that Hansen made known to the latter the wishes of the French Government. In addition, being in touch with Mohrenheim and with the Foreign Minister, he conveyed unofficial messages to both parties whenever it was necessary to remove difficulties or explain away misunderstandings.[1]

Relations between the two Governments grew more intimate in 1890. The Russian Government, being aware that the French Ministers were anxious to show their readiness to oblige, instructed Mohrenheim to request them to arrest certain Nihilists in hiding in Paris who were alleged to be hatching a plot against the Tsar. Constans, the Minister of the Interior, undertook to comply with the request, with the result that twelve Nihilists were shortly afterwards thrown into prison. The Emperor, on hearing the news, exclaimed: "At last there is a Government in France"; and sent an expression of his gratitude. This incident marked a considerable step forward in the direction of an alliance, and Hansen records that the steps taken "helped greatly to bring the two Governments closer together".[2]

[1] Hansen, pp. 127–129. Cf. de Freycinet, *Souvenirs*, pp. 488–489.
[2] Tardieu, in his *La France et les Alliances*, p. 12, calls this a "trump card".

At the request of Laboulaye, the French ambassador, General de Boisdeffre, the deputy Chief of the General Staff, received an invitation to attend the Russian army manœuvres at Narva, which were also witnessed by the German Emperor and his Chancellor, Caprivi.[1]

In 1918, as the result of the publication by the Bolsheviks of certain secret documents in the archives of the Russian Foreign Ministry, the French Government decided to publish a "Yellow Book" of documents relating to the conclusion of the Franco-Russian Alliance, under the headings of Origins, Agreement, and Military and Naval Conventions.[2] We propose to defer our comments on these papers until a later chapter, merely remarking here that it is at present impossible to check them by the originals, since the archives of the French Foreign Ministry for the period in question are not accessible to the public. In the meantime we will summarize the facts as they are presented in this official collection.

The first document in Chapter I of the "Yellow Book" is a dispatch from Laboulaye to Ribot, the Foreign Minister, dated August 24, 1890, in which the ambassador reports the date fixed for Boisdeffre's return and affirms that "the *rapprochement* between France and Russia, which barely three years ago seemed to be a mirage, an illusion, has gradually assumed such a genuine solidity that even a propaganda visit like this of the Kaiser's is not regarded in any quarter as likely to weaken it". But "we could not rest content with welcoming these evidences of platonic affection; we required some tangible result". After the active good will France had evinced towards the Russian Government, "but little remained to consummate the union". It was Boisdeffre's mission that represented this

---

[1] The Tsar is reported to have said to Caprivi: "There is a great deal of talk about an Entente Cordiale between Russia and France, but believe me, I shall never form an alliance with a Republic."—Eissenstein to Kalnocky, August 27 and September 5, 1890 (Vienna Archives), quoted by Langer in the *Slavonic Review*, March 1925, p. 561.

[2] Cf. Margaine, *Rapport sur le Livre Jaune relatif à l'Alliance franco-russe* (Paper No. 6036 of the Chamber of Deputies, 1919 session.)

final step, and the hopes that had been reposed in it were now realized, for his conversations with the Russian War Minister and with the Chief of Staff, Obruchev, were sufficient grounds for stating that henceforward the two Staffs would be in direct contact.

But Laboulaye was somewhat over-confident as to the "genuine solidity" of the Entente, and an incident which took place immediately afterwards showed that the "union" was not yet "consummated". E. Daudet relates that in that same month of August—apparently arising directly out of Laboulaye's dispatch—de Freycinet and Barbey, the Minister of the Navy, conceived the idea of instructing the ambassador to ask the Tsar if he would view with favour an official visit from the French Northern Battle Squadron to Kronstadt. Alexander III sent an evasive reply, however, and the visit, which had been provisionally fixed for September, had to be postponed. Laboulaye did not find it possible to reopen the subject until January 1891, when the Russian Government agreed to the visit taking place in the following July.[1] The "Yellow Book" contains none of the dispatches dealing with this incident.

About the same time tentative inquiries were made by Laboulaye with a view to President Carnot being made a member of the Order of St. Andrew. Hansen states that he was entrusted with the task of putting the suggestion first to the Russian Government.[2] Here again the French Government were made to wait, the Tsar having been put out by the attitude of the French Ministers in connection with the banning of Sardou's play *Thermidor*.[3] The decoration, when it did arrive some months later, was represented to the French public as a spontaneous tribute from Russia. De Giers had some justification in saying as he did to Ghika, the Roumanian Minister at St. Petersburg: "The French are at our feet, and

---

[1] Daudet, pp. 299–300.—Hansen, p. 115. In an article in the *Nouvelle Revue* of November 15, 1893, Flourens claimed to have initiated the idea of this visit.

[2] Hansen, pp. 129–130.      [3] Daudet, pp. 302–303.

it would be ungracious to grumble. They have been making endless efforts to get us to sign an agreement, but they have not succeeded for all their entreaties." He added caustically, referring to the Cross of St. Andrew that had been conferred on President Carnot: "Little presents keep a friendship alive."[1]

The second document in the "Yellow Book", after a gap of nearly seven months, is a dispatch from Ribot to Laboulaye, dated March 9, 1891, notifying him that Mohrenheim had communicated to him (Ribot) the contents of a dispatch from de Giers regarding the Empress Frederick's stay in Paris. De Giers had stated in the course of this dispatch that "the *entente cordiale* now so happily established between France and Russia is the best possible guarantee of peace. While the Triple Alliance continue their prodigal expenditure on armaments, an intimate understanding between the two nations is essential in order to maintain a suitable Balance of Power in Europe." Ribot had at once expressed his cordial agreement.

Laboulaye sent no reply to this, and document No. 3 in the collection carries us forward more than four months, to July 18th, when the ambassador reported to Ribot that he had had a confidential talk with de Giers, in the course of which "the conversation turned on the renewal of the Triple Alliance and the indirect adherence of Great Britain", and they discussed "whether the new situation thus created for France and Russia did not render it desirable that the Entente should be developed one stage further". Laboulaye asked Ribot to let him know his (Ribot's) view and to instruct him as to the attitude he should adopt in the next interview with de Giers.

A *rapprochement* had, it is true, taken place between Germany and Great Britain. Britain had surrendered to Germany the island of Heligoland in exchange for compensation in East Africa, and, following a friendly visit by the Kaiser to London, the British Mediterranean Fleet had called at Fiume and Venice. At the same time the German Emperor had annoyed

[1] *Die Grosse Politik*, VII, p. 205: Bülow to Caprivi, May 2, 1891.

the Tsar by favouring the Polish party in Posen. At this period Russia was feeling the need of French support in Asia against Great Britain—with Austria Russia's chief adversary. In addition, her need of money was growing more and more urgent, while a famine and an outbreak of cholera supervened to increase her embarrassment still further. All these facts help to explain the change in Russia's attitude, especially as France on her side stood in no need of support from Russia in the Near East. To understand Russia's policy aright, it must be remembered that, ever since the Seven Years' War, it had been based on alliance with Prussia. "If there is any one dominant tradition at the Court of St. Petersburg", wrote Leroy-Beaulieu in 1888, "it is that of favouring an alliance with Prussia."[1] For Russia, the enemy was not Germany, a protagonist of the monarchist principle, but Austria and, still more, Great Britain, at odds with Russia both in the Balkans, over the question of the Straits, and in Central Asia, where, with the aid of French capital, the Transcaspian railway was just being completed. On the other hand, the renewal of the Triple Alliance had been announced at the end of June.

On July 21st the French Battle Squadron, under the orders of Admiral Gervais, entered the harbour of Kronstadt, where a magnificent reception was accorded. The Tsar stood to attention at the sound of the *Marseillaise*, the playing of which had been prohibited in Russia up to then and remained prohibited subsequently. Poincaré, speaking in 1921, "could not recall without emotion the profound effect which the Tsar's friendly gesture produced on French public opinion at the time. . . . For France", he said, "it marked the end of a prolonged period of isolation and was clear evidence of her revival."[2] Looking back with a full knowledge of the circum-

---

[1] *Revue des Deux Mondes*, February 15, 1888. The *Journal des Débats* also admitted that the traditions of Russian diplomacy were "in favour of a close relationship with Prussia" (February 3, 1887).—Cf. Bülow, *Deutsche Politik*, pp. 76–81.

[2] From a speech on the causes of the War, February 16, 1921.

stances surrounding this episode, one is mildly astonished at
his enthusiasm, but the French people, being unaware that
the visit had been first suggested by their Government and
deferred by the Tsar, and knowing nothing of Russia's real
situation, may be excused for imagining at the time that the
Alliance was an accomplished fact. "Through an obvious misunderstanding", remarks Debidour, "they took this one incident for the prelude of the *revanche* of which they had been
passionately dreaming for two decades." The French man-in-
the-street was all too ready to believe that, by listening to the
*Marseillaise* at Kronstadt, the Tsar had protested against the
Treaty of Frankfort and announced his intention of tearing
it up. In a conversation at the time with Debidour, Léon Say
deplored this misunderstanding on the part of the French
public, fearing that it might have calamitous results, either in
the direction of inciting the nation to embark prematurely on
a war of revenge, or else, by a natural reaction, leading it to
accept fatalistically the fact that the Tsar really intended to
maintain the peace of Frankfort.[1] Charles Maurras admits that
all patriotic citizens, all adherents of Boulanger, were passionately in favour of an Alliance with Russia, because they
imagined that, through her aid, France would be enabled the
sooner to take her stand again on the Rhine.[2] Poincaré alone
continues to assert that "there was nothing in this universal
elation which could have been suspected of being inspired by
the spirit of revenge".

Ribot replied on July 24th to Laboulaye's inquiry, referring
bluntly to the suggestions made by de Giers as "overtures",
although the latter had deliberately dealt in vague generalities.
Taking full advantage of the opportunity, obscure as were the
motives which gave rise to it, Ribot proposed that, now that
the Triple Alliance had been renewed, "we must endeavour
to strengthen the guarantees for the maintenance of peace and
an appropriate Balance of Power in Europe which our *entente*

[1] Debidour, II, pp. 177 and 178 (footnote).   [2] *Kiel et Tanger*, p. 15.

with Russia provides". He added: "We shall therefore be prepared to give the most favourable consideration to any *proposals*
that may be made to us", and went on to refer to the possibility
of an alliance, and even to suggest definite points on which it
might be based:

In our view it might be sufficient if the two Governments pledged
themselves on the one hand to take counsel together on every question
which is calculated to jeopardize the maintenance of peace, and on the
other hand, in the event of the definite threat of an outbreak of hostilities coming from one or other of the Triple Alliance Powers, to
take without the least delay such measures as would obviate any
danger of a surprise. In other words, France and Russia would
agree in advance to mobilize their forces simultaneously as soon as
any one of the countries of the Triple Alliance should mobilize hers.
The details of such simultaneous mobilization might suitably form the
subject of an agreement to be discussed and signed between the
General Staffs of the two countries.

Here already appears the essential framework of a treaty such
as was actually concluded. One of the two contracting parties
had put forward in general terms a suggestion of co-operation;
the other had immediately seized upon this to propose the
definite lines of a binding agreement, and began at once to
speak of military conventions (Documents No. 4 and No. 5).
Without losing a moment, Ribot sent to Laboulaye a draft
instrument of this nature which he had drawn up in conjunction with de Freycinet and President Carnot.

Several days elapsed without bringing a reply from St.
Petersburg. On July 29th, Ribot gave Laboulaye peremptory
instructions "to have a *decisive conversation* with M. de Giers,
for it would be most unfortunate" if he were "to miss the
opportunity of ascertaining quite definitely the attitude of the
Russian Government". Ribot insisted that, if time did not
admit of coming to a formal agreement, at least an exchange
of views should take place defining without further delay the
main lines of such an agreement. (No. 6).

It was not until August 5th that Laboulaye was able to
notify the Foreign Minister that the Tsar agreed in principle

to an *exchange of views* taking place between the two Governments. De Giers, however, desired to widen the scope of the understanding to cover the maintenance of peace in general, not merely in Europe, since threats to peace might arise in Egypt or even in China. (No. 8.) Russia, said Ribot in reply, seemed to be chiefly concerned to secure French support against Great Britain, whom she affected to regard as already linked up with the Triple Alliance. (No. 10.) In the upshot, de Giers and Laboulaye managed to agree on a formula which provided that the two Cabinets should take counsel together on every question calculated to menace the peace of the world, and, in the event of either country being threatened with aggression, that they should, "if they deem it necessary, consider the best means of agreeing in advance on such measures as the two Governments might be forced to adopt immediately and simultaneously should the threat materialize". (No. 9.) This formula contained no obligation to agree upon the steps that would be taken in joint self-protection. It is clear that de Giers was reluctant to pledge himself definitely and was aiming at securing all the advantages of an agreement without making any real concessions himself. But the French Government was not to be caught. Ribot replied on August 7th with the proposal to substitute for the phrase, "would consider the best means", etc., the phrase, "undertake to agree upon the measures. . . ." (No. 11.) He wanted a precise and binding pledge. Already he regarded "the agreement now concluded as a far-reaching act of state, with great potentialities".

But Ribot was going too fast. The agreement was not yet signed and sealed, and in successive dispatches from Laboulaye two obstacles were reported: first, that de Giers was raising objections to the revised formula on the ground that it seemed to go rather further than his own draft (No. 13), and, secondly, that the Tsar, while concurring in substance, was not pleased with the procedure that had been adopted, being unwilling to keep Mohrenheim outside the negotiations. (No. 14.) "Let us not be in too great a hurry", said Alexander III to Laboulaye; "draft agreements cannot be hammered out by telegraph; *that would be a very dangerous proceeding*. Baron Mohrenheim, who must be consulted, is coming to St. Petersburg shortly, and I think that by October or November we shall have a clearer view of the position." This was tantamount to an open criticism of the way the negotiations had been conducted under pressure from the French Government. The Tsar was struck, as de Giers had been, by the precise and far-reaching nature of the terms that had been suggested by the French, and did not intend to be rushed into a decision or to have his hand forced. He determined first of all to ascertain from his ambassador in Paris the actual state of public opinion there, especially the real strength of the party of "*la revanche*".

The negotiations thereupon came to a standstill for a short time. "It is obvious", wrote Ribot to President Carnot on August 11th, "from the involved wording of the second paragraph, that M. de Giers is making every effort to avoid committing himself definitely as regards the idea of a military convention. . . . It is also not improbable that the Emperor may have had scruples at the last moment as to the effect that might be produced by the announcement of an agreement between the two countries." As a matter of fact the Tsar was undoubtedly anxious to ensure that Germany should have no grounds for feeling herself directly threatened, and Mohrenheim had shown Ribot the day before a private letter from de Giers in which that anxiety was clearly expressed. The Emperor was especially concerned lest the French "*revanche*" party should find themselves in a position to involve him in a military adventure. (No. 16.)

Mohrenheim, who had received instructions from the Tsar to return to St. Petersburg, came back to Paris on August 27th with a letter from de Giers authorizing him to notify the French Government that the Tsar had "graciously approved of the principles of the agreement" as previously drafted, including the amendment proposed by Ribot to the effect that "the two contracting parties undertake to agree upon the measures . . .", and that he (de Giers) desired to make it clear that the two Governments remained "free from any sort of Alliance". (August 21st—No. 17.) Ribot replied to Mohrenheim on the same day that the French Government fully accepted the two points formulated by de Giers. He took the opportunity of adding: "The Imperial Government will doubtless agree that it would be advisable to entrust to a special delegation, to be appointed as soon as possible, the task of working out in practical detail the measures designed to meet the eventualities envisaged by the second half of the agreement." (No. 18.) The finally approved wording of the agreement was as follows:

With a view to intensifying and reinforcing that cordial understanding which now unites them, and to promoting by their joint efforts the maintenance of peace, which is the object of their sincerest desires, the two Governments hereby affirm that they will take counsel together on all questions which are calculated to jeopardize the peace of the world. In the event of peace being actually endangered, and more particularly in the event of one of the two high contracting parties being threatened with aggression, the two contracting parties undertake to agree upon such measures as the two Governments might be forced to adopt immediately and simultaneously should the threat materialize.

De Freycinet had no scruples in declaring that this agreement was in harmony with aspirations that had been seeking expression for many years past. "The peoples, by a deep-seated instinct, had led the way for the diplomats."[1] Where and in what way had the two peoples ever given expression to their wishes in this respect?

Such was the agreement by which the foundations of the Franco-Russian Alliance were laid. Though it implied the concurrence of the two Governments, it is noteworthy that it was signed neither by the Tsar nor by the President of the Republic, but merely by the two Foreign Ministers, de Giers

[1] Op. cit., p. 467.

C

and Ribot, the latter not even being Prime Minister. It is obvious that the intention of the Russian statesmen was simply to lay down certain principles, which would not actually commit them to definite action in specific circumstances. They were clearly anxious not to allow themselves to be led away willy-nilly into some adventure in which Russia's vital interests might not be at stake. They were, in point of fact, solely concerned at that time with Great Britain, and it was against Great Britain that they were anxious to secure the support of France.

The German Government showed no signs of alarm at the *rapprochement* between France and Russia. The Chancellor Caprivi, who had received every possible friendly assurance from Russia, expressed the opinion, in speeches which he delivered at Osnabrück and in the Reichstag in September and November 1891, that the demonstration at Kronstadt and its sequel had merely tended to strengthen the restoration of a proper equilibrium in Europe, and that peace was not in any way endangered.

# CHAPTER III

# THE MILITARY CONVENTION

From the very outset the French Government considered the agreement of August 1891 as insufficient in itself. De Freycinet in particular, while under no misapprehension as to its far-reaching implications, regarded it as merely a stepping-stone to further negotiations. The terms of the agreement seemed to him to be *too theoretical*. In his view, a military convention, laying down in advance the lines on which the joint action contemplated by the agreement should proceed, was the indispensable logical complement of the agreement itself. He had pointed out this deficiency from the very first. Accordingly he attached the greatest possible importance to the two General Staffs getting together without delay to work out the best means of achieving such joint action. He feared that, if war came, Russia would leave France to bear the full brunt of the attack from Germany and Italy, concentrating her own efforts entirely against Austria, and he therefore recommended that Russia should be compelled to allocate a considerable force to the German front. (No. 16.)

Accordingly, de Freycinet, then Prime Minister and Minister of War, sent Hansen at the end of August on a mission to Fredensborg, where the Tsar was then staying on a visit to his father-in-law, the King of Denmark. Hansen took with him a sort of memorandum which he had drawn up after his conversation with the Prime Minister, explaining "the urgent necessity of arranging a military convention between the two countries, the essential feature of which should be that, the moment the Triple Alliance was known to be mobilizing, Russia and France should immediately mobilize the whole of their forces". In addition, it was proposed that an agreement should be framed between the two General Staffs to regulate the strength and relative movements of the various Army

Corps according to circumstances, so far as they could be foreseen. De Freycinet regarded it as "of the greatest importance that this convention should be kept strictly secret". Thus the Tsar was not the only one with a disinclination from publicity.

The position was, therefore, that the agreement had no sooner been signed than, with one accord, Ribot proceeded to sound Mohrenheim as to the framing of a military convention, and de Freycinet dispatched his confidential emissary to Alexander III to expound the necessity of such a step. Hansen set off for Denmark on September 1st, and on the 4th had an interview with Price Obolensky, who submitted his memorandum to the Tsar and brought him back an answer in the following terms: "M. Hansen may tell M. de Freycinet that the Emperor is giving serious consideration to the request, and will make a point of dealing with it as soon as he returns to St. Petersburg."[1] Shortly after this, Mohrenheim wrote to Ribot that the Tsar

considers that the needs of the situation are fully met for the present by the principles formulated and established in the agreement between the two Governments, and would prefer to defer further action on the important question of military co-operation until he has had an opportunity, after his return to Russia, of making a preliminary detailed examination of the problem himself, in conjunction with his Ministers of War and Foreign Affairs. (No. 19.)

This was almost a rebuff; at all events it was clear that the Tsar was evading the issue. De Freycinet and Ribot were somewhat damped, and it is not surprising that, speaking, the one at Vendeuvre on September 16th, on the conclusion of the army manœuvres, and the other at Bapaume on the 28th, they should have referred with the strictest reserve, in vague, almost cryptic terms, to a "new situation which enables us to seek peace and ensue it with greater self-respect"—and this to audiences who were convinced that the Alliance was already an accomplished fact.

[1] Hansen, pp. 133–136.

Alexander III returned to St. Petersburg, and the matter remained at a standstill. In fact, Ribot had two important interviews with de Giers during November in which the latter reiterated that "the Tsar thinks that the principles laid down in the agreement of last August are sufficient for the present, though he is prepared to go into the question of the possible steps to be taken to supplement them in an emergency". (No. 20.)

The Russian Government was all for peace, the Tsar was perfectly sure Germany would never make a hostile move, and de Giers, anxious to enlarge upon Russia's pacific intentions, took pains to assure Ribot that all she desired in the Balkans was to maintain the *status quo*. He added:

Some people imagine that we have designs upon Constantinople. On the contrary, our view is that nothing would be more embarrassing for Russia than to have her centre of gravity shifted. What would be the effect on our northern provinces and on St. Petersburg? We prefer that the Turks should remain the appointed guardians of the Straits. As for the Freedom of the Straits, we are satisfied with the arrangements settled a few months ago, and want nothing more than was then conceded to us, as you are aware, that is to say, the right of sending transports through the Straits in certain circumstances.[1] (Nos. 21 and 22.)

Both Ribot and de Freycinet returned to the charge in the matter of the military convention, but de Giers, who was not a

---

[1] In reporting this interview to Paul Cambon, then ambassador at Constantinople, Ribot wrote: "M. de Giers gave me a definite assurance that the Tsar had quite made up his mind not to embark on any further measures against the Porte. 'It is not in our interest at all', he said to me, 'to saddle ourselves with Constantinople. . . . It would be a rash undertaking for the Russian Empire to take up a position on the Bosphorus. What would be the effect on St. Petersburg if we did that? It is better for the Turks to continue to guard the Bosphorus.' " (No. 22.)

In a note dated December 14th to Nelidov, de Giers draws particular attention to the fact that "the Balkan situation is governed by the Treaty of Berlin. . . . Our chief concern ever since has been to ensure that the state of things set up by that international instrument shall be maintained inviolate. We have no intention ourselves of suggesting any change in the situation then created, and . . . we must therefore concentrate our efforts on maintaining the *status quo*." (No. 24.)

believer in Germany's warlike intentions, evaded the point. He touched discreetly on the difficulty of entering into too great detail and parried all arguments with the plea that he had no authority to deal with the question independently, as the Emperor had expressed a wish to go into it personally with the War Minister and himself. He did, however, go so far as to admit that it might be possible to consider some supplementary agreement for giving more definite shape to

(i) The mutual obligation of the two countries, already recognized, to support each other in the event of external aggression;

(ii) Their obligation to order the mobilization of their armies if either Germany or Austria were to mobilize;

(iii) The steps necessary to render the military effort of the two countries as effective as possible.[1] (No. 21.)

In short, de Giers persisted in his policy of nebulosity, and declined to go beyond general principles. Meanwhile the Tsar, in a conversation with Montebello, without referring to what had just been taking place, expressed the view, with regard to the proposed convention, that there was no object in "introducing an element of haste, which might well prove dangerous". The first two points seemed to him, in any case, to be already implicit in the second paragraph of the agreement, which, he said, guaranteed peace, and hence ample time to devise the necessary plans. (No. 23.)

Alexander III was shuffling, playing for time, encouraged in this course by the fact that loans were still being successfully floated. Suddenly, on the eve of the issue of a new loan, the Rothschild Bank, which had been undertaking the issues since 1889, cancelled the arrangements under the terms of a clause relating to the persecution of Russian Jews. The Crédit Lyonnais, with Rouvier's express permission, was then given the

---

[1] Touching, at the same time, on French internal politics, de Giers expressed the hope that France would adhere as closely as possible to Thiers' ideal of Conservative Republicanism.

task of floating the loan with the co-operation of a syndicate of French bankers, and the issue was speedily subscribed. The German banks then organized a campaign against it; wholesale unloading led to a rapid fall in the quotations, and a serious crisis was imminent. The Russian Finance Minister was able, however, to arrange for the repurchase of the stock, and the price rose again. The French financial houses had once more saved the Russian Treasury.

In these circumstances the Tsar was in no hurry to investigate the necessity of a military convention. He was convinced of Germany's peaceful intentions and was particularly anxious not to antagonize her, hoping that the Russo-German tariff war would soon end in a commercial treaty favourable to Russia. The British menace in the East, too, was showing signs of relaxing, and Gladstone's return to power shortly afterwards was an additional guarantee of Great Britain's pacific outlook.

The causes of the delay in the negotiations over the military convention were thus totally unconnected with French internal politics or with any lack of continuity in her foreign policy due to changes in Governments, despite the suggestions to this effect made by certain partisan historians who take their inspiration from the Quai d'Orsay. The facts are clear. The persistence and pertinacity of de Freycinet and Ribot are unmistakable, and the Russian Government was quite obviously becoming restive under their importunity.

Paris went on waiting for some sign from St. Petersburg. Surely the Tsar would at last make up his mind to agree. But no. Alexander III and his Ministers still declined to implement, by means of a military convention, the undertaking contained in the second paragraph of the agreement. They maintained the attitude that the protocol of August 1891 was sufficiently binding. It was clear that they had made up their minds that Russia's liability to armed intervention should be limited to cases of entirely unprovoked aggression, and that they were not going to tie their hands by too precise a formula, for fear of being involved in some rash venture instigated directly or indirectly by the *revanche* party.

At this stage a note was drawn up, based on a draft by General de Miribel, with amendments by de Freycinet, setting out clearly and definitely the main features of the proposed military convention, including the disposition of troops on the various frontiers, and demonstrating the necessity of concentrating on the overthrow of the chief enemy, namely, Germany. Ribot forwarded this on February 4, 1892, to Montebello, with the request that he would submit it to the Tsar, adding that de Freycinet "was prepared to send anybody they liked to St. Petersburg or to see anybody they liked to send to Paris". (No. 28.) But the French ambassador, knowing the conditions on the spot and appreciating de Giers' peculiarities, gave rather careful consideration to the tone and phrasing of the note before delivering it, and decided to modify the wording so as to bring out the principal ideas more strikingly and prevent the detailed figures from distracting attention from the main argument. He also deemed it advisable to insert a direct appeal to the Tsar's sense of probity and fairness. The Miribel note, thus modified, was placed before the Emperor on March 8th. He expressed a wish to examine it carefully and discuss it with de Giers, and concurred with the principles of mutual assistance and simultaneous mobilization (these being points which had already been agreed to), but had to leave for Denmark before he could find time to pass any definite opinion on the draft convention.

De Freycinet now lost all patience, and instructed Hansen to submit a letter to the Tsar reiterating the desire of the French Government to set the seal on the Entente by elaborating a military convention and requesting Alexander III's consent to their sending a responsible officer to St. Petersburg to work out a draft convention with the Russian War Minister and Chief of Staff. Hansen's letter was duly dispatched to Rachkovsky, who laid it before the Tsar.

No reply was received to this, but Montebello reported on May 4th that the Emperor had shown the Miribel note to the Minister of War and instructed him to draw up a draft military convention. The inference was that he was not prepared to accept all the ideas of the French Chief of Staff, and, in fact, instead of sending for the latter, or for his deputy, Boisdeffre, specially in order that their Russian colleagues might discuss the details with them at St. Petersburg, he merely proposed to invite one of them to the July manœuvres. (No. 32.) Ribot then urged Montebello to "do everything possible to expedite the signature" of the convention. "Europe is at rest now, but who would venture to assert that the present state of peace will be of long duration?" (No. 34.) At this juncture Mohrenheim, who had already been the subject of attacks on the part of the *Défense Nationale*, was accused of having taken half a million francs from the Panama Canal Company to meet his private debts. This attack, combined with the many scandals connected with the Panama affair, had the effect of antagonizing the Tsar.[1]

On June 23, 1892, as the Russian Government still showed no signs of furnishing a reply, Ribot wrote to the French ambassador in St. Petersburg again, drawing attention to the terms of the 1891 Agreement and emphasizing the necessity of losing no further time.[2] He referred to de Giers as

an unenterprising individual who is afraid of clear-cut decisions and delights in circumlocution. . . . Give him to understand that if need be you will be constrained to approach the Emperor direct. Make good use of the fact, too, that the War Minister is favourably disposed. . . . You may use your discretion as to the means to be adopted, but it is important that the matter shall be cut and dried by

---

[1] Hansen, pp. 145–149.

[2] There must have been another dispatch from Montebello in the interval which is not reproduced, explaining the point of view of the Russian War Minister, as Ribot now writes: "General Vannovsky is entirely right in wanting everything to be clearly set down in black and white," whereas no mention had been made in the ambassador's last recorded dispatch of this special desire on the part of the General.

the end of July at latest. . . . Boisdeffre will be ready to start whenever the word is given.

Boisdeffre, added Ribot, would be fully primed and authorized to discuss with the Russian General Staff all technical questions arising out of the military convention.

You will not need to go into these administrative details, which are outside your province. We must confine ourselves to laying down principles and leave it to the soldiers to draw up the consequential operation plans. The simpler and shorter the actual convention which lays down the broad lines of joint action, the better. I should be glad to see it limited to the few lines which we jotted down together before you left. (No. 35.)

It must not be forgotten that the Tsar had still not definitely agreed even to consider a military convention. It is evident that the French were endeavouring to insure against his constant hesitation and shuffling by negotiating a convention which, taken in conjunction with the main agreement, would commit him irrevocably. It was an attempt, in short, to force his hand. And Ribot was even instructing the ambassador that

it goes without saying that a convention of this nature must be regarded as primarily a political instrument. If it is not actually signed by the Heads of the two States, it must at least bear the names of the Foreign Ministers, on behalf of the Emperor and of the President respectively. But this question of procedure should not be raised until the whole of the material points have been settled. (No. 35.)

On July 1, 1892, being still without definite news of the Tsar's intentions, Ribot urged Montebello to "take vigorous steps, if necessary requesting an audience as soon as the Emperor gets back" (No. 36); but Montebello reported that de Giers was unwell and inaccessible to visitors, while the Tsar was still away. Ribot thereupon gave vent to his irritation and annoyance at the long-drawn-out delay. He was

determined to put an end to this period of inaction, which has lasted much too long. The need for a military convention was generally recognized and even stated in as many words as long ago as last August, and M. de Giers pledged himself to hasten its completion.[1] Months have passed since then and nothing has been settled . . . the matter must be brought to a head. I find it extremely difficult to explain to the President and to the Minister of War why it is taking so long.

He fixed a time limit. "If by the end of August we have no definite results to show, I shall be obliged, in order to safe-guard my own position, to bring the matter before the Cabinet." Ribot was aware that the Tsar was anxious to keep the pro-ceedings a dead secret, and was therefore trying to intimidate him by the threat of publicity. He added, in obvious vexation: "How can I explain that the conduct of the affairs of two great nations is at the mercy of chances like one Minister's indisposition, or questions of etiquette which prevent an ambassador, with such serious matters to discuss, from going straight to the Emperor?" He recommended Montebello, in the event of his being dissatisfied with the result of his inter-view with de Giers, to consider very seriously the desirability of requesting an audience of the Tsar, or at any rate submitting a note reminding him of the many reasons for urgent action and of his own pledged word. (Nos. 38 and 39.)

Just at that time the *Figaro* (July 14th) published an article entitled "Marriage or Flirtation?" The article was signed "Conscius", and was obviously officially inspired. The writer urged the two Powers to call a truce to coquetry and to make up their minds to pass from empty preliminaries to the signing of a marriage contract. France was entitled to claim that her diplomats should be allowed to come into action and leave the realm of pretty phrases.

This exchange of vague promises, these half-hearted assurances of co-operation, these fitful demonstrations of Platonic attachment—all this tends to arouse the susceptibilities of certain Powers and to mobilize against us certain interests which imagine, quite mistakenly, that they are threatened. Our diplomacy would be gravely to blame if, in the event of such susceptibilities flaming into hostility, we were to find ourselves isolated as we have been in the past. The wooing

---

[1] N.B.—This was not correct.

has lasted over a year; now let us proceed with the nuptials without more ado, as is customary in respectable families. The match is a highly suitable one, but to prolong this flirtation without a definite conclusion would be unwise.

The article seemed to draw the conclusion, obviously reflecting the state of mind of French official circles, that a good dose of Franco-Russian military convention was required to allay German uneasiness! Any expedient would serve to bring pressure on Alexander III, but this one must have put a strain on his credulity.

De Giers' indisposition dragged on, while the Tsar was not due back from his prolonged absence until the middle of July. Montebello was beginning to expect that he would meet with a certain amount of opposition when he started to press for a decision. On July 22nd Ribot made it clear that, when Boisdeffre, who had been invited to attend the Russian army manœuvres, came to St. Petersburg, it would not be merely to discuss with the General Staff the best distribution of troops. He was afraid that the Russians would want to confine themselves to exchanges of views or to bare statements, but these could not be permitted to take the place of a formal convention.

Our responsibilities are too grave to allow us to agree to treat the subject with anything but the strictest realism. Two points are already established: first, France and Russia have agreed to take counsel together on all questions affecting the peace of the world, and secondly, they are pledged to come to each other's assistance in case of attack. What we must now aim at securing is an unequivocal declaration that—

> (a) In the event of the Triple Alliance mobilizing their forces, Russia and France will do likewise without needing to consult with or notify each other;
>
> (b) If war ensues, Russia will bring to bear on the German frontiers the whole of her available forces other than those required to hold the Austrians, the numbers so available being estimated at 700,000 men;
>
> (c) The troops employed against Germany will not be merely used for reconnoitring, but will launch a vigorous offensive so as to prevent the Germans from transferring reinforcements

*Forty divisi[...]
which they
would do
under any
circumstances*

to the Western front to overwhelm our army. In return, we would undertake to place the whole of our forces on the Rhine except those required for holding the Italians.

In contrast to the clause inserted later on, in 1899, at the instance of Delcassé,—an amendment which by the light of this earlier history is revealed in its true colours,—Ribot proposed that the convention should have a definite time limit, the same as the treaties by which the Triple Alliance was constituted. "By this means we shall emphasize in the plainest possible way the *defensive character* of our *rapprochement* with Russia." No more striking condemnation could be uttered of the initiative taken by Delcassé six years later.

Both Ribot and de Freycinet attached the greatest importance to the negotiations being completed before the end of September. "Nothing could be more detrimental than to prolong this uncertainty. . . . It is essential that the Emperor should know as soon as possible what we regard as indispensable, and that we on our side should know where we are." (No. 45.)

On July 28, 1892, Ribot wrote that Boisdeffre had left for Russia, taking with him a draft military convention which had been drawn up at a conference at which de Freycinet, Miribel and Boisdeffre had been present. "In the event of Germany not joining in the war", he added, "we should prefer that each side should reserve full liberty of action, and that our hands should not be tied by a mutual pledge of too binding a nature. This consideration was in our minds in preparing the draft, a copy of which I enclose." The draft read as follows:

France and Russia being alike animated by a sincere desire to preserve peace, and having no other object than to provide against the eventualities of a defensive war forced upon either of them by an attack by the armed forces of the Triple Alliance, the two Governments have deemed it advisable to elaborate and supplement in this respect the principles agreed upon between them by protocol dated August 15, 1891.

In consequence, the Foreign Ministers and Ministers of War of the two countries, with the authority and on behalf of their respective Governments, have agreed to the following arrangements, viz.:

(i) In the event of the mobilization of the armed forces of the Triple Alliance, or of Germany alone, France and Russia will, immediately the news reaches them and without waiting to consult together, forthwith and simultaneously mobilize the whole of their forces and move them as near as possible to the frontiers.

(ii) In the event of either France or Russia being actually attacked by the armed forces of the Triple Alliance, or of Germany alone, both Powers will bring to bear against Germany the whole of their forces which are not absolutely indispensable on other fronts. These troops will proceed to launch a vigorous and determined offensive, so that Germany will be forced to give battle in the East and in the West simultaneously.

(iii) In the most unfavourable circumstances, that is to say, if the whole of the forces of the Triple Alliance are brought into action, France estimates that the number of combatant troops she will be able to place in the field against Germany will be about 1,300,000, and that these troops will be concentrated at the frontier by the 14th day after the order for mobilization has been given. In the same circumstances Russia estimates that the number of combatant troops she will be able to place in the field against Germany will be about 800,000, and that these troops will be concentrated at the frontier by the ......th day after the order for mobilization has been given, approximately equal numbers being employed against Austria.

(iv) France and Russia will not conclude a separate peace with the Triple Alliance. Whatever the outcome of the events of the war, each of the two Powers will at the final settlement uphold the interests of the other as if they were her own.

(v) The General Staffs of the armies of the two countries will at all times keep in close touch with the object of jointly planning and carrying out the measures referred to above.

(vi) This convention shall remain in force for so long as the Triple Alliance exists and shall be renewable under the same conditions as the latter. (No. 47.)

Ribot again emphasized in this dispatch the necessity of arriving at an "early decision". But Russia did not intend to abandon the independent control of her political destiny. Alexander III went on a visit to Kiel and had an interview with the Kaiser. Poincaré remarks that the French Government did not always learn with entire exactitude the details of these conversations, which "remained somewhat of a mystery to them".[1] It is to be remembered that at that time the military convention had not yet been discussed, let alone signed.

Boisdeffre left Paris in advance of schedule time and reached St. Petersburg on August 1, 1892, when he at once called on the War Minister and the Chief of Staff, Obruchev. On the same evening, after a long conversation with the latter, he wrote that he "must at once report with regret that the situation is not so well advanced as we had reason to believe when I left Paris". The *Figaro* article "Marriage or Flirtation?" had provoked certain retorts in the Russian press and had altogether created a decidedly bad effect, some individuals quoting it as evidence in their suggestions to the Tsar that France was trying to force his hand. Boisdeffre had put forward the view that, so long as nothing definite was settled, Germany might be tempted to take high-handed action,[2] but Obruchev had replied that, on the contrary, the delays were all in favour of the maintenance of peace. He had opposed the mention of simultaneous mobilization, for that would involve defining the precise moment at which a mobilization can be said to have begun—a most delicate question. He had also objected strongly to the inclusion of the phrase "or of Germany alone", wishing to apply the same distinction to Austria. In the event of war with Austria, her chief enemy, Russia could not order a partial mobilization, but would mobilize completely. Lastly, the Russian Chief of Staff refused to fix a definite figure for the number of troops to be employed against Germany. Boisdeffre had gone away from this, his first interview, "with a distinct feeling of depression, and distinctly uneasy at my interlocutor's policy of reserve and evasion".

He was but at the beginning of his troubles, however. On the following day, August 2, 1892, he was received by the Minister of War, General Vannovsky, and the uneasiness he had felt the day before was confirmed and intensified. Although

---

[1] *Au service de la France*, I, p. 285.
[2] This was the gist of the *Figaro* article.

Montebello had reported on July 19th that the War Minister was definitely favourably inclined to the French views and that his attitude was such as to inspire the utmost confidence, he now said to Boisdeffre: "Why sign a military convention? Conventions signed and sealed in advance are never carried out. It is much better to have a 'gentlemen's agreement', based on verbal assurances only." The Emperor was very loath to agree to a signed compact, for fear of leakages. Vannovsky also pleaded that the collaboration of the Russian Foreign Minister was necessary, the question at issue being just as much a political as a military one; but Boisdeffre assured him that the political side could be regarded as settled, the whole thing being based on principles which had been formulated by de Giers, who "need not therefore be consulted again. Besides, he may be ill a long time, and it seems to me only natural that you should carry on the negotiations." This airy advice from the delegate of a Republic to an Imperial Minister of State is not without its piquancy.

Vannovsky then made a point of the "Emperor's known reluctance to enter into any further written obligations", for fear lest, if they were divulged, the resulting sensation might lead to war. He went on to refer to the frequent changes in the French Cabinets and to the constitutional dogma that a treaty was not binding on the French nation unless it had been ratified by the two Chambers. When, however, Boisdeffre, who was well aware of the Tsar's desire for complete secrecy, at once suggested that the treaty should be brought before Parliament, the Russian Minister "was loud in his protests, saying that there was nothing the Emperor feared more than an open sensation". In this light, a reduction to the minimum of Cabinet changes in France seemed to be demanded as a patriotic duty. Boisdeffre's mission seemed fated to end in failure. "The foregoing", he wrote, "summarizes in a very expurgated form the substance of the conversation. I have toned down certain features which strike me as almost indicative of ill will, sometimes nearly amounting to a desire to pick a quarrel."

The Tsar's feeling was that France "might be only seeking to obtain a treaty in order to publish it to the world, or at least parade it more or less openly, in either case involving him in the risk of war". Montebello therefore counselled extreme moderation and a special effort to prevent Boisdeffre from getting from Alexander III himself the next day an endorsement of the views that had been expressed by his Minister.

On August 4, 1892, the French Deputy Chief of Staff was invited to lunch with the Emperor and Empress, but the conversation, stiff with formality, was of no importance. (No. 50.) Three days later he saw Obruchev again, who asked him to be patient, apologized for his inability to discuss the second clause of the draft in the absence of de Giers, who was still unwell, but hinted that there was every hope of settling the whole matter satisfactorily. The chief point was to come to some agreement and then get the Emperor's verbal approval; "after that we might consider the question of signatures".

Boisdeffre reiterated with the utmost emphasis how dangerous all these delays were, that the Tsar's bare word was not sufficient guarantee for the French Government, and that it was essential for the convention, as finally agreed, to bear the signature of Ministers on both sides. In regard to the phrase "of the Triple Alliance, or of Germany alone", Obruchev refused to agree to the inclusion of the last four words, since from his point of view the Austrian army was the chief enemy. He also declined to fix a figure of 800,000 as the number of troops to be put into the field against Germany, and, finally, he insisted on the need for complete secrecy being specifically mentioned.

Negotiations seemed bound to end in a deadlock when suddenly, on August 8th, Boisdeffre found the Russian Minister "quite differently disposed, in fact entirely cordial". It was obvious that the financial and internal situation in Russia was

D

not unconnected with this change of attitude. Vannovsky was, however, still unwilling to agree to the inclusion of the words "or of Germany alone", being convinced that Russia would be attacked first of all by Austria in conjunction with Italy. Boisdeffre then put a written proposal before him, again pressed for a signed agreement, which the French Government regarded as a necessary and indispensable guarantee, and asked him to use his influence with the Tsar in support of the French proposals. The Russian Minister then said: "Now, there is one other thing that is worrying me, and that is: once you have got your signed convention, won't you be wanting to hurry things up and go to war?" Like the Tsar himself, his Ministers were obsessed with this fear. But Boisdeffre assured Vannovsky that the French Government was as pacifically inclined as the Emperor of Russia, adding that in France everyone was unanimous in approving of an alliance with Russia. "The sentiments of the whole nation in this respect are notorious, and guarantee the sincerity of the French assurances." The Russian Minister also expressed the fear lest the Germans might hasten to declare war when they knew that the agreement had been signed.

On August 9, 1892, Obruchev was definitely authorized to negotiate with Boisdeffre. The latter reported that he had every hope that the French draft would be adopted, with the exception of the clause regarding an attack by Germany alone, but that he feared that he would be unable to secure the signature of Ministers, since the Tsar would do nothing without de Giers, who was still unwell. Montebello suggested that it would be best to trust the Emperor's word and accept the delay in signing, so as not to jeopardize, by showing undue haste, the results that had been attained. Obruchev's advice was that the agreed draft should be signed in the first place by himself and Boisdeffre, as that would be the best means of ensuring that the Emperor gave his approval. (Nos. 53 and 58.)

On August 10, 1892, Boisdeffre notified Paris of the amended

wording. For the phrase "or of Germany alone" Obruchev
had insisted on substituting "or of one of its constituent
Powers", which would imply that France would be bound to
mobilize if Austria alone mobilized, even partially, but seemed
to conflict with the first clause in the draft, which stipulated
that France would only take part in the struggle at all if Russia
were attacked by Germany or by Austria with Germany's
support. (Nos. 56 and 57.) Ribot accepted the amendment,
although he would have preferred to leave France a free hand
in the event of Germany holding aloof.

Montebello suggested that Boisdeffre should be authorized
to sign the document on behalf of the French Government.
The Foreign Minister agreed, and submitted the proposal to
de Freycinet, who approved. "We have met with so many
difficulties of all sorts up to now that I fully appreciate his
impatience to get the matter over." (Nos. 47, 52, 62, and 65.)
He gave way also on the first clause, for fear of jeopardizing
the whole agreement, and expressed the belief that "we shall
soon be at the end of all our anxiety and trouble", unless
de Giers tried to hold up the settlement. He thanked Montebello for all that he had done, in company with Boisdeffre,
to ensure the success of "these wearisome negotiations".
(No. 68.)

The Tsar, however, still insisted on de Giers being consulted,
and sent Obruchev to Finland to discuss the matter with him.
He demanded a pledge of the strictest secrecy, and proposed,
in his fear of upsetting Germany, that if any of the details of
the convention were divulged, the whole agreement should be
null and void. He also requested, in order to avoid comment,
that Boisdeffre's stay should not be prolonged beyond the last
day of the manœuvres. (No. 67.)

In his final report, Boisdeffre stated that the Tsar had
expressed a desire, on August 15th, to insert an additional
clause providing for the cancellation of the agreement in the
event of France declaring war without provocation, but had

withdrawn the proposal on General Vannovsky's pointing out
that the treaty was designed to deal with a defensive war only.
The French Deputy Chief of Staff added: "The Russians are
everlastingly harping on the necessity for secrecy, and there
is a reason for this in addition to what I have already reported,
namely, *their need for concluding a treaty with Germany to get
favourable terms for the transport of grain.* This is essential if
it is to command a ready sale." The Russians further proposed
that, if a crisis should arise which France regarded as affecting
the national honour, such as the Schnaebelé case, she should
not declare war without first consulting the Tsar. The Russian
General Staff was desperately anxious to have another two
years of peace in order to complete the arming of the troops.
"What with the expenditure caused by the famine and the
cholera epidemic, they are certainly hardly in a position at
present to pursue any active policy."

The Tsar gave an audience to Boisdeffre on August 18, 1892,
and once more emphasized the necessity for maintaining
absolute secrecy. He was afraid that, if the convention were
brought up for discussion in the French Cabinet, it would
inevitably become public property, "in which case", he said,
"the treaty falls to the ground so far as I am concerned". The
French delegate asserted warmly that cancellation was unthinkable. "When a country unanimously desires an Alliance, it is
naturally inclined to jump to the conclusion on the slightest
evidence that its desire has been realized. The French nation,
so openly eager for a treaty of Alliance with Russia, would be
simply intolerant of any suggestion that the Cabinet were
unable to bring it to fruition." Alexander III then requested
that the French Government should at least keep the military
convention a secret. He was all for peace, and could see, for
his part, no war-clouds on the horizon. Moreover, it was
essential that Russia should complete the arming of her troops
and her strategic railways, and should recover from the famine
and cholera. "In short", he concluded, "it is our duty to

assume that peace will last a long time yet. Let us hope it will."
On the question of mobilization being raised, Boisdeffre pointed
out that *"to mobilize is to declare war, to force one's neighbours
to follow suit. Mobilization necessarily entails the strategic movements of troops and their concentration."*[1] Otherwise, to allow a
million men to be mobilized along one's frontiers without
simultaneously doing likewise would be to cut off all possibility
of taking active steps later on, would be, in fact, comparable
to the position of a man who, having a revolver in his pocket,
allows another man to cock his and put it to his head without
taking out his own. "That is my view of the matter, too",
replied the Tsar.

At this point in his report, Boisdeffre saw fit to make a
strange observation, which was without any foundation, but
which sheds a strong light on his own outlook: *"I have a
feeling that, although the Emperor may genuinely desire peace,
he is not particularly alarmed at the idea of war, especially with
the support of France."* This remark seems to have been brought
in to allay the qualms of the French statesmen. What else could
have been the object? In any case, it is amazing to hear words
like these from a man who, like his superiors, was always
talking of nothing but peace. (No. 71.)

As Alexander III had now approved the whole of the convention in principle, all that remained was for the two Governments to ratify it formally. Boisdeffre's mission was ended.
He signed the draft convention, of which the following was the
wording finally adopted:

France and Russia, being alike animated by a sincere desire to preserve
peace, and having no other object than to provide against the eventualities of a defensive war forced upon either of them by an attack by
the armed forces of the Triple Alliance, have agreed to the following
arrangements, viz.:

---

[1] The Russian Chief of Staff was also quite clear that the mobilization
of France and Russia would be followed immediately by active steps, by
warlike acts, "would be, in short, indistinguishable from an *attack*".
(No. 42.)

(i) If France is attacked by Germany or by Italy with Germany's support, Russia will bring all her available forces to bear against Germany. If Russia is attacked by Germany or by Austria with Germany's support, France will bring all her available forces to bear against Germany.

(ii) In the event of the mobilization of the armed forces of the Triple Alliance, or of one of its constituent Powers, France and Russia will, immediately the news reaches them and without waiting to consult together, forthwith and simultaneously mobilize the whole of their forces and move them as near as possible to the frontiers.

(iii) The number of troops available to be placed in the field against Germany will be 1,300,000 by France and from 700,000 to 800,000 by Russia. These troops will proceed to launch a vigorous and determined offensive, so that Germany will be forced to give battle in the East and West simultaneously.

(iv) The General Staffs of the armies of the two countries will at all times keep in close touch with the object of jointly planning and carrying out the measures referred to above.[1]

They will keep each other informed in peace-time of all particulars regarding the armies of the Triple Alliance that are now available or may hereafter come to their knowledge.

They will investigate and agree in advance on the best ways and means of keeping in touch with each other in war-time.

(v) France and Russia will not conclude peace separately.

(vi) This convention shall remain in force for so long as the Triple Alliance exists.

(vii) All the foregoing clauses shall be kept strictly secret.

Montebello wrote on August 19, 1892, to Ribot with great satisfaction: "We have reached a result which exceeds our expectations, and in a surprisingly short space of time. I did not dare to hope for as much as this." (No. 70.)

The conclusion of the negotiations now seemed to be in sight, when de Freycinet announced that he contemplated making certain suggestions in regard to the wording of some of the clauses. (No. 73.) At the same time Ribot wrote to Montebello with reference to the second clause:

[1] The French and Russian Chiefs of Staff subsequently decided (on August 31, 1911) that the words "defensive war" could not be interpreted in the sense of "war to be conducted defensively", and placed on record the absolute necessity of the two armies taking the offensive simultaneously and vigorously. This point was confirmed in 1912 and 1913 (*Livre Noir*, pp. 419–437).

There seems to be no doubt that, in the mind of the negotiators, the text was only intended to cover the case of a general mobilization on the part of the Triple Alliance or of one of its constituent Powers, which would constitute a threat of aggression against either Russia or France. If, for instance, some incident occurred in the Balkans which led Austria to take certain precautionary measures, such as mobilizing two or three army corps, it would obviously be unnecessary and contrary to our joint interests to insist on France immediately moving the whole of her forces as near as possible to the frontier. It is only in the event of Germany or Austria or Italy, even if it be only one of them, proceeding to mobilize the *whole* of their forces that Russia and France would be justified in placing all their available forces on a war footing forthwith and without waiting to consult together. Such a step would be fraught with such grave consequences that every precaution must be taken to eliminate any ambiguity in the clause in question.

He consequently proposed, after consulting Boisdeffre, to re-word the clause as follows:

In the event of the Triple Alliance or one of its constituent Powers ordering a *general* mobilization of its armed forces, France and Russia will, etc. etc.

Further, de Freycinet pressed for the alteration of the number of available troops to be placed in the field by France against Germany from 1,300,000 to "from 1,200,000 to 1,300,000".

To ensure secrecy without violating the Constitution, an ingenious line of argument was adopted. It was a matter of principle with the President of the Republic that he could not conclude a *secret* treaty, i.e. one which had to be concealed from Parliament, but the Tsar's wishes could be met and the scruples of President Carnot respected if clause vii were worded as follows: "The foregoing clauses shall only be divulged by and with the consent of both parties."

Ribot next took over from the Tsar his bugbear of the danger of French ministerial changes, and used it as an argument in the opposite sense, to enforce the need for a prompt and definite settlement of the convention:

Should we not be obliged to inform the members of the new Ministry of the state of the negotiations? Is it not quite enough to have to bring the draft agreement before our present colleagues at an early meeting of the Cabinet and to reply to the objections which one or another of them may raise? How can we hope to keep the thing a strict secret if it drags on for several more months? . . . To leave the matter where it is without a definite conclusion after having got so far would be a colossal blunder. The Emperor must realize this, if only his attention is once drawn to the point . . . We cannot remain where we are. (No. 75.)

Obruchev, somewhat taken aback by these last-minute amendments,[1] accepted the first, regarding general mobilization (at the same time putting on record his conviction that Austria would never stop at partial mobilization), and also the modification in the number of the French troops, but would not agree to eliminate the word "secret", saying that "if the Tsar had had his way, he would only have negotiated with one man, and that without telling anyone else". The Russian insistence on this word was somewhat surprising, as the proposed amendment would have had the same effect in ensuring secrecy, contrary to the spirit of the French Constitution. Ribot wrote to Montebello that it was only a form of words after all, as everyone was quite clear that the military clauses would be kept secret. President Carnot's scruples about entering into a secret agreement only related to the political side. (No. 77.)

On September 5, 1892, the French Foreign Minister had an interview with de Giers at Aix-les-Bains. His attitude was that Europe was at peace, that Germany was just as pacifically minded as Russia herself, and that he had no intention of looking for trouble in the Balkans. "The Emperor", he said,

has come to the definite conclusion that it would not be to the interest of Russia to pursue an active policy in the Near East. He was not always so prudent. When he was only a Grand Duke he was at the head of the forward movement, sending Russian agents into Roumania, Bulgaria, and so on. He now recognizes that we sometimes blundered,

---

[1] Montebello pointed out later that the alterations were particularly unwarranted, since the final draft was actually based on the original French note of March 1892.

that we were too eager and also too prone to dictate to the minor nations whom we had helped to liberate themselves. Russia's hand was sometimes heavy and clumsy. Rest assured that we are not now disposed to stir up any further complications, but are sincerely animated with a desire for peace. You can absolutely rely on the Emperor in this.

Ribot concluded that "we shall have to reconcile ourselves to taking our pace from the Emperor. We may consider the convention as settled, since he has given his word. . . . It is annoying not to be able to finish it off once and for all, but I agree with you that it would not do to show too much impatience." (No. 79.) But it was not long before his patience gave out. On October 31st he wrote to de Giers to remind him of the necessity of signing the convention, as "too long a delay might give rise to serious difficulties". He went back to the argument, which he seemed to regard as a cogent one, of the risk of leakage through a change of government. "Can we be sure that our successors would be prepared to accept the agreement in all its details, and that it would not be necessary to reopen negotiations on all these delicate matters? And again, how risky it will be from the point of view of secrecy, which we both regard as indispensable, if we have to bring the matter up again for discussion at a Cabinet meeting." By thus harping on the danger of leakage—the Russian Government's chief fear—Ribot was running the risk of seeing the latter back out of the convention altogether, but he knew very well that, in the state the Russian finances were in, the Tsar could not possibly venture to do that. This is one of the most striking instances of the decisive influence of the French financial backing of Russia, which was at the bottom of the military convention, as it had been of the 1891 Agreement.

Ribot asserted that the proposed amendments did not in any way affect the substance of the convention, and had in fact been recommended by Obruchev himself to Vannovsky, and was sure it would be the easiest thing in the world to settle the whole matter in a few moments. "You will, no doubt,

agree with me that it would be a pity not to bring it to a conclusion." (No. 80.) On November 5, 1892, de Giers replied
from Monte Carlo that he had not yet resumed his duties as
Foreign Minister and could not, therefore, in his present
circumstances, pursue the discussions with Montebello on the
subject of the convention. "Moreover", he added, "events are
not likely to take us unawares, and it will be perfectly simple
when the time comes to reach a definite agreement on details,
provided, of course, that the Entente so happily established
between our two countries still persists." (No. 81.) This vague
letter made it clear that the convention would not be signed
just yet, and a distinctly cooler tone entered into Franco-
Russian diplomatic relations and lasted for several months.
The Panama scandals and the charges levelled against Mohrenheim seem to have made a considerable impression on
Alexander III, who, according to de Giers, was reluctant to
"ally himself with a nation so eager for a revenge which had
no interest for Russia".

In November the Cesarevich paid a visit to Vienna, where
he was cordially received by Francis Joseph, who later, in
1893, also gave a warm welcome to de Giers. In January 1893
the Cesarevich visited Berlin, where the Kaiser took pains to
persuade him of the peaceful intentions of the Triple Alliance,
and made the most of the Panama scandals to set him against
France. It almost seemed as if another *rapprochement* between
Russia, Germany and Austria were taking shape.[1] The "Yellow
Book", in any case, contains no documents of dates between
November 5, 1892, and May 20, 1893. On the latter date
Montebello wrote to Develle, who had taken Ribot's place at
the Quai d'Orsay on the fall of the de Freycinet Ministry in
January, pointing out the need for being prepared in case
Russia should show any sign of agreeing to embody the draft
signed by Boisdeffre and Obruchev in an official convention.
Although "there are no grounds at present for reopening the

[1] Cf. Langer, in the *Slavonic Review* for June 1925, pp. 93–94.

negotiations with a view to giving them final shape", and in fact he saw no chance of reopening them, the ambassador expressed his regret at the amendments suggested by de Frey-cinet and Ribot as calculated to delay the ratification still further, and pressed for their reconsideration. (No. 82.)

Gradually the course of events began to take a direction more favourable to France. Mohrenheim was publicly exon-erated by Ribot, the Panama crisis blew over, Russo-German economic relations grew strained, the negotiations for a com-mercial treaty fell through, and, lastly, the German Govern-ment introduced in the Reichstag a new Military Service Bill increasing the army by 60,000 men, which, at first rejected, was passed in July by a fresh Reichstag. At this juncture, Develle, making use of Hansen as an intermediary, notified the Russian Government that France would welcome a visit from a Russian Battle Squadron, in return for the Kronstadt reception,[1] and on June 11, 1893, a favourable reply was received, leaving the date open. This was fixed in August, with the request that the news should receive as little publicity as possible.[2]

Montebello was concerned to seize the earliest opportunity that offered of pressing for the definite confirmation of the draft convention. On August 17, 1893, at his suggestion, Develle took the opening afforded by the new German Military Service Act and forwarded a note prepared by Miribel for transmission to the Tsar, drawing attention to the substantial increase in the German army, in the hope that Alexander III's reaction to the news would induce him to ratify the convention. The note was submitted to the Tsar by de Giers, after having been touched up by Montebello. (Nos. 84–88.) Meanwhile urgent representations were being made to the Tsar, both by

[1] Hansen, pp. 157–159.
[2] The Russian Squadron, under the orders of Admiral Avelan, was composed of the battleship *Imperator Nicholas I*, the cruisers *Admiral Nashimov* and *Pamyat-Azova*, and the scouts *Teretz* and *Rynda*. It arrived at Toulon on October 13, 1893.

his confidential advisers and Ministers, who were favourably impressed with French policy, and by "more or less indirect agents of the Republic", to the effect that it was high time to take advantage of the cordial good-will manifested by France towards Russia by concluding "if not an offensive Alliance, at least a definite agreement which would form an effective insurance against war".[1] Added to this, France's action in Siam in July 1893, which provoked serious differences with Great Britain, showed the Emperor that he could rely on French co-operation in Asia, where Russia's persistent penetration since 1879 had brought her into conflict with British interests. The visit of a British squadron to Italy enhanced the risk of a Quadruple Alliance, and, finally, the financial support of France in the precarious state of the Russian Treasury was of prime importance. All these considerations, taken together, removed the last remaining hesitations of the Russian Government, for it became clear that, without France, Russia would be isolated.

The festivities at Toulon and Paris also impressed the Tsar favourably, although the French *chargé d'affaires*, de Vauvineux, spoke with regret of "the extravagant raptures which certain sections of the public saw fit to indulge in and which might easily have been turned to ridicule in Russian eyes". (No. 89.)

The French Government now began to get really impatient. According to Paléologue, Casimir-Périer expressed the opinion that, from the points of view of self-interest and self-respect alike, France could not wait any longer for a decision on the part of Russia. It was an unheard-of thing that negotiations of such importance should remain in abeyance for sixteen months. "I am not prepared", he said, "to put up with such treatment. If the Tsar is no longer in favour of an Alliance with France, let him say so, and we will adapt our policy accordingly." He instructed the French ambassador to request an audience and

[1] Debidour, p. 189.

persuade the Tsar to make some definite statement. Montebello, however, was insistent that Russia ought to be left to
take the initiative in these concluding stages of the negotiations.[1] He returned to Russia, and an exchange of decorations
took place, the Grand Cross of the Legion of Honour being
conferred on the Grand-Duke Paul, the Tsar's brother, and
the Order of St. Andrew on the French ambassador, to whom
the Emperor stated that he was now fully reassured as regards
the strength of the idea of "*revanche*" in France. Finally, on
December 30, 1893, Montebello was able to report to Casimir-
Périer that the draft military convention had been approved.
(Nos. 90 and 91.)

Alexander III had been waiting, before agreeing to the
convention, until France had shown herself ready to stand up
to Great Britain and to abandon the idea of a war of revenge
against Germany. De Giers made the following statement in
October to the Danish Minister:

We have entered into an *entente* with France, but with a pacifically
minded France. We have but one aim—peace, lasting peace. I am well
aware that behind these manifestations of joy and enthusiasm for
Russia the idea of revenge is still lurking. But this popular aspiration
finds no echo in the entirely pacific policies of the two Governments.
. . . You may rest assured that we have made it perfectly plain to
the French that the Entente must be an Entente of peace or no
Entente at all.

Von Werder, the German ambassador at St. Petersburg,
reported that, in his view, the Franco-Russian Entente was a
danger to the peace of the world and might well produce
serious political complications, and that in the future, when
Alexander III and de Giers were no longer in control, the
agreement would have awkward repercussions. The German
Government, however, showed no sign of uneasiness. The
English press seemed chiefly to fear that Russia would
endeavour to take advantage of her Entente with France to

---

[1] Paléologue, *La Russie des Tsars pendant la grande guerre*, Vol. II,
pp. 128–130.

force the Straits and compel Great Britain to evacuate Egypt.[1]

From the documents published in the "Yellow Book", it is clear that the French Government was originally responsible, not only for the form and the precision of the 1891 agreement, but also for the very idea of the military convention, as well as for the naval visits to Kronstadt and Toulon and the bestowal of the Order of St. Andrew on President Carnot. In both cases, the agreement as well as the convention, it was the French Government who proposed the basis and drafted the wording, insisting always on pledges which the Russian Government was at pains to evade. It was Ribot and de Freycinet, assisted by Boisdeffre and Montebello, who emphasized the necessity of a military convention, returning incessantly to the charge when the Russians adopted every possible device of procrastination, and who finally succeeded, by dint of unremitting pressure, in forcing it through after more than two years of laborious negotiations, which at one time nearly fell to the ground, and after making full use, it is fairly easy to guess, of the most varied forms of influence, especially that of financial support, with which Russia could not dispense.

There are numerous and important gaps in the French "Yellow Book". For instance, it does not contain

(a) Any correspondence prior to August 24, 1890, while the earliest *pourparlers* go back to 1886–1887;

(b) Any dispatches between August 24, 1890, and March 9, 1891, or between the latter date and July 18, 1891;

(c) Laboulaye's dispatch on Franco-Russian relations, referred to by Ribot on July 29, 1891;

(d) The telegram mentioned by Ribot in his dispatch of July 9, 1892 (No. 40);

[1] Aehrenthal to Kalnocky, December 20 and 21, 1893 (Vienna Archives), quoted by W. L. Langer in the *Slavonic Review* for June 1925, p. 100. *Die Grosse Politik*, VII, p. 254 (Werner to Caprivi, November 27, 1893), and the whole of Chapter XLVII, pp. 191 to 259.

(e) Montebello's replies to Ribot's dispatches of July 22nd and 28th (Nos. 45 and 47);

(f) The correspondence between Montebello and the French Foreign Minister from September 8, 1892, to May 20, 1895;

(g) Develle's answers to Montebello's dispatches of May 20, June 27, and July 29, 1893.

Moreover, there is no guarantee that such documents as have been vouchsafed to us (as a result of the Russian Revolution) have been published in full without cuts or touchings-up. It would be necessary to check them by the originals, which will be impossible until the archives of the Foreign Ministry are thrown open, as has been done in Russia and Germany. It is, moreover, very doubtful whether they will ever be thrown open completely in France, so long as the policy followed hitherto is allowed to continue unchanged. Throughout the documents, too, no mention is made of the financial factor which, nevertheless, is the whole explanation of the abrupt changes of attitude on the part of the Russians and dominates the situation throughout, playing as it did an outstanding part in the minds of all those engaged in the negotiations. It is, in fact, essential to bear this constantly in mind to follow what is said, written, and debated.

The question arises, why should so much haste have been displayed to conclude this convention at a time when the Tsar and his Ministers were convinced of Germany's peaceable intentions, and when the representatives of France only pretended to believe in an immediate danger of war which did not in fact exist? The Russians had no real sympathy for the Republic, which stood for democracy and disestablishment. They were, moreover, averse to the idea of a military convention for fear of offending Germany, whose good will was necessary economically, and of provoking a war, which was the last thing Russia wanted. Yet they had to swallow this convention by reason, primarily, of the lamentable state of their finances, and, secondly, of their need, isolated in Europe as they were, of French support in Asia against Great Britain, their chief enemy along with Austria. They would have preferred to confine the Entente to a vague expression of general principles which would have left them free to intervene only with their eyes open, after considering all the circumstances. Their aim was to enlist the support of France against Great Britain without committing themselves to any hostility to Germany, for they were obsessed, as appears at every moment, by the fear of being dragged into a war of revenge.[1] At the eleventh hour, as mentioned earlier in this chapter, the Tsar was anxious to stipulate that the convention should be null and void in the event of aggression on the part of France. But the French Government was out for bigger game, and was determined, with the bait of French financial support, to secure a proper convention in black and white, pledging Russia in unequivocal terms to take part in war with Germany when it came.

Obviously the Tsar was afraid of France developing an aggressive attitude towards Germany, for he had no reason to be on bad terms with Austria, having abandoned his designs on Constantinople and in the Balkans.

Notwithstanding Boisdeffre's strange remark,[2] the French Government of the day were sincerely animated with a desire for peace. They had no desire to go to war if Austria should merely mobilize two or three Army Corps for a Balkan expedition, providing Germany made no move. In a spirit very different from that which was to inspire Delcassé in 1899, they suggested that the convention should have the same duration

---

[1] In spite of this, André Mévil, of the *Echo de Paris*, in his book *La Paix est malade* (1914), asserted that "to Alexander III's mind, the Franco-Russian Alliance represented a weapon pointed constantly at Germany, who remained the chief enemy in Europe of both the allied Powers" (p. 101). Cf. also General Bonnal, in *Paris Journal* of February 1, 1911.

[2] See page 53.

as the Triple Alliance, and were quite satisfied that the Russian aims on Constantinople should be abandoned, whereas in 1912–1913 these same aims were encouraged by the French governing class, who were decidedly disconcerted when they were definitely abandoned in 1917 as a result of the Revolution.

The main object of the treaties of 1891–1893 seems to have been to prevent an unprovoked attack on the part of the Triple Alliance. As France was bound to come to the assistance of her ally if the latter was attacked by Germany, Alfred Fabre-Luce, in his striking book *La Victoire*, has suggested that she might have been automatically obliged to intervene in the event of an attack by Russia on Austria provoking a counter-attack from Germany. In our view the agreement was not susceptible of this interpretation. The preamble to the convention assumed that it only entered into force in the event of a defensive war provoked by an attack from the Triple Alliance. Moreover, the military convention was inseparable from the 1891 agreement, of which it was merely the corollary and supplement. Now the agreement stated specifically: "in the event of peace being actually endangered, more especially if one of the two high contracting parties is threatened with aggression, the two parties agree", etc. etc. This wording, which explicitly covered the case of one of the two countries being threatened with aggression, excluded the contingency of an unprovoked attack by Russia on Austria, in which case France would have been entitled, in the spirit of the pact, to refuse to intervene, just as Russia would have been free to remain neutral if her ally had delivered an attack on Italy which had provoked a counter-attack from Germany.

Any other interpretation would be at variance both with the text and with the intentions of the signatories, whose chief concern, on the Russian side, was to avoid a war provoked by France. The convention could not be separated—French statesmen have been guilty of forgetting this—either from the agreement or from the declared intentions of the negotiators;

E

otherwise there was a risk of violating both their expressed wishes and the pact itself, for to make no distinction as regards the original aggression would have transformed the defensive treaty into a definite instrument of offensive policy. In the same way, it imposed no obligation on France, in the event of war between Austria and Serbia, to intervene on the side of Russia if Russia should see fit to go to the support of her fellow-Slavs in the Balkans. On the contrary, it is as clear as daylight that the convention only applied if one of the two countries was threatened with aggression, and there was nowhere any provision specifying that Russia was obliged to support Serbia in a war with Austria. In fact, the contrary was generally assumed, since de Giers of his own accord had announced that Russia had "abandoned her aims on Constantinople" and that he was not in favour of going to war over purely Balkan questions. On the other hand, Ribot was anxious that France should retain a free hand if Germany were not involved.

Furthermore, the agreement by implication prohibited either of the two parties from mobilizing before the enemy had done so. There was a loophole here, certainly, in the fact that even a partial mobilization by Austria might involve mobilization by France, and Ribot, as we have seen, endeavoured at the last moment to insert in the draft a specific reference to the *general* mobilization of the Dual Monarchy. But the alternatives are clear: either Austria would have been mobilizing against the Balkan nations, in which case France would not have been concerned, or else she would have been planning an unprovoked attack on Russia before the latter had mobilized, in which case it would have been perfectly natural for France to take all steps to assist her ally. Moreover, as a matter of actual fact, mobilization by Austria in 1909, and again in 1912–1913, did not produce any corresponding measures on the part of France.[1]

---

[1] This was in accordance with decisions at joint military conferences held between 1906 and 1913; vide *Livre Noir*, II, pp. 420–437.

The real peril lay in the secrecy in which the pact was shrouded, which actually allowed statesmen, unchecked by any informed criticism, or even by any indiscreet inquiry, to place their own interpretations upon it—interpretations of a most misleading character and entirely contrary to the letter and the spirit of the original treaty. It should, incidentally, be noted that the French Government was just as intent on keeping the matter dark as the Russian Government. It was the former that first proposed that the military convention should be kept secret, and, in the discussions on this point at the end of 1892, General Obruchev did not seem to grasp that the French Minister was merely endeavouring to circumvent the difficulty by a drafting expedient, but did not intend any more than he himself did to run the risk of having the essential clauses made public property. After the death of Alexander III, the French Government never made any serious effort to get the ban of secrecy lifted. The pledge of secrecy demanded by Delcassé for the modification introduced at his suggestion in 1899 was of course another and even more serious thing.

At intervals Ribot would get up in Parliament and deliver himself oracularly and dogmatically of his version of the Alliance without anyone being in a position to question his assertions. Thus on two separate occasions, in the Chamber of Deputies on January 23, 1903, and in the Senate on April 6, 1911, he affirmed that in the period 1891–1893 the Tsar had made *offers* to France, proposals that the French Government had accepted, allowing his hearers, who had been kept in ignorance of the facts, to assume that Russia had suggested both the 1891 agreement and the convention of 1893. He was even then giving to the Alliance a sense which had never been contemplated by its signatories.

This fundamental blemish of secrecy permanently prevented the French people from discussing the precise meaning of the agreement, from expressing doubts as to the interpretations of its clauses, from contributing their own suggestions, from keeping their rulers on the alert—in short, from watching the clearly defined interests of the nation. They were obliged to follow blindly in the wake of the sacred oracles, which were sometimes controlled by questionable forces and which, secure from contradiction, could involve the country in all kinds of risks with impunity.

With treaties even more than with constitutions, it is fatal to adhere to the letter, which may sometimes lead to complete stultification, and it is essential to investigate the spirit in which they were negotiated and concluded. In 1891–1893 the motive underlying the Franco-Russian pact was the maintenance of peace, and all depended on the way in which the governing classes would carry it out and the end which they would make it subserve. For any treaty, even of the most defensive nature, can be read in different ways, according to whether the statesmen whose duty it is to put it into effect are determined to use it for purposes of peace or willing to allow it to lead to war. In 1891–1893 the Tsar's object was, firstly, to procure the funds necessary to restore his shattered finances, and, secondly, to prevent France, in pursuit of her peaceable and moderate aims, from being crushed or weakened. It is beyond a doubt that, if any threat of a Franco-German war had arisen from some dispute over colonies, such as Dahomey, which France was then engaged in conquering, he would have recoiled in horror. It is a significant fact that the word "Alliance" was never officially used by Ribot until after Alexander III was dead, and even then only in vague terms which left it doubtful whether a treaty really existed.[1]

We shall see in a later chapter how the whole aim and scope of the Alliance were modified by the supplementary declaration of 1899, and how the partisans of the new forward policy isolated the military convention from the 1891 agreement with

[1] "We have linked the interests of France with those of another great nation", said Ribot in the Chamber of Deputies on June 10, 1895; "we have done this to safeguard the peace of Europe and to maintain the Balance of Power."

a view to its being applied in all circumstances, even if the original provocation were to come from Russia, and hence gave Russia assurances of unconditional support from France, in a spirit definitely opposed to that in which the pact of 1891–1893 was negotiated and signed.

From the outset the attitude adopted by the French Government was a mistaken one and could not fail to produce disastrous effects. Whereas Tsarism had approached France under the spur of necessity, French statesmen had the bad taste to receive it with a profusion of servile flattery, and set out to persuade that tottering empire that the support of its army was a vital need for France. They hailed the Tsar as a saviour, suggested visits from his navy, and then represented these as spontaneous acts of graciousness and so forth. Worse still, they led the public to believe that this Alliance, which was based on a recognition of the European *status quo*, would have as its fruit the return of Alsace-Lorraine.

Under such conditions all equality between the two parties to the contract disappeared, and they became patron and dependent. This fundamental defect vitiated the Alliance from its inception and was fatal to its growth. Both French public opinion and the Tsar's own Government gained a false impression of the strength of the Russian Empire, and nothing was done to render it efficient. France sent her gold without real security and without participation in control, and Russia was enabled to put off from day to day that salutary internal reformation which might have restored her to vigour. For France, instead of allowing her complete freedom of action in foreign affairs, as her statesmen claimed, the Alliance meant, on the contrary, a very definite subordination to Tsarist interests.

This pernicious attitude rendered it incumbent upon the leaders of the nation to underestimate the resources of France in order to magnify their achievement and emphasize the necessity of the Alliance. Jaurès demonstrated very clearly what a blunder it had been to exaggerate the benefits of the Alliance to such a degree that it was made to seem that France could hardly breathe apart from this symbiosis, which should have been a commensalism of mutual advantage. When, in 1903, Paul Deschanel, in a public speech, said that Russia had brought back the warmth of life into the heart of France with her loyal embrace, and when Ribot contrasted the "peace of humiliation the country had known up to the time of the Franco-Russian Agreement with the peace of self-respect which it had enjoyed ever since", the Socialist orator ventured to inquire whether the *rigor* of cold or of death had actually seized upon the heart of the nation to that degree, and he felt bound to remind those two great patriots that, between 1870 and 1892, France had succeeded, without humiliation, without panic, and without despair, in reconstructing her finances and her army, in consolidating her Republican liberties, and in building up a vast colonial dominion—all this during a most difficult period when everything had to be started afresh and refashioned, and "the Alliance which was said to have been our salvation had in fact supervened after we had demonstrated that we were capable of saving ourselves".

The mistake made by the French Government, from 1890 onwards, was to regard Russia, in spite of the warnings of experts, as a modern Western Power, whereas Tsarism was an Asiatic growth, was not even an efficient autocracy, and had for long stood in need of thoroughgoing reform to bring it up to the standard of the major European nations and to be able to meet them on an equal footing in the event of war.

# CHAPTER IV

## HONEYMOON (1893–1898)

THE welcome given to the Russian sailors in October 1893, first at Toulon and more especially later in Paris, was unparalleled in its enthusiasm. A brief résumé of the chief press comments and of the statements of the most prominent public men will show the degree of emotional excitement aroused among the French people at the time. The *Journal des Débats* asserted that the ardent mutual attachment of the two nations arose not merely from harmony of political interests, but also from a distinct similarity of racial characteristics between the two peoples, who had gradually grown to think and feel alike on many important points. "The genius of the Slav race has opened its heart to us; and we have responded with comprehension and with love." (October 13, 1893.) The *Echo de Paris* argued that hatred of the Teuton was "perhaps stronger among the Russians than among ourselves, and of older growth". (October 19th.) Paul de Cassagnac, in the *Autorité*, recognized that, notwithstanding glaring divergencies in the customs, traditions, and principles of the two peoples, "events have drawn them together with irresistible force, and heart has called to heart". (October 18th.) Hector Depasse wrote in all seriousness that there was in Russia "an active, fertile public opinion which finds free expression. The Emperor takes pains to imbibe and study this public opinion, and ruler and ruled are as one mind."[1] Professor George Duruy, of the *École Polytechnique*, went so far as to exclaim: "All honour to our press, which has spread throughout the land the true picture of the great Russian nation."[2]

The *revanche* party took no trouble to conceal their real thoughts. Cassagnac, describing the unprecedented infatuation of the French public for the Russians, wrote:

---

[1] *République Française*, October 30, 1893.　　[2] *Figaro,* November 4th.

Not even the leaders of a victorious army or the representatives of a nation which had saved us from destruction could have been acclaimed with greater unanimity. And the sole cause of this fervour is that inextinguishable hatred of Germany which impelled us to declare war in 1870. . . . In the Russian Alliance our patriotism sees a vision of the future with its revenges, and is gloating over it in advance.[1]

And it would be a mistake to imagine that vapourings of this description were only turned out by extravagant individuals like the Bonapartist writer just quoted. Alfred Rambaud, who became Minister of Education in the Méline Government, had written some weeks earlier:

Within a measurable time, sooner or later, but with inexorable certainty, Germany will reach a stage when she will be unable, both from the financial and the military point of view, to maintain her hegemony, and then the day of reparation will dawn. France has only Alsace-Lorraine to demand from her; but the claims of our neighbours beyond the Vistula may perhaps be more exacting. The racial consciousness of the Slavs, so long repressed by the German race, has reawakened. . . . The period of the *Drang nach Osten* is over for Germany. The turn of the tide, the *Drang nach Westen* of the Slav nations, has begun.[2]

Thereupon the amazing notion began to spread, even in the Radical press, that after these festivities the Alliance was no longer a secret, that Russia and France had concluded an open covenant over the heads of the statesmen and diplomatists, and that, for the future, written agreements and treaty clauses were of minor importance. Public rejoicings, popular enthusiasm, must surely remove the scruples and dissipate the fears of the most timorous. Clemenceau, the fiery Radical, who had just been defeated at the polls as a result of the Panama scandals, bluntly asserted in *Justice*:

This is not one of those secret treaties, such as nations like the Triple Alliance contract. No, it is an open-hearted covenant, an ingenuous understanding, above-board, *coram populo*, which masks no rash dreams, no reckless designs, no traps for any third party. This is

---

[1] *Autorité*, October 25th. See also the article entitled "L'Ennemi" in the *Petit Journal* of October 28th.    [2] *Revue Bleue*, October 7, 1893.

diplomacy in the light of day, a little boisterous perhaps, but in its very simplicity and candour unsubject to the errors and dangers to which the other kind of diplomacy is exposed. (October 15th.)

Flourens, the ex-Foreign Minister, asserted with imperturbable gravity:

This is an Alliance concluded in an atmosphere far removed from the misty formulae of diplomatic protocols, from the stealthiness of Foreign Office procedure, couched in language of simple grandeur, each word of which tells and hits the mark. It is an Alliance between two great nations, each the mistress of her own destiny, with nothing to conceal. This is open, sincere, *plein-air* diplomacy, free from guile, with all its cards on the table. The aims of the Tsar, the embodiment of the will of the Russian people, have converged with those of the French nation, and we have formed ties that nothing can now dissolve. . . . War has become impossible. The Franco-Russian Alliance means the final and lasting triumph of liberal ideals throughout Europe, and a checkmate to all hopes of a revival of Reaction. . . . For the Slav peoples it heralds the dawn of an era of progressive emancipation and peaceful development along the paths of civilization and freedom.[1]

George Duruy tried to go one better:

The Franco-Russian Alliance has one absolutely novel, unique feature: it is not the result of the schemings of official diplomacy. . . . This Alliance can fitly be termed a triumph for popular diplomacy. Statesmen rejected it. Thinkers dreamed of it. The people have achieved it.[2]

In Conservative quarters the Alliance was hailed with joy as holding out an unexpected chance of rehabilitation. The party fortunes were then at a low ebb, the 1893 election having brought into Parliament no less than fifty Socialist deputies, led by Jaurès, Guesde, Millerand, Viviani, and Rouanet. The Conservatives looked to the Alliance to cure France of all the diseases that the Republic had brought her. J. Delafosse wrote in *Figaro*: "We owe a great deal to the Tsar, who at the present

---

[1] *Le Journal*, October 30, 1893. See also Henri des Houx's article in the *Matin* for October 31st: "The Emperor of Russia has placed the French people in their true and proper rank—the rank of sovereign."

[2] *Figaro*, November 4th.

moment is virtually our ruler." France had to thank him for the reappearance in her people of qualities such as discipline, good manners, self-respect, decency, harmony, justice, and even piety. In short, the Alliance implied a rigid reorganization of her material and moral resources which could be summed up in the single word: Order. It was this virtue in all its aspects that had been clearly endangered by the revolutionary policy of the country, and the swing of the pendulum was overdue. "The Tsar", Delafosse added, "has signed a treaty of Alliance with France direct, over the heads of our political leaders and the Government—a treaty deposited in the very heart of the nation." (October 28, 1893.) Piou claimed that the Franco-Russian Entente was a result of Vatican policy, and added: "It is high time that our rulers grasped that religious peace is the *sine qua non* of France's good reputation and the only guarantee of her influence abroad. Rome is the pivot of our foreign policy."[1] Finally, Bishop Gouthe-Soulard, who had recently attained some notoriety as the result of an impertinent letter he had addressed to Fallières, the Minister of Public Worship, drew attention to the fact that the clergy had played a large part in all the celebrations, together with the chief civil authorities, and had been the object of the most respectful courtesy, and asserted that the festivities had had the effect of bringing the name of God into prominence before the eyes of the whole official world. "France is a Catholic country, and her spirit cannot be rightly understood if this fact is forgotten." He then proceeded to denounce the scholastic profession as tools in the hands of fanatical local Governors, gave expression to his conviction that the decision to laicize the hospitals would have to be revised, and demanded the exemption from military service of all seminary students.[2]

An anti-parliamentary campaign began to take shape. The man in the street, said the *Echo de Paris*, had not even troubled to wonder what his representatives were doing. He felt that

---

[1] *Figaro*, November 13th.          [2] Ibid., November 6, 1893.

some big event was happening without their co-operation, and
that they would quite probably only have placed obstacles in
its way. "The best qualities of our race suffer eclipse in the
polling-booth, and are not much more in evidence in Parliament." (October 26th.) The leading newspapers and the politicians of the Right and Centre, supported by the Church and
the Services, cleverly exploited the idea of a German Peril
and the hopes of recovering the lost provinces in the interests
of sheer reaction, political and social. The country must show
a bearing worthy of the ally of the mighty Emperor who was
graciously offering his friendship. The Tsar must not be
estranged by any radical measures; internal dissensions must
cease; political quarrels must be patched up, and all this
mania for reform, all more or less revolutionary, must be
abandoned, so as to present to friend and foe alike the united
front of a great and strong nation, ready for the struggle which
might come at any time and which would bring back Alsace
and Lorraine. The Tsar had been persuaded to enter into
closer relations with the French Republic because he hoped
to find guarantees of order and stability; but if France were
unfortunate enough to fall into the hands of Radical and
Socialist agitators, the Autocrat of All the Russias would lose
all faith in her, and her great friend and ally would be hers no
longer. That would be a clear proof that the parties of the Left
did not really desire to get back the lost provinces.

In this style, little by little, the Alliance was exploited in
the interests of party politics and social reaction. This was
the genesis of that fatal misconception which prevented France
in later years from urging upon the Tsar a policy of internal
reform which might have been the salvation of Russia. It is
easy to see the priceless advantage which the reactionary
parties, who had been defeated each time the nation had been
consulted electorally, gained by this policy. It became the
main plank in their political platform. The moderate "progressive" parties were also well served. Did not this ideal of

"national union" coincide with the New Spirit that Spuller had recently been preaching? As we shall see, the leading representatives of this particular political sect—Barthou, Raynal, Méline—all maintained that the Franco-Russian Alliance could not fail to be seriously weakened by the adoption of a policy of reform as advocated by the Radicals and Socialists.

The Socialists were practically alone in standing out against the universal infatuation.[1] In the *Petite République*, which Millerand was then editing, Rouanet wrote how humiliated he felt to witness the orgy of fulsome flattery, with its spate of jejune, ridiculous addresses, all tending to misrepresent France as a degenerate nation which could only keep its head above water with the aid of Russia. Anyone expressing even the slightest hint of dubiety in the face of these vociferous demonstrations was howled down, insulted, and accused of treachery. Millerand himself wrote that the nation had lost its sense of proportion. What more ecstatic welcome could have been given to the Russian officers if, instead of merely symbolizing as they did to the French people a hoped-for but uncertain future, they had come bringing with them in the folds of their tunics the provinces France had lost? He referred warmly to the violent contrast which was all too apparent between these festivities and the tragic scenes in progress at the same time in the industrial North, where the Government was treating the strikers with the utmost brutality.[2] This was the way the Third Republic was commemorating the centenary of 1793. Jaurès put the antithesis in this way:

[1] The *Siècle*, representing moderate Radicalism, had warned the public against excessive enthusiasm. "True patriotism", said that journal, "threatens to be swamped almost entirely by the big drums of the circus showmen and the childish extravagances of some of our Chauvinists."
[2] *Petite République*, October 22, 1893. At a public dinner on October 2nd, Millerand had said that the news of the Russian naval visit to France, a land where of old it was said to be fatal to be ridiculous, had given rise to hundreds of programmes, each more absurdly comic than the last. He warned his fellow-countrymen of the danger of allowing France to become, on any pretext, the mere tool of the policy of a foreign Power.

The value of the Franco-Russian Alliance is conditioned by the precise circumstances in and for which it was framed, whether these are clearly recognized or not, and whether they are explicit or merely implicit in the bargain. An Alliance negotiated by a self-respecting, democratic, courageous Government might well increase our immediate security and the chances of future peace without sapping that revolutionary ardour which is the true and undying source of our strength as a nation, far above the region of bargaining. If on the other hand the Alliance is accompanied by a kind of self-abnegation of the spirit of republicanism; if consciously or unconsciously it forms part of a system of hypocritical reaction; if it threatens the French Socialist movement with paralysis, then it weakens and enfeebles our country, or rather betrays her. It is the duty of our responsible Ministers to inform the nation in which spirit, with what aims, they negotiated this pact, if indeed they negotiated it at all.

He added a phrase which the political leaders of the Third Republic would have done well to retain as their motto: "Just as the Revolution saved its soul alive by remaining revolutionary, so we can only preserve France from all dangers by holding fast to the revolutionary spirit."[1] Shortly afterwards Jaurès drew attention to the fact that the powers of reaction were continuing, on the basis of the Franco-Russian celebrations and with the semi-complicity of the Government, their plan of gradual penetration with a view to capturing the Republic, while the pundits of the Centre were looking to the same source for a welcome weakening in the popular control of affairs. He already perceived that certain individuals would not be sorry if these transports of popular emotion were to lead to war.[2]

Thus, by the efforts of the French governing classes themselves, Russia and the Tsar were being held up to the French people as their saviours, as their protectors from invasion and utter defeat. What, it may be asked, was the real opinion of the Russian people in all this affair—the people who, according to the French press and political leaders, were rushing into the arms of France? Lavrov pointed out that Alexander III's internal policy, particularly since the Kronstadt visit, had

---

[1] *Petite République*, October 15, 1893.       [2] Ibid., October 29th.

shown no signs of liberalism, but that, on the contrary, very definite evidence had been forthcoming of reaction and the systematic destruction of the reforms initiated by Alexander II. He added that, for the numerous Russian Liberals, who were all Francophile in sentiment, the Entente had been a painful disillusionment, and that when they came to the head of affairs in Russia they would remember that the French Republic had supported with its moral authority the enemy of Russian liberty.[1] Tolstoy was even more emphatic. He condemned the Alliance root and branch. Writing in 1894 of the Franco-Russian celebrations the previous year, he said:

The whole thing is based on a lie. . . . It is a stupid lie to assert that the object of these unseemly and silly orgies was to create respect for peace in Europe. . . . The Franco-Russian Alliance can stand for nothing but what it is in reality, that is to say, an association of war-mongers. . . . The proceedings at Toulon and Paris can have but one sequel—wholesale murder. You will see the same familiar story beginning over again. A number of crack-brained individuals will start spreading hatred and fratricidal mania in the newspapers under cover of patriotism. There will be great activity among the factory owners and the generals, and then you will see processions of hundreds of thousands of inoffensive, kind-hearted men, equipped with instruments of slaughter, driven like herds of animals. . . . We regard it as a sacred duty to protest with all our strength, on behalf of the millions of men and women in Russia, against what the journalists, politicians, military and naval leaders and ambassadors are saying. We cannot admit the right of such people to pledge our words by what they say and write. . . . Notwithstanding our undeserved reputation as a nation especially loyal to religion, the Tsar and patriotic ideals, the working class in Russia, numbering perhaps one hundred millions, is as free as possible from the illusions of Jingoism and the ideas of devotion to the Faith, to the Emperor, and to Russia. They are almost entirely ignorant of the meaning of Faith, they are profoundly indifferent towards the Tsar, and as for patriotism, if by that is understood anything more than a feeling for the *mir*, or perhaps the *volost*, they either do not know what it is or else they make no particular distinction between Russia and the other nations of the world.[2]

---

[1] *Petite République*, October 14, 1893.
[2] From "Christianity and Patriotism." Ludovic Naudeau drew attention, in *Illustration*, April 2, 1924, to the accuracy of this forecast in the Russo-Japanese War and the World War. In 1901, G. Savich, one of the most

The French Government and ruling class ought to have known what was the real truth about Tsarism, but they preferred to shut their eyes to facts, refused to pay any attention to reliable witnesses, and persisted in displaying a disgraceful degree of credulity. Years passed, and all that occurred went to show, even to the most wilfully blind, that the organism of the Russian State was positively cancerous. But in vain; apart from a handful of intellectuals and Socialists, everyone kept their eyes resolutely closed. The industrial magnates, army leaders, university professors, diplomats, business men, politicians of all shades of opinion, seemed to be in a conspiracy to conceal from the French people the truth about this idol with feet of clay. With what object? it may be asked. There were very definite political and social reasons, which became manifest, as we shall see, at those periods of crisis when it might still have been possible for France to draw back, or at the very least to exercise some check on the expenditure of the credit she was allowing to run to waste in a practically unknown land. The historian Debidour felt justified in saying that France, a free nation,

made every sacrifice to gain the friendship of an ignoble Government whose barbarism and corruption stank in the nostrils of the civilized world. . . . This *rapprochement* had the fallacious attraction of an act of retaliation, but our statesmen were unwilling to recognize what an illusory, costly, and discreditable step it was for the Republic to enter into such a pact with a Government like that of the Tsar, execrable, bankrupt, and rotten.[1]

---

brilliant writers of the younger generation in Russia, whole-heartedly endorsed Tolstoy's remarks. National feeling in Russia was practically non-existent. Wars, politics, and foreign relations were the concern of the governing class only; the nation as a whole was simply not interested. There was no solidarity, no connection even, between the Russian people and their Government. The Franco-Russian Alliance only evoked, and continued to evoke, mild surprise in Russia, where the idea of nationality was an empty phrase hardly ever used except by official speakers. The only real patriotism in Russia was the brotherly love of the toiling, suffering masses, full of humanity, but with no tinge of nationalism (*La Revue*, May 1, 1901).

[1] *L'église catholique et l'Etat sous la Troisième République*, Vol. II, pp. 10–11, 156–57.

Charles Maurras, too, has since said with truth:

One could conceive France acting as teacher and adviser to Russia.
. . . But the result of this policy was to place the chief standard
bearer of the world's culture under the tutelage of a semi-barbarous
empire still torn by profound racial and religious dissensions, exploited
by a Court and a bureaucracy whose corruption has been the bane of
the nation ever since the time when Joseph de Maistre exposed its
ingrained spirit of unbelief, venality, and prodigality. The Alliance
was a perverse affair, and both parties were fated to suffer from it.
For France to be led by Russia was like a party of semi-paralysed
men with good eyesight being guided by a quarrelsome and spiteful
blind man, or a flock of adults shepherded by a child.[1]

Yet the slightest acquaintance with Russian conditions ought
to have been enough to put France on her guard against the
Russian legend. What was wrong with the politicians and the
financiers in France that they could overlook the fact that a
budgetary deficit was as regular an occurrence in Russia as a
famine? The national accounts were divided into two parts,
"ordinary" revenue and expenditure and "extraordinary". The
"ordinary" budget showed a surplus, but the "extraordinary"
budget always showed a more or less serious deficit, and only
the former was published in the press. The whole thing was a
mere juggling with figures. The deficit was due to extravagance
of a kind only rivalled by that of the old French monarchical
régime, and the State actually only continued to exist financially
by means of expedients which the German bankers had
made up their minds to put an end to, when France came
forward to free Tsarism from its servitude to Berlin, without,
however, herself demanding any guarantees. This system, in
point of fact, only came to an end when the Empire itself
disappeared.

The bonds of friendship uniting the two Governments grew
closer and closer. Successive French ministries, under Dupuy,
Casimir-Périer, Ribot, Méline, representing the élite of the
Catholic bourgeoisie, could not do enough to curry favour

[1] *Kiel et Tanger*, p. 18.

with Tsarism. By 1895 the Alliance had reached the point of forcing France to support Russia against Japan in connection with the treaty of Shimonoseki, to send three warships, the *Hoche*, the *Dupuy-de-Lôme*, and the *Surcouf*, to attend the opening of the Kiel Canal (June 1895),[1] and to refrain from intervening to put a stop to the Armenian massacres because Russia's interests required that the reform of the Ottoman Empire should be deferred; and the infatuation went on growing with the years. The propertied classes in France realized the effective use that could be made of the Alliance for the purpose of side-tracking measures of political and social reform, and found it a thoroughly reliable bulwark against the inroads of any real democracy. The nation was told that it must be good, modest in its ideas, humble in its demands, firm in its avoidance of any suspicion of anti-clericalism, so as not to antagonize the Autocrat, who might otherwise withdraw the protection of his invincible army. The Government, the banks, the press, all urged the French public to take up the Russian loans which followed one after the other, with barely a year's interval. The Alliance became the chief subject of popular interest, as was shown by the prevailing fashion in books, toys, ornaments, flags, portraits of the Tsar in every cottage, etc. etc. Such was the gullibility of the French "democracy" that, while the name of Russia was in everyone's mouth, nobody even thought of insisting upon

[1] Poincaré, who at that time was Minister of Education, has given us his recollections of the acute embarrassment which the Kaiser's invitation caused to the Foreign Minister, Hanotaux. He "was inclined to refuse, but feared that Russia would accept and send representatives to Kiel without us . . . so that the Franco-Russian friendship would droop and fade. . . . He begged Montebello to ascertain the Tsar's intentions. Nicholas II wrote a brief marginal note on his Minister's report to the effect that he failed to understand our hesitation, and that, as Russia was sending warships to Kiel, she naturally counted on seeing ours there too. Hanotaux informed the Cabinet of the reply, which disposed of all objections."—*Au service de la France*, Vol. I ("Le Lendemain d'Agadir"), p. 286. Jaurès drew the moral that "the first effect of this Alliance was to induce France to blunt the edge of her national demands". Cf. *Die Grosse Politik*, Vol. IX, pp. 335 sqq.

F

having precise details of the agreements made with the Tsarist Government. Only the Socialists seemed uneasy, and yet when Millerand challenged the Government on June 10, 1895, he was chiefly concerned with reproaching it for having, by appearing with Russia at Kiel, seemed to acquiesce in the Treaty of Frankfort.

With the object of strengthening still further the ties of friendship between the two countries, arrangements were made for Nicholas II and the Tsarina to pay a visit to France in October 1896. The Méline Government, flouting the very spirit of the Constitution, though this was not hostile to monarchism, kept this visit a secret so long as Parliament was sitting, and avoided any opportunity of explaining to the representatives of the people the significance and purpose of the step. Further, no steps were taken to obtain Parliamentary sanction for the expenditure of five million francs which the festivities involved. The Council of State authorized the necessary credits, and the Chamber of Deputies could only ratify the expenditure after the event. The Conservative press took upon itself to reveal that it was the behaviour and judgment of the Deputies that failed to inspire the necessary confidence. Parliament was like a quarrelsome, compromising acquaintance who must be kept out of the way as far as possible when important international questions were being decided. "When the presence of Parliament is found embarrassing in the settlement of these big questions", remarked Jaurès, "it means that the Republic itself is beginning to become an embarrassment."[1]

---

[1] *Matin*, October 1, 1896. Jaurès went on to say: "Can Ministers have the audacity to assert that our debates would have offended or disturbed the Tsar? That would mean that he does not accept as ally the real France, with all her institutions and liberties, with that right of free speech which is the very breath of the Republic; in which case the Alliance simply spells servitude for us. When one is trying to establish diplomatic co-operation and popular friendship between two countries of very different political structure, it is extremely unwise not to give from the outset the fullest scope to each party to the agreement. . . . M. Félix Faure and M. Méline did not know

At this juncture the *Figaro* published a curious warning which shows to what a level of absurdity the French public had descended. The organ of cultured opinion wished to put the French people on their guard against extravagant enthusiasm, urging that tact and moderation were called for. "The utmost circumspection is indicated, the utmost sobriety, the utmost self-discipline, in short. To welcome the Emperor and Empress in a worthy fashion, our demonstrations must obviously be of a superior and more restrained character than those which we quite rightly lavished a few years ago on the gallant officers of the Tsar's navy." And to avoid all misunderstanding, the paper reported next day, on reliable authority, that its previous remarks had correctly interpreted the feelings of the Imperial visitor. The Tsar's *entourage* and Russian society generally had been much concerned as to the kind of welcome that would be given in Paris, and "what they had been inclined to fear was precisely an excess, a redundance of enthusiasm".[1] It was clear that the Tsar and Tsarina had no desire to be welcomed in the same style as the Russian sailors in 1893. It was a humiliating lesson. Clemenceau especially found it hard to swallow.[2]

Before proceeding to France, the Tsar met the German Emperor at Breslau, and had a long interview with the Chancellor, Prince Hohenlohe, in the course of which he asked whether the latter saw any objection to his forthcoming visit to Paris. Hohenlohe reassured him by replying that the visit seemed to him to be *unavoidable*. The Tsar emphasized the fact that he had refused to take up his quarters at the Quai d'Orsay or anywhere else but in the Russian Embassy, which was his own property. He conferred on Prince Hohenlohe the

how to receive guests as republicans should, with the result that they are receiving them like flunkeys. The French people will not submit much longer to being committed without their sanction. . . . When these festivities are over the Government will have to tell us where France now stands and whither she is being led."

[1] *Figaro*, August 15 and 16, 1896.         [2] *Dépêche*, August 25th.

Order of St. Andrew, and assured him that relations between Russia and Germany would "always remain good".[1]

What actually occurred at the celebrations of October 1896 is a matter of history. The output of enthusiasm far exceeded that of 1893; it may be said to have reached delirium. The *Figaro's* phrase was that "the French nation had been struck by lightning". (October 5th.) Doumer asserted that a true "intimacy" had been established between the Tsar and the French people.[2] Henri Rochefort maintained that it was the people who had formed the Franco-Russian Alliance. (October 6th and 7th.) In the opinion of Abbé Garnier, editor of the *Peuple Français*, the Alliance was an event specially determined by Providence:

Shame on those who refuse to see in what is now taking place anything but the result of human devices or even of chance. The Franco-Russian Alliance came into being, despite strong opposition, at a time which clearly shows its providential character. It was shortly after that blessed day on which the Church of the Sacred Heart at Montmartre was first opened for public worship. The inaugural ceremony took place on June 5, 1891. It was followed closely by the Kronstadt celebrations, on July 18th of the same year. It is true that the Alliance was then only in an embryonic stage, but it has developed *pari passu* with the progress of the sacred edifice towards completion.

Mme Adam also expressed the view that the Alliance was "a mystical union transcending ordinary human associations". (*Matin*, October 13th.) J. Delafosse proclaimed that the Tsar's visit had revealed to France the secrets of her own heart. The French nation was monarchist to the core. It had a Parliament, to be sure, but would any day welcome the news that it had been disbanded. (*Gaulois*, October 13th.) P. de Cassagnac observed that the authorities seemed to "blush at the thought of being in a Republic", and added that the platform erected for the Tsar was "a dais for the coming French monarch". Cornély summed up the situation by saying that "we are all

---

[1] *Memoirs of Prince Hohenlohe*, II, p. 470.    [2] *Matin*, October 9th.

turning into Cossacks". (*Matin*, October 11th.) François Coppée
wrote in the *Journal*:

> Let us show the Russians that we are still a warlike nation. With the
> coolness of a man conscious of his strength, we display our glorious
> battle array without boasting, merely saying "Ready, aye ready!"[1]

The Radical press, too, contained very definite incitements to
a war of revenge. Just like the Nationalists of the "Patriots'
League", on whose behalf Sanbœuf had only agreed "with
reserves" to participate in the celebrations because the Alsace-
Lorraine question was not sufficiently stressed, the most
prominent Radicals looked to the Alliance to realize their
hopes of a war which they passionately desired. Clemenceau,
not yet fully recovered from his defeat in 1893, wrote: "It
must be our aim to make Russia, who was an accomplice in
our overthrow, the instrument of our complete rehabilitation,
that is to say—to call a spade a spade—of our revenge. If we
asserted the contrary, nobody would believe us. It is simpler
to admit the fact." He went on to say, with bitterness: "The
peace of the *status quo* on which the Alliance is reputed to be
based is for us a peace of dismemberment, a German peace."[2]
And in the *Voltaire*, L. L. Klotz wrote: "If the Tsar had
linked the idea of peace with the word 'Alliance', he would

[1] In a book entitled *Hommage au Tsar*, produced in collaboration by Jules
Claretie, Albert Sorel, André Theuriet, Armand Silvestre, d'Esparbès,
Léonce Bénédite, René Maizeroy and J. de Mitty, a foreword by François
Coppée contained these words: "We hold Central Europe between the jaws
of a vice. At the first insult, we shall turn the screw. . . . Let us keep our
rifles at the slope, but ready for use on the frontier at any time. . . . Does
this young Emperor cherish secretly in his heart the traditional ideal of
the Slav race? Does he dream of hurling the Turkish barbarians beyond the
Bosphorus and setting the Greek Cross to gleam on the dome of St. Sophia?
Why not? But let it be understood that, on the day when the Cossacks
gallop through the narrow streets of old Stamboul, a French battalion will
be presenting arms in front of the Kléber statue in Strassburg. Such were
the thoughts that thronged the brains of the four million Frenchmen who
had assembled to cheer Nicholas II as he passed by; such were the thoughts
that gave such a solemn tone to the five days of festivity in October last. . . ."
[2] *Dépêche de Toulouse*, August 25th and October 13th. Cf. also René
Goblet's speech at Limoges, October 11, 1896.

have dashed our dearest hopes to the ground." (October 11th.) Charles Bos expressed the view that "the Quai d'Orsay is now in an excellent strategic position". But it was Lucien Victor Meunier who chiefly excelled in warlike ardour. On October 5th, in an article in the *Rappel* entitled "France Rediviva", he wrote:

The Franco-Russian Alliance has been formed to inspire Germany with proper respect, formed—oh, let us have courage and say aloud what we really think—against Germany. . . . Shame on those who stand aloof and turn their backs. . . . Where is their heart, where is their courage, these renegade sons of France whom France will, must disown? Nothing can forbid us to dream of the day when this all-powerful Alliance shall snatch his prey from the rapacious conqueror and restore to a radiant France our beloved Alsace and Lorraine.

On October 10th he returned to the charge:

All hopes, all ambitions are now possible for France. . . . In our hearts there is the living hope of revenge. If the Franco-Russian Alliance were to have no other result than to maintain this atrocious armed peace, every patriotic heart would be bitterly disappointed. . . . We are keeping watch and ward. If the Tsar has understood us aright, he will know that all the shouts of enthusiasm which have surrounded him as he passed can and must be summed up in one brief, telling phrase: "Sire, France is ready."

We need spend no more time over such ridiculous braggadocio, but what is one to think of the politicians who were prepared to allow the war feeling to develop without even troubling to ascertain the degree of readiness of the Russian army—that army which, eight years later, was to crumple up before Japan in circumstances which are now a matter of history? What would the result have been in 1896 in face of the Triple Alliance?

What was the attitude of the French Government at that time? Drawing its strength from the parties of the Right and Centre, its policy was on the one hand to refuse to supply any detailed information regarding the treaty, and on the other to

make use of the Alliance to combat Socialism. Its Parliamentary
majority was fully in sympathy with this line of action. Immediately after the Tsar's visit, Barthou, Minister of the Interior,
in a speech at Oloron, asserted that a moderate policy in home
affairs was an essential prerequisite of lasting agreement with
Russia. Raynal, in a big speech at Bordeaux, declared that the
Alliance imposed on France a "new duty", that of fighting
Socialism more vigorously than ever. Europe expected from
France "resolute hostility to these wild doctrines; she looks
to us to stamp out Socialism, the inevitable and fatal sequel
and consummation of which is Communism".[1] Raynal's speech
laid bare the reactionary trap laid by the bourgeoisie and the
ruling class under cover of their Russian policy. It was a very
adroit manœuvre and extremely convenient. The Alliance
became in this way an admirable weapon against the extreme
Left, whose reputation was thus besmirched in the name of
patriotism. Henceforth Socialism could be represented as a
danger to the stability of the Alliance. If the Tsar cooled in his
attitude to France, the democratic party could be stigmatized
in advance as those responsible for war, if it should come;
while if peace were not endangered, they could equally well
be held up to obloquy as those who prevented France from
recovering Alsace-Lorraine, since the masses were allowed to
think that the Alliance implied the return of these provinces
to the mother country. In this light, Socialism, all advanced
ideas, became a sort of treason. And in fact the struggle
against the Socialists was growing more acute day by day. The
serious labour troubles at Fourmies in 1891 had been followed
by strikes at Decazeville and in the coal-mines of the Pas de
Calais. Jaurès had had the courage to say, on the eve of the
Imperial visit, that opportunism and reaction were counting
on the low intellectual and moral level of the people of Paris
in calling upon them to cheer the Tsar, who was the pre-
eminent symbol of reaction in Europe. The only fit and proper

[1] *Temps*, October 17, 1896.

thing to ask of the French Socialist population in the circumstances was to keep silent.[1]

Immediately after the celebrations, Jaurès protested against
the warlike tone adopted by various newspapers and demanded
vigorously that the Government should give a full explanation
of the Franco-Russian Alliance:

It is essential that Parliament should be sufficiently well informed to
be able to prevent French liberties from ever being pledged without
its knowledge. If Parliament were to relinquish the control of France's
destinies to a clique of diplomatic mandarins, the Republic itself
would soon be a mere empty word. What! shall we tolerate a situation
in which shadowy statesmen beyond the borders of France dictate
what her future shall be and in which she marches with blind enthusiasm along a path she has not chosen?"

He continued, driving in his point:

If there is a definite treaty of Alliance which pledges Russia and ourselves in certain hypothetical conditions, what right have the Government to conceal its terms from the nation? If it exists, no doubt the
treaty involves responsibilities as well as privileges. Is France doomed
one day, as the result of some unforeseen event, to be called upon
suddenly to keep a promise she has never known was made in her
name? . . . If it is claimed that the French Government is at liberty
to conceal from the French people a treaty which perhaps pledges
their very existence, all their resources, their whole army, then it
means that they are in a state of tutelage, that they have no concern
with questions of vital import to them. . . . The time has come when
Parliament and the nation must be told the facts. Our elected representatives would be betraying their constituents if they did not now
insist on the whole truth.[2]

On October 14th Millerand gave notice of a question in which
he proposed to ask the responsible Ministers to furnish par-

---

[1] *Petite République*, August 14th and September 1st. "Our governing
classes", he said, "have allowed friendship to degenerate into servility,
because they have lost sight of the real significance of France by losing sight
of the significance of Republicanism. They imagine that the Republic must
make excuses for its very existence, both to its allies abroad and to its enemies
at home, and they have subordinated the Republic to Tsarism in foreign
affairs as they have already subordinated it to reaction in home politics.
They have no sense of equality in their relations with other Powers. They
negotiate as inferiors on behalf of a France in the garb of a penitent, ready
to offer any guarantees of good behaviour."    [2] *Matin*, October 12th.

ticulars of how the Franco-Russian Entente arose and in what
terms it had been established.

> For the Government to maintain silence on this point would be not
> only to flout Parliament in a way that could not be tolerated, but to
> imperil the nation. What we want to be able to do is to weigh up the
> benefits and the responsibilities of a contract of which we have only
> been given the bare title up to the present. It is impossible to accept
> the position that France may be compelled to take up arms one day
> on account of some squabble in the Balkans without having even
> been permitted to consider the terms of the agreement under which
> she is called upon to draw the sword.[1]

But the press, the Parliamentary majority, and the Government all opposed this request for details. Even Arthur Ranc
declared that Jaurès and Millerand would be affronting the
feelings of the immense majority in the Chamber of Deputies
and in the nation. It was rumoured that, if the Socialists
insisted on demanding explanations as to the nature of Franco-
Russian relations, the Chamber would, by a unanimous vote,
indignantly prevent their spokesmen from continuing; to which
Jaurès retorted that he hoped the Chamber would be chary
of following the example of the servile majorities of the *Corps
Législatif*, which led France to the verge of ruin by substituting
unanimous resolutions in favour of the administration for the
free discussion of the vital interests of the country.[2]

The question duly came up in the Chamber of Deputies on
November 21, 1896, when Millerand asked the Minister of
Foreign Affairs whether there existed between France and
Russia any special agreements, whether of the nature of a military convention, or a simple memorandum or a formal treaty,
and if so, what was the extent and scope of such agreement.
"What!" he said, "is not the very definition of a Republic
the government of the people by the people? Shall a nation
which in theory controls its own destinies be forced to hand
over that control blindly to a man or to a Government whose
ability or good intentions I do not question, but who cannot

---

[1] *Petite République.*          [2] *Matin*, October 20th.

be infallible? And there is no question as to the price to be paid in such case for a false step: the prosperity of France and her territorial integrity are at stake. Very well! I contend that there is no one in the world who has the right to dispose of these things, save only France herself. No one can pledge her without her consent." And he continued, amid the applause of the Extreme Left:

If, by some unlucky chance, to honour undertakings concluded over the head of Parliament and without the knowledge of the country, France were involved to-morrow in a warlike adventure which she had neither foreseen nor desired, I ask you, gentlemen, what would be the judgment on that gross dereliction of, I will not say our constitution, but of any free constitution, the essence of which is that the right of making war and peace shall be reserved to the elected representatives of the nation, freely consulted? . . . What benefits have we contracted for in return for our obligations? Have not speakers and newspapers on the Government side created dangerous illusions in the minds of the people? Is not the enthusiasm of certain patriotic gentlemen sustained by the belief which they hold and propagate, the belief in an Alliance which is not merely defensive? We call upon you to explain clearly what is the actual position of the country, for we have a right to know where we stand. We ask you not to allow, by your silence, legends to form and illusions to strike root which would inevitably be the source and the starting-point of the most bitter and deplorable disappointment.

All that was vouchsafed in reply by Hanotaux, the Minister of Foreign Affairs, was this:

All that can and ought to be stated in public has already been expressed in measured, agreed, and definite terms by H.I.M. the Tsar and the President of the Republic, firstly at Cherbourg, to the officers of the navy, then in Paris to the representatives of the people, and finally at Châlons to our army leaders. The Minister of Foreign Affairs adheres to these statements. The duties of his office and the higher interests of the nation, as the House will understand, forbid him to add anything further on the subject of an understanding the existence of which no one now dreams of denying or doubting.

Jaurès' comment was: "On behalf of the nation we take note that, from the silence of the Foreign Minister, it is clear that the French Government has lost the right of speaking openly to the people of France. . . . It is our bounden duty to remind our countrymen that now, more than ever, they can count on no one but themselves"; and Viviani observed: "If it was for this that the Republic was founded, there has surely never in the course of history been such a melancholy delusion."[1]

The position of the Government in replying to this question had been made all the more awkward by the fact that only a few days before, on November 16th, Baron Marschall von Bieberstein, the German Secretary of State for Foreign Affairs, had stated in the Reichstag that the relations between Germany and Russia were founded on respect for treaties and on the desire the two countries shared to ensure that they were carried out universally. He had even referred to the moderating influence which Russia's friendship could not fail to exert on France.[2]

Thus both Parliament and public opinion acquiesced in this absolute silence and were content to remain in complete ignorance of the terms and scope of the agreement. What is more, no inclination was shown to exercise any check on the expenditure of the milliards of francs which found their way to Russia each year through the French banks. Patriotism and national honour required that Frenchmen should approve of everything with their eyes shut: this seemed to have been a dogma which had impressed itself on the conscience of the nation. Moreover, the private investors themselves seemed to be perfectly satisfied with this state of things. There was never the slightest movement of serious inquiry with regard to the mighty Empire, no disposition to get at the real facts about Russia. This is one of the strangest phenomena ever observed in the mentality of a nation.

This refusal of information on the part of the French Government, this policy of secrecy, was all the more serious as the Russian Government was at that moment preparing

[1] *Petite République*, November 24, 1896.
[2] Cf. *Die Grosse Politik*, XI, pp. 337 sqq.

an expedition on a large scale to take forcible possession of Constantinople and the Straits. Once before, in 1895, when, as a result of the massacres at Constantinople, Great Britain had seemed to be on the point of intervening to help the Armenians, the Tsar, at the instigation of Prince Lobanov, the new Foreign Minister, had decided to take energetic action in regard to the occupation of the Dardanelles and the partition of the Ottoman Empire. Preparations for the mobilization of an Army Corps of 100,000 men had been made, but the move had not received France's support. In 1896, having in view the difficult situation in which Turkey then found herself, and the fresh Armenian massacres, which seemed bound to bring about intervention on the part of Great Britain, the Tsar called a conference on his return from France to review the position again. Nelidov, the Russian ambassador at Constantinople, suggested that "incidents should be engineered which would furnish Russia with legal grounds or pretexts for seizing the Bosphorus". He asserted that circumstances were very favourable at that moment because of the state of anarchy in Turkey and the fact of Germany's goodwill. He was strongly supported by General Obruchev, the Chief of Staff, and the Emperor finally came over to his point of view, despite warnings by the Minister of Finance, Count Witte, who was alarmed at the possible outcome of such a venture. The military authorities at Odessa and Sebastopol began to make preparations for disembarking in Turkey a force of 200,000 men. Nelidov was to give the signal for the raid as soon as he considered the appropriate moment had arrived.

But the French Government, on being informed by Mohrenheim, who was instructed to request France's support, did not conceal its opposition to the scheme. Hanotaux stated to Mohrenheim that, if a conflict arose on the subject of the Black Sea and the Straits, France was not at all inclined to take any active part in the warlike operations that might conceivably follow, seeing that the risks would be so great and the advantages for France were not apparent. The French Foreign Minister wrote at the same time to Count Muraviev, who had just succeeded Lobanov: "We have been considering with feelings of some apprehension the tendency of the Russian Government to seize an opportunity for taking swift and decisive action in regard to the Straits and Constantinople." He promised diplomatic support, but not military co-operation on the part of France. "The best service we could render to Russia would be to maintain strict neutrality and thus compel Germany to do the same." He also wrote to the French ambassador at St. Petersburg on January 12, 1897, that the odds were too great, French interests too little involved, and the chances too doubtful of seeing this most serious of international questions settled equitably "for us to desire anything but the maintenance of the *status quo*". This prudent counsel, definitely deprecating any complications on the subject of Constantinople, inevitably had its effect on the Russian Government. Witte, on his side, induced Pobedonostsev, Procurator of the Holy Synod, who had not previously been consulted, to use his influence, and he persuaded the Tsar to reverse his decision, after demonstrating to him the dangers such an enterprise would involve for the dynasty and for Russia. The expedition, which would have set all Europe in a blaze, was abandoned on the score (according to Sazonov) of insufficient transport and defects in the mobilization arrangements on land.[1]

In the following year the President of the French Republic returned the Tsar's visit. Félix Faure set out for Kronstadt in August on board the *Potuau*. Elaborate festivities took place at St. Petersburg and especially at Peterhof Palace. For the first time references were made in the toasts to the two "allied" nations, and all French hearts beat at the news. The Tsar used the words "justice" and "equity", and everyone took them as a guarantee of the early restoration of Alsace-

---

[1] Witte, *Mémoires*, pp. 164–166. E. Judet, *G. Louis*, pp. 145–147. *Livre Noir*, II, p. 367. E. J. Dillon, *The Eclipse of Russia*, pp. 235 sqq.

Lorraine.[1] The *Temps* proclaimed that the union rested on the threefold basis of unanswerable political expediency, overwhelming reasons of State policy, and instinctive sympathy of temperament. "'The Russian and French peoples, loving each other and understanding each other, even speaking if need be the same language, are united henceforth in an unshakable fraternal friendship." It called upon the Socialists to abandon "their absurd and unconstitutional demand for the immediate publication of the treaty, for the soul of the nation is wholly engaged in the contemplation of the great event which is so propitious for the future destiny of France". (August 24th and 31st.)

As in the previous year, the Radical leaders distinguished themselves by their bellicose attitude. "Peace founded on justice and equity", wrote Lucien Victor Meunier, "that must mean that if crimes have been committed, the perpetrators must make amends, give up their prey, and suffer humiliation in their turn. The hour of reparation is at hand. The wheel of time has gone full circle. Lorraine, Alsace, you shall become French again!" On Félix Faure's return, Meunier exclaimed:

An overwhelming pious emotion fills my heart; I am on my knees, I kiss thy soil, oh my country! May my blood flow for thee, as my tears have flowed. Take me; I am still strong, I can stand long marches, put up with fatigue, cold or heat, and I can fight. Land of my fathers, take me![2]

Simultaneously Déroulède was expressing the keenest anxiety lest the Alliance should have been diverted from its main object—to keep watch on Germany—and become a more generalized association in which the most diverse interests and factors might come into play,[3] while Clemenceau was

---

[1] See the *Correspondant*, October 10 and 25, 1897; *Die Grosse Politik*, XIII, pp. 49 sqq.

[2] *Le Rappel*, August 28th and September 2nd. He added: "When the hour strikes, the nation will rush forward as one man, and fear will seize upon those who attempt to bar our path;—nay, they are already trembling."

[3] *Le Gaulois*, August 27, 1897.

renewing his protest, this time in the *Echo de Paris*, not against the secret character of the Alliance, but against the fact that it seemed to perpetuate the present peace, that is to say, the *status quo*:

> In Europe, Russia needs peace, and the unfortunate thing for us, as I have often pointed out, is that the peace she requires to maintain is called the Peace of Frankfort. . . . What peace is this that Félix Faure and Nicholas II are celebrating? It is not clear why the two countries should enter into a close compact if they wish to maintain the same peace as the Triple Alliance. They might just as well, for this purpose, combine with the three allies. (September 1, 1897.)

And when, later on, the *Vyestnik Evropi*, the organ of the enlightened Russian bourgeoisie, declared that the Alsace-Lorraine question was now eliminated from the field of practical politics, and that the Franco-Russian Alliance was a guarantee, not only against the political predominance of Germany but also against possible ebullitions of the bellicose spirit of revenge amongst the French themselves, Clemenceau was dumbfounded by the blow, and wondered how the Government could possibly be solemnly celebrating a diplomatic achievement which had only ended in the open avowal of our country's decadence. Tony-Révillon, in the *Radical*, echoed Clemenceau's plaint. At last he had realized that Russia had not the slightest intention of going to war with Germany over Alsace-Lorraine.

Going on from discovery to discovery, it was soon found that, while the French showed every sign of obsequiousness towards the Tsar, the Russian people were far from feeling the same enthusiasm for the Alliance. When the *Temps* averred that, at the festivities at St. Petersburg, the Russian heart had "thrilled with joy",[1] the *Vyestnik Evropi* took a malicious

---

[1] The journalist Latapie reported with surprise that while the President was in Russia he was very seldom allowed to come into contact with the masses. "The public saw nothing of him, and hardly knew he was there." (*Télégramme*, August 31st.) Yet Hector Depasse could write: "France is a name the sound of which goes straight to Russia's heart, like the breath of spring and the soft warmth of the sun." (*Echo de Paris*, September 6, 1897.)

delight in destroying the French illusions, declaring hard-heartedly:

It is excusable for French journalists to attribute to our people joys and hopes which are quite foreign to them, but . . . *the Russian heart cannot "thrill with joy" at the thought of the Alliance, because the people have not the least idea of what it means.* Our Parisian contemporary has evidently been taking at their face value some of the customary fine phrases of our patriotic press, which always purports to speak, in its pompous style, in the name of the Russian nation.[1]

Russians were less cultivated than the French, but also evidently less liable to gusts of unreasoning emotion. Instead of replying to the Russian publicist, the French official press maintained a discreet silence.

This, then, was the gist of the criticisms directed against the Alliance by the Radicals: they did not complain of its secrecy, the result of which might have been to risk the very life of France in some rash escapade or for a dispute in which she was not interested, but of its one-sidedness, benefiting Russia without restoring Alsace-Lorraine to France. "In looking round for alliances", wrote de Lanessan, later Minister of Marine in the Waldeck-Rousseau Cabinet, "we had always in mind that they should assist us to regain our lost territory and to avenge our defeat, but the very first price we have had to pay for Russia's friendship is Alsace-Lorraine". This Alliance was in fact an imperfect and unfinished example of diplomatic action, concluded too hastily. Many points had been overlooked which ought to have been taken up and settled in the best interests of France, which had up to now only been a satellite to Russia.[2]

It will be seen in a later chapter how regrets and anxieties of this description crystallized to form the basis of the modification introduced into the treaty by Delcassé during his visit to St. Petersburg in August 1899.

As regards the Socialists, they were pertinacious in con-

[1] Quoted by Clemenceau in the *Dépêche de Toulouse*, November 2, 1897.
[2] *Le Rappel*, September 3, 1897.

demning both the atmosphere of mystery in which the treaty was enveloped and the way in which it was applied.[1] At the beginning of July, Jaurès had drawn attention to the chief objection to the President's visit, namely, that it was one more glaring token of the advent, in French foreign politics, of a frankly monarchist demeanour in place of a truly national and Republican one. Moreover, by entrusting to a handful of men the secrets of high politics by which the very life of France might be imperilled, all reality of self-government was destroyed. At St. Petersburg, the office of Chief Magistrate of France would be held up to all the world as a travesty of a monarchy. Jaurès went on to denounce the shifty policy of the governing class, who entered into mysterious undertakings, "possibly running directly counter to the best instincts of the nation", and refused to disclose their terms to the very people most affected. Their foreign policy was, moreover, warped and degraded by a home policy inspired by fear of democracy, and this nullified what elements of liberal thought there might be in the Alliance, which "was thus wantonly reduced to the level of a party manœuvre based on reactionary aims". It was, he must admit, a skilful move to give this policy a popular veneer by throwing to the thoughtless masses sops such as showy rhetoric, joy-bells, Chinese-lanterns, and gaily flying bunting, while all the time concealing from them all the truth, all the reality of what was happening.[2]

Millerand pointed out that there was not one single instance in recent foreign politics in which the Cabinet had not confronted Parliament with a *fait accompli*. It was unnatural and wrong that France should be left in complete ignorance of the

---

[1] For this they were vilified by the journalist Judet as "self-importantly displaying their treacherous oratory in floods of unseemly interpellations. . . . Thanks to the good sense of the majority, the trap basely set by these unworthy councillors, these indecent stirrers-up of disorder and panic, was resolutely unmasked and consigned to ignominious oblivion." (*Petit Journal*, August 29, 1897.)

[2] *Dépêche de Toulouse*, July 10, 1897; *Matin*, August 30th; *Petite République*, September 4th.

G

policy by the light of which the treaty had been concluded. The Franco-Russian Alliance was merely a means to an end, not an end in itself. It was an important part in a complete mechanism. But what was that mechanism? What function was it intended to perform? These questions were shrouded in mystery. France alone through her neglected representatives had the right to decide her future, to fix the general lines of her policy both at home and abroad.[1]

On February 7, 1898, Millerand again raised the question in the Chamber of Deputies. With even greater firmness than in 1896 he pressed the Méline Government to say definitely whether or not the toasts on board the *Potuau* implied the inauguration of a new phase. "What is this Franco-Russian Alliance? I do not mean, what is its detailed wording, but its essence, which is something you have no right to conceal or to disguise from the nation. What is the aim, scope, and significance to us of this contract? We are in league with Russia. With what object?" If the Alliance merely resulted in the maintenance of the Treaty of Frankfort, it was questionable whether we had not made a bad bargain. In that case, the Alliance was of doubtful utility, and it was much to be feared that the upshot would bring bitter disappointment to the illusions in which certain sections of the French public were indulging. Millerand further attacked the Government for agreeing to the Kiel visit, "a mark of deference towards a Power in respect of which no French Government had the right to forget for one moment the tacit sentiments of the nation".

Méline endeavoured to allay the fears of the Socialist spokesman by declaring dogmatically that Russia would one day be in the position of laying down the law to the whole world, and that when that time came problems which might now appear insoluble would be automatically removed. Leaving it thus open to conjecture, according to individual predilec-

[1] *Lanterne*, September 22, 1897.

tions, whether the solution would be a peaceable one or attained through war, the Prime Minister, in his profound ignorance of the outlook of the Russian people, knowing in fact as little about Russian affairs as he did about the Dreyfus Case (and he remarked on one occasion that "there *is* no *affaire Dreyfus*"), declared with perfect equanimity that the friendship which united the two countries was no superficial or transitory passion, but "a deep and lasting emotion" which had its foundation in "the very roots of our sense of patriotism". And when Goblet argued that no information had been given in Parliament about the Franco-Russian Alliance, Hanotaux replied:

Now that the Entente has been solemnly proclaimed, there is a demand for its terms and conditions. Now, it is perfectly well understood that such information cannot possibly be divulged. (*"Hear, hear ! Hear, hear !"* from the Centre.) I repeat once more, we cannot allow ourselves to be inveigled into such a course. This political achievement, which may now be regarded as a historical fact, was designed and developed by many successive Governments. The public acknowledgment of its existence by the two high contracting parties is a great event in the world. But we are precluded from adding anything to that solemn announcement. The facts speak for themselves, and we need say no more.[1] (*Applause from the Centre, Left, and Right.*)

By refusing all requests for particulars of the Treaty, the Government left a free field for all the misleading interpretations which had already gained currency owing to the official policy of silence, unsettling the public mind and threatening, on the one hand, to disturb the peace of the world, and on the other, to reduce the real value of the Alliance. What influence did this policy exert on the opinion of the outside world

---

[1] When de Lanessan, in the *Rappel*, called upon the Government to lay the Treaty of Alliance before Parliament, since France was able and willing to govern herself, the *Temps* replied by reminding the country that Bismarck had expressed approval of this demand for the publication of the agreement, adding that it would be criminal levity to ignore traps set by the man who had garbled the Ems telegram. Any advice by Bismarck was *a priori* under suspicion. (September 10, 1897.) That line of argument speedily led to the accusation that all who demanded the publication of the treaty were in German pay. (September 10, 1897.)

regarding the French Republic?[1] In general, foreign comment
on the French Alliance with Tsarism was decidedly hostile.
In response to an invitation from the *Figaro* to express his
views, Lombroso replied: "The enthusiasm displayed for the
Tsarist Government, whose main function is to repress human
liberties, and which is based solely on militarism and bureaucracy, demonstrates that France is really only a Republic in
name, and is actually ultra-Conservative and an enemy to all
progressive aspirations—that she, too, is a militarist nation."
J. B. Eustis, a former ambassador of the United States in
Paris, in an important article in the *North American Review*,
argued that a liberal nation like France could not contract
an alliance with an autocratic, semi-Asiatic Power like Russia
without losing a great deal both in self-respect and in her
essential interests. In his view there could be no affinity of
moral outlook, nor community of ideas, nor real sympathy,
nor solidarity of interests, between France and Russia. He
expressed his fears lest France's democratic vigour should be
gradually exhausted by her deliberate subordination to the
Russian Government.[2]

---

[1] The moderate press continued to maintain that the Alliance required
a Conservative policy in home affairs if it was to be entirely fruitful. The
elements of disruption must be kept in check, the power of the Executive
strengthened, and the anti-religious campaign stopped. (*Correspondant*,
October 10 and 25, 1897.)

[2] *North American Review*, July 1897, pp. 111 sqq.

# CHAPTER V

# DELCASSÉ'S VISIT TO ST. PETERSBURG

As we have seen, many very diverse sections of public opinion in France, from the Right to the progressive Left, agreed in regarding the Franco-Russian agreement as insufficient. They were not unduly concerned at the fact of a secret Alliance existing between a Republic and an autocrat, but feared that this Alliance would tend to perpetuate the *status quo* in Europe and thus favour the maintenance of the "German peace". They considered that Russian interests stood to benefit from it almost exclusively and that it failed to take into account France's legitimate aspirations. Matters could not be left in that position: it was essential that the agreement should be revised, and this could be done without provoking indiscreet comment from the representatives of the nation by taking advantage of the secrecy in which it had become the practice to conduct the negotiations.

On August 1, 1898, a somewhat peculiar unsigned article appeared in the *Revue de Paris*, in which the writer complained that, while the Alliance, by guaranteeing France against aggression, had lessened the nation's anxiety, it had not gone far enough to remove all cause for uneasiness. Phrases were used which, in the light of more recent events, take on an ominous significance; for instance:

The Alliance will not have proved its value beyond all doubt until it has succeeded in putting an end quite conclusively to Germany's predominance in Europe. . . . Are not the Balkan States obviously destined, by the sheer pressure of events, to co-operate in the execution of this policy? At all events, should not their parts be allotted to them in advance? . . . In the event of an international conflict, the part played by Serbia would assume an importance out of all proportion to the apparent strength of the Serbian army. From a racial point of view, Serbia, Montenegro, and Bosnia-Herzegovina make up as it were a Serbian entity, the present disunion of which can only be temporary. . . . The crux of the matter is the question of nationality. Russia has a great function to perform from the point of view of European civilization; oppressed races are only waiting for her to assume it; a defeated nation is hoping she will fulfil it; Germany's overweening ambitions are calling aloud for her to realize it. Duty as well as self-interest demand that France should remind her ally of this.

The article is altogether very enlightening. The old idea of breaking the isolation in which France found herself and being able to cope with a possible attack from Germany is abandoned, and the question is approached more broadly and from a different angle. The Alliance was worthless if it merely perpetuated the "German peace"; it must be turned into an instrument of definite activity. And as it was not feasible to reveal one's full aims officially, they must be realized indirectly *via* the Balkans, where Russia had traditions and duties which would impel her to intervene, and if necessary France would remind her ally of these duties.

This new tactic was particularly adroit in that France, instead of being a kind of satellite to Russia, became the ringleader. To put it into actual practice was the self-imposed task of Théophile Delcassé. The victory of the Radical Party in the 1898 elections brought this man into the Foreign Office in succession to Hanotaux, and he remained at the Quai d'Orsay until 1905. Successive Prime Ministers—Brisson, Dupuy, Waldeck-Rousseau, Combes—were too preoccupied by problems of home politics to interfere with the Foreign Minister, who was free to direct the foreign policy of France as he thought fit.

One of his first actions, in 1899, was to introduce a modification into the Franco-Russian Alliance. At a time when scores of Frenchmen, running the gauntlet of unbridled mendacity and calumny, were staking their future careers and their very lives in an unequal struggle for truth and justice, in August 1899, on the eve of Dreyfus's retrial at Rennes, Delcassé set out for St. Petersburg, without a word to Parliament, without even notifying most of his colleagues in the Cabinet, to consult

with the Tsar with a view to introducing into the Treaty of
Alliance a new element which completely changed its orienta-
tion and scope.

The existing basis of the French agreement with Russia
was twofold: on the one hand, there was the general diplomatic
*entente* contained in the letters exchanged on August 21 and 27,
1891, which stipulated that the two Governments should take
counsel together on all questions calculated to endanger the
peace of Europe, and on the other hand there was the military
convention of December 23, 1893, which was designed exclusively to cover a case of aggression by one of the Powers of
the Triple Alliance and was only to remain in force as long as
the Triple Alliance itself. Now Delcassé's uneasiness expressed
itself in the following speculation: "What would happen if
the Triple Alliance came to an end otherwise than by the
free choice of its members—if, for example, the Emperor
Francis Joseph suddenly disappeared from the European stage
and Austria found herself threatened with dissolution—which
might not be unwelcome in certain quarters, and which, at all
events, would furnish a tempting opportunity for self-interested
action? Can any situation be imagined which would be more
likely to endanger the peace of the world or to upset the
equilibrium of power in Europe—and hence more appropriate
for France and Russia to confront not only with unanimity of
purpose, but also with joint readiness for action? And yet the
military convention would have automatically ceased to exist
at the very moment at which it ought most fittingly to be
coming into effect: the Triple Alliance had given it birth, and
it would pass away with the Triple Alliance."

Delcassé had resolved, as soon as he assumed the direction
of foreign affairs, to arrange for this gap, as he saw it, to be
filled in. With the approval of the President of the Republic,
he proceeded to St. Petersburg and laid before the Tsar all
his arguments as to the necessity of assigning to the military
convention of 1893 the same duration as the 1891 Agreement,

namely, so long as the general and permanent interests of the
two countries should remain in harmony. The Tsar having
expressed his approval, Delcassé at once submitted to him a
draft declaration which he had drawn up that very morning.
In this, according to Delcassé's own account, the agreement
of 1891 was solemnly confirmed, but its scope was very
strikingly widened. Whereas in 1891 the two Governments
only stated that they were concerned with the maintenance
of peace, this draft provided for their paying just as much
attention to the "maintenance of the Balance of Power in
Europe". Further, it was decided that "the terms and the
actual existence of this new undertaking should be kept strictly
secret". The agreement was embodied in letters exchanged
on August 9th between Delcassé and Count Muraviev, the
Russian Minister of Foreign Affairs. ("Yellow Book", Nos. 93,
94, and 95.) Thus, on his own showing, on the plea of merely
extending the duration of the military convention to correspond
with that of the main diplomatic instrument, Delcassé had
completely altered the significance and the scope of the Franco-
Russian Alliance. It amounted in fact to an extension of the
treaty, and it is obvious that the adjustment of the duration
of the military convention to that of the diplomatic agreement
was only suggested as a blind to cover the other modifications.
Delcassé had taken a defensive treaty which only came into
operation in the event of aggression on the part of the Triple
Alliance, and imposed upon it as its chief aim the maintenance
of the Balance of Power in Europe, or rather what a handful
of rulers, diplomats, generals, and politicians might in their
own interest regard as the Balance of Power—a formula with
a fine flavour of *ancien régime*. And this balance could be upset,
as Delcassé himself clearly foresaw, by the disruption of
Austria-Hungary, and in particular by any expressed wish on
the part of the German Austrians to join with their mother
country. In that event France and Russia would be bound to
intervene to prevent, if necessary by force, the realization of

this desire. Thus a purely defensive treaty, designed to guarantee the freedom of a certain nation, was not only turned into a partially offensive weapon, but also into a menace to the right of self-determination of other nations.

Similarly, it goes without saying that any alteration in the territorial *status quo* of the Balkan States could be interpreted by the Pan-Slav party, if they saw fit, as an infringement of the Balance of Power, and hence an excuse for intervention. Albert Mathiez has pointed out with much justification that the seeds of the World War lay hidden in the secret agreement of August 9, 1899, since the monarchist policy of the Balance of Power was bound to lead to war sooner or later.

What was Delcassé's motive in effecting such a drastic transformation in the Alliance? Mathiez has suggested that his chief aim was to detach Russia from Germany. To do this, he had to offer sufficient inducements to the Tsar to compensate him for the loss of German friendship. These concessions were contained in the new agreement, which completely reassured the Tsar as to his interests in the Near East being safeguarded, since France, in the sacred name of the Balance of Power, would afford armed support for Russia's Balkan ambitions. "Thus the secret agreement of August 9, 1899", says Mathiez,

was the price France—or rather M. Delcassé—paid for the abandonment of the policy of amicable relations with Germany which M. Hanotaux had pursued. The agreement meant that M. Delcassé did not relinquish the hope of regaining Alsace-Lorraine, while Russia was determined, when an opportunity arose, to realize her traditional ambitions in the Balkans. It was, in fact, a bargain—the Straits for Alsace.[1]

This seems to be perfectly true, and the whole of Delcassé's policy since 1899 fully confirms the eminent historian's view.

[1] *Internationale*, August 2, 10, and 26, 1921. Mathiez points out that none of the semi-official historians of the Alliance—neither Schefer, nor Delcassé's friend Reynald, nor even Debidour—made any mention of this secret agreement of 1899. It remained unknown until 1918.

It is to be noted, further, that this modification in the terms
of the treaty introduced an element of contradiction, for,
though it legislated for a new reason for intervention, namely,
the disturbance of the Balance of Power in Europe, the conditions under which the intervention would actually take place
remained as specified in the military convention, and the latter
was only designed to operate in the event of aggression on the
part of the Triple Alliance. But the terms of the military
convention were henceforth of secondary importance only.
The apparent contradiction could be removed by simply
attributing aggressive motives to the enemy, and the convention would then come into force *ipso facto*. From this time
onwards, therefore, not merely would the Alliance set in
motion all the machinery of armed intervention whenever one
Government, in the hands of some oligarchy, decided that the
state of European equilibrium was not in its favour, but,
worse still, the destinies of France were bound up with the
idiosyncrasies of possibly one man—a Stolypin, a Sazonov,
an Isvolsky, or even some individual spokesman of a clique
dominated by a Rasputin—and with the way such a man
would interpret the European equilibrium.

The capital importance of the agreement of August 1899 is
thus clear. Yet Delcassé had the audacity to declare that there
was nothing in his visit but "simply the returning of a call".[1]
The *Temps*, too, made out that the visit was quite a normal
occurrence without any special importance.[2] As for the Nationalist papers, they asserted that Delcassé had only gone to
Russia to carry on intrigues to save Dreyfus and the Waldeck-
Rousseau Government. They regarded the visit as another
proof of Dreyfus's guilt. This is the amount of knowledge that
France, under a Republican régime, possessed of an event
which was destined to exercise a profound influence on the
whole of her future destiny. Even Ernest Lavisse, with all the
authority attaching to his name, could assert in 1901 that

---

[1] *Temps*, August 9, 1899.          [2] Ibid., August 6th and 10th.

the essential character of the Franco-Russian Entente remained as it had been fixed by the circumstances of its genesis:

There is a danger of falling into serious errors of judgment and of conduct if it is forgotten that the chief aim of the Alliance is not clinical, but prophylactic—not to do, so much as to prevent. It does not visualize such and such steps being taken as a joint offensive by the two high contracting parties, but merely envisages the possibility of some such offensive action being taken against one or the other party.[1]

[1] *Revue de Paris*, September 15, 1901.

# CHAPTER VI

## PRESAGES OF REVOLUTION

WE are now entering upon a period during which it became particularly difficult to sustain the spirit of the Alliance in France. Hitherto the Government and the ruling class generally had been able to maintain that the Tsar and his people were closely united and that the Emperor of All the Russias was the object of unanimous adoration, but from now onwards the statement began to fail to carry conviction. Events soon demonstrated, even to those most unwilling to see, that Tsarism was a yoke under which the Russian people chafed. About this time the *Revue Blanche* inquired of Tolstoy what was the attitude of the Russian people towards the Alliance, and the great novelist replied as follows:

The Russian people, the people proper, have not the slightest idea that such an Alliance exists. If they did know about it, I am sure that their common sense and humanity would tell them that an exclusive alliance with one nation rather than another can have no other object than to lead them into unfriendly relations, perhaps war, with other countries, and for this reason the Alliance would be in the highest degree distasteful to them.

In reply to the question whether the Russian people shared the enthusiasm of the French, Tolstoy had no hesitation in saying that not only did the Russian people not share the enthusiasm of the French, but if they knew all that was being said and done in France *à propos* of the Alliance they would, on the contrary, be filled with distrust and dislike of a nation which could suddenly and without any reason profess a spontaneous and exceptional affection for them. To a third question: "What is likely to be the influence of this Alliance on civilization in general?" the author of *War and Peace* replied:

I believe I am justified in assuming that, since the Alliance can have no other object than war or the threat of war against other countries, its influence can only be a harmful one. As regards its effect on the

two nations whom it allies, it is clear that it has done nothing but
mischief to them both up to the present and that it will undoubtedly
do the same in the future. The French Government, the press and
all that section of the French public which belauds the Alliance have
already had to make great concessions and compromises, and will
have to shed still more, in the future, of their traditions of freedom
and humanity, if they are to be, or to appear to be, at one in outlook
and sentiment with the most despotic, retrograde, and cruel Government in Europe. This is, and will be, a great loss to France. On
Russia the Alliance has had and will have, if it lasts, an even more
baneful influence. Since concluding the treaty with France, the
Russian Government, which used to feel some shame and was chary
of offending European public opinion, takes no more notice of criticisms and, deriving a feeling of security from this unnatural friendship
with a nation reputed to be the most cultured in the world, goes on
growing more and more despotic, retrograde, and cruel. Thus, in my
opinion, this strange and ill-omened alliance cannot but have a most
pernicious influence on the welfare of the two nations and also on
civilization in general.[1]

Thus with astonishing accuracy Tolstoy described the inevitable consequences of the Alliance, and subsequent events
confirmed his judgment only too fully.

From 1900 onwards the revolutionary movement in Russia
took on a more intensive form. Intellectuals, business men,
peasants, workers, all were discontented to the point of exasperation, and it began to grow more and more evident that
Tsarism could not exist for a moment without the financial
support of France. The movement developed first of all in
the Universities, and the Government had recourse to brutal
and ferocious measures of repression, the number of persons
executed, shot down, or exiled to Siberia growing apace. A
protest was addressed by forty-five Russian men of letters
and Professors to their foreign colleagues in the following
terms:

We the undersigned, deprived of the possibility of expressing freely
our ideas on the needs of our unhappy country, prevented by the

---

[1] *Revue Blanche*, October 1, 1901.

censorship from describing what is happening under our very eyes, appeal to our colleagues abroad to inform the civilized world of the atrocities that are being perpetrated here. . . . Filled with horror and anguish at the prospect of the future which lies before our country, we entreat the press of the entire world to give the utmost publicity to this mournful record of facts of which we have been eye-witnesses.[1]

All the best minds throughout the world received the appeal with emotion, and expressions of sympathy with the Russian intelligentsia were heard in every country. Numerous French writers, among them Zola, Anatole France, Jules Claretie, Octave Mirbeau, Paul Adam, Maeterlinck, L. Descaves, Paul and Victor Marguéritte, Séverine, J. H. Rosny, Brieux, and Lucien Besnard, placed on record their indignation against Tsarism and their disgust at seeing their own country support such a régime. Clemenceau, who had fought nobly for truth and justice in the Dreyfus case, asked: What did the word Russia connote? Politically speaking, the Tsar and nothing else. Russia was the only country where the views of the governed were regarded as non-existent. None the less, no people had ever furnished more numerous instances of stoical resolution, of lavish expenditure of untiring energy in the cause of Justice by men in the prime of life. It was inspiring, at a time when other nations were enamoured of "autocratic imperialism, to find Russia offering the spectacle of idealism and love of liberty in vigorous and determined action."[2] Shortly afterwards Clemenceau pointed out that the French people were not much better informed on their own affairs than the subjects of the Tsar on theirs. . . . Blue Books sometimes shed an unfortunate light upon the "*eyewash in our 'Yellow Books'*". He added that the Russian ambassadors Mohrenheim and Yurussov had consistently treated the French

[1] The *Correspondant* wrote on January 10, 1905: "Whoever lived in Russia towards the end of 1903 knows that one phrase was heard in every quarter, from the highest to the lowest: 'It cannot go on like this'."
[2] *Le Bloc*, March 31, 1901.

Governments with the off-handedness of barbarian chiefs, which was nothing short of a political scandal.[1]

General André relates that, when he was offered the post of War Minister by Waldeck-Rousseau in 1900, and found it necessary to dismiss certain officers for disloyalty, the Russian Military Attaché, Colonel Count M——, called on him one day and requested him to cancel his instructions. When the Minister declined to do so, the Attaché declared: "Then I must tell you, Sir, that you have violated the Alliance." André showed him the door, and then went and reported to Waldeck-Rousseau what had happened. The Prime Minister concurred in the line he had taken, assuring him that there was nothing in the Treaty of Alliance which had any bearing on the subject, and requested him to mention the matter to Delcassé, who would put it right. But the Foreign Minister seemed to be greatly upset over the incident, and did not conceal from his colleague that in his view it "would have been better if this had not happened", even going so far as to add: "You must be very cautious and discreet in your reforms. We must not offend people. Let us avoid quarrels anyhow; that is always the best thing."[2]

Delcassé was anxious not to antagonize the Autocrat of All the Russias by carrying out democratic reforms. He had his reasons. At the very moment when Tsarism was imposing the most savage of repressive measures on those intellectuals who had committed the crime of reaffirming their faith in the principles of the French Revolution, Delcassé set off on a fresh visit to Russia, and returned plastered all over with decorations and bursting with pride at the welcome he had received. It was this incident which led Henry Bérenger to

[1] According to Clemenceau, the Russian Embassy under Mohrenheim had become a hotbed of monarchist agitation, and the ambassador thought nothing of intervening in French domestic affairs on the slightest provocation, offering advice to Ministers, or even to the President. The Prime Minister had to request Carnot, during a Cabinet crisis, to close the doors of the Elysée to Mohrenheim. (*Dépêche*, September 26, 1901.)

[2] *Cinq ans de Ministère*, pp. 33 and 37.

denounce the "crazy hypocrisy which lay at the root of the official Franco-Russian Alliance"—never more clearly revealed than in the last few days, when the representative of the French Republic had been making his obeisances to the Russian autocrat and exchanging complimentary speeches with those who were beating down with the knout all advocacy of justice and freedom. "The essential vice of the Franco-Russian Alliance is that it is directed against the most sacred impulses of the human conscience. Would any honest man conceive the idea of protecting himself against a robber by joining forces, on terms of equality, with a murderer and calling him friend and ally?" A little later Bérenger wrote:

The Alliance and friendship between the French Republic and the Tsar of Russia is one of the strangest phenomena in history. It is one of the essential conditions of the maintenance of their association that each party to it shall solemnly play the hypocrite or the innocent the whole time. Official Paris must applaud things done in St. Petersburg which would be regarded as monstrous if they occurred in Paris and *vice versa*; the execution of Louis XVI and the Marseillaise must be swallowed without a shudder on the Tsar's side, while the mass deportations to Siberia and the massacres of students must be accepted without flinching by the French. The Alliance and the official friendship between the two nations are, in fact, poised above the twofold abyss of pretended and real ignorance. It is surely no light thing for a nation to pursue a foreign policy which gives the lie to its domestic policy, and to deny as a Great Power the very principles which it stands for as an organized community.[1]

At that time, immediately after the crisis of the Dreyfus case, it seemed hardly possible that the Alliance could stand the shock of the revolutionary events that were taking place in Russia. Consciences were sorely tried, and Frenchmen who had just been struggling so manfully for justice at home were driven to ask themselves whether they could tolerate in the

[1] *Dépêche de Toulouse*, April 29, May 3, and May 13, 1901. Bérenger asked in conclusion: "How can the ideals of 1789 be reconciled with the requirements of the Franco-Russian Alliance? Is it desirable that they should be? Is it possible? We will examine this problem in our next article." But his campaign came to an abrupt end. The "next article" is not to be found.

foreign policy of the nation a daily and public denial of the principles for which they had been fighting.

One of the objects of Delcassé's second journey to Russia had been to make arrangements for the Tsar and Tsarina to pay another official visit to France. The Imperial couple landed at Dunkirk at the end of September and proceeded to Compiègne, where sumptuous festivities were held, the temper of the capital being no longer to be altogether trusted. Count Witte remarked one day to Tardieu: "For the last ten years now you have been arranging Franco-Russian demonstrations on every pretext, and sometimes on none." Tardieu adds the comment: "An excess of festivities—too many bouquets, one might say—weighted down the Franco-Russian Alliance. Neither side was the gainer by this." In his view, "France's courtesies savoured a little too much of obsequiousness."[1]

By 1901 the Alliance had lost a good deal of its popularity with all sections of opinion in France. Paul de Cassagnac complained that it was not only barren of any useful result, and terribly expensive at that, but also perpetuated past humiliations and condemned the French people to everlasting renunciation.[2] Clemenceau, in his pacifist zeal, pointed out that the Tsar, as autocrat, could plunge into adventures none had bargained for, and his people had no choice but to follow him resignedly in all the consequences—ruin or death—that might be involved in his irresponsible caprice. "When a susceptible people like ourselves acquires a potentate like that as travelling companion, elementary prudence dictates that we should keep ourselves constantly informed as to the vicissitudes of the journey and should not lose sight of the horizon."[3] But Delcassé, rapt in his dreams, did not perceive the oncoming storm in the Far East.

Sigismond Lacroix, who had remained uninfected by the general infatuation in 1897, pointed out that a notorious

[1] Tardieu, p. 19.   [2] *L'Autorité*, September 12, 1901. See also *Le Soleil*.
[3] *Le Bloc*, September 29th.

H

oppressor of people like the Tsar was ill-qualified to commend
the "principles of international equity", as he had recently
done in a banquet speech. Lacroix drew attention to Russia's
arbitrary occupation of a section of Chinese territory.[1] Edgard
Milhaud observed that the Conservatives were delighted at
the spectacle of "the country which gave birth to the Revolution hampered in its every movement by the fetters of association with counter-revolutionary Russia".[2] Jaurès and Aristide
Briand supported the resolution proposed by the executive of
the Socialist Party, declaring solidarity with those who were
"carrying on in Russia a heroic struggle against Tsarist
despotism, that permanent menace to the world-wide Social
Revolution". In the Chamber of Deputies and the Senate,
however, none got up to ask the questions that should have
been put. Jaurès was not there, having been defeated at the
General Election of 1898. Apart from that, the personalities
of the men who held the position of Prime Minister in 1901
and 1902 were such as to inspire public confidence. It was
felt vaguely that, with such men at the helm, France would
never be swept away into a war by Tsarism. Hypnotized by
the anti-clerical reforms which were the logical outcome of
the Dreyfus case, the Democrats never dreamed that, in the
background, a conflict might be brewing for the more or less
remote future; still less that the Foreign Minister had been
allowed full scope for committing the country to a modification
of the Alliance.

Yet there is reason to think that, at that very moment, while
men's minds were still tempest-tossed by the repercussions of
the Dreyfus case, it might have been possible to extract from
the Government sufficient enlightenment to force them to
reconsider what Delcassé had done. Jaurès seems to have had
a glimpse of the right solution when he wrote, on April 11,
1901, that the French policy ought to be to "relax slowly and

---

[1] *Le Radical*, September 24th and 25th.
[2] *Petite République*, August 30th.

gently all the ties of obligation which bind us, and also those by which others are bound".[1] But his hands were tied by his support of the Combes Government, and he was not in a position either to exercise the necessary check on French foreign policy or to demand information regarding a treaty which, in the hands of any other man but Combes or Rouvier, was capable of involving the country in commitments of the most serious nature. This fact is all the more regrettable since Jaurès was the one man who, by his prestige and his splendid courage, might have been able to effect France's release from her degrading entanglement, so ensuring that she should not be plunged into war over some Balkan question, and at the same time, perhaps, bringing about the downfall of Tsarism. It is true that Jaurès had not the slightest reason to suspect the tremendous changes that Delcassé had introduced into the Alliance in 1899. If he had lived to learn this, with what a flood of indignation he would have denounced the men who had pledged France's word in disloyal secrecy at the very moment when, after endless efforts, she had succeeded in crushing the machinations of fraud and reaction within her borders. It is true, too, that Jaurès trusted certain individuals; but how quickly one politician takes the place of another and how chameleon-like they all are under the influence of changing motives! He might have learned, from examples quite close at hand, a salutary lesson of scepticism in regard to all men, whatever their characters. "Let us put our trust in no man", says Anatole France. The best of them are sometimes subject to the worst lapses, when their faculties begin to fail or their conscience nods under the stress of ambition.

In his ignorance of the modification of 1899, Jaurès even declared as late as 1903 that the Socialist Party had no objection in principle to the Franco-Russian Entente, seeing that, if kept to its proper sphere, it remained a purely defensive measure, calculated to assist in the maintenance of peace in

[1] *Petite République.*

Europe. He stipulated, however, that all due precautions must be taken, and that many points that were obscure must be cleared up. He reminded his hearers that the nation had at first believed that the Alliance was not solely a defensive one, and that, a few years back, Méline's newspapers had treated the Alliance as a weapon to be employed on the side of reaction in the arena of party politics.[1]

All this time Delcassé was pursuing his own line of policy undisturbed. Not satisfied with having altered the character of the Alliance, he signed a new agreement with Russia on March 19, 1902, shortly after the first Anglo-Japanese treaty, dealing with Far Eastern affairs, and providing for joint consultation, if necessary, in the event of aggressive action by a third party (Japan or Great Britain), to ensure that the interests of the two allied Governments were safeguarded. Thus the field covered by the Alliance was now extended to the Far East.

On March 25th a Conservative member, Denys Cochin, asked Delcassé for information on the subject. He called attention in strong terms to Russia's penetration of Manchuria and the risks thereby involved, to the regular campaigns of annexation that were being carried on by General Grodekov, to the seizure of towns and arsenals. Russian detachments were overrunning the whole country, and the Chinese could send no troops of their own into Manchuria except forces for purely police duties, and even with these the number and type of weapons carried were subject to Russian approval and the officers chosen by Russia. All railway and mining concessions were reserved to Russian subjects. Cochin foresaw that conflict with Japan would be inevitable, and emphasized with great vigour the difference between the interests of France in the Far East and those of Russia. "These disputes", he said,

are entirely foreign to us. The scene of the troubles lies in Asia. We are not directly concerned with Northern China at all. . . . Never-

---

[1] Chamber of Deputies, January 23, 1903.

theless a Franco-Russian Asiatic Entente is growing up in opposition
to the Anglo-Japanese Entente. How far are we committed? That is
what I am asking . . . An alliance must be operated with egoism
by the representatives of the countries concerned. They have no right
to show generosity. The national interests that are confided to their
care are not their personal property, and they have no right to lose
sight of them. The object of the Alliance was to give each party
security in Europe. Is it to be transformed into an undertaking
whereby each of the parties can call upon the other for assistance in
any and every detail of the most remote concerns and would in
fact embark on nothing independently of the other?

He mentioned briefly a number of instances in which France
had had to extricate herself from awkward positions without
assistance, such as Fashoda and the unfortunate Armenian
affairs, and concluded by addressing to the Foreign Minister
the direct question: "What exactly is expected of us nowadays?
To what extent are we committed to action under this latest
agreement?"

Delcassé replied that both Russia and France had but one
desire: to preserve the integrity of China. But if China's
integrity were threatened, would not "inactivity, hesitation
even, on the part of a Great Power like France be equivalent
to forfeiting her prestige"? And he went on coolly to declare,
though Russia was at that very moment violating her engagements by occupying Manchuria, that

the fact is that all the Powers are equally concerned to ensure that the
principles which they have solemnly enunciated shall be respected
equally by all, so that China may remain intact and independent, an
open field for the free play of intelligence and capital from all parts
of the world.

Denys Cochin rose again to express his disappointment that
Delcassé had not replied to the direct question he had put to
him regarding the extent of the French commitments in case
of war. "I regret to see France, whose aims are most sincerely
pacific, involved, and so unnecessarily involved, in the affairs
of an allied Power whose interests are far removed from ours,
and who, moreover, has no need to require from us this token

of obsequious zeal." Denis Guibert then vainly endeavoured to turn the question into a vote of non-confidence, but the Chamber resolved that the Minister's explanations should be accepted as satisfactory.[1]

It was not long, however, before Delcassé's categorical statements were to be tested in the fire of events and found wanting. On December 26, 1903, in a speech before the Senate, he was still vaunting with undiminished pride the magnificent results of the Alliance, which he termed the "ideal Alliance", as in 1887. Disregarding the repression behind the scenes, he spoke of the "keen and deep-seated popular sympathy" which had shown itself in the demonstrations in St. Petersburg, as in Paris, and praised Russia's organized forces and the Alliance which "gives us complete and fruitful security". A few months later, the real truth as to the strength of the Russian Empire and the security that the Alliance afforded was to be made manifest.

[1] In May 1902 the President of the Republic went to Russia on board the *Montcalm*, and the Alliance was again renewed.

# CHAPTER VII

# THE RUSSO-JAPANESE WAR

THE Russo-Japanese War was regarded by the Russian Government as a means of diverting the threat of revolution. Count Witte relates that Plehve, the Minister of the Interior, said one day to his colleague Kuropatkin, who had been reproaching him for his desire for war: "You do not know what the internal situation in Russia is like. We need a little victorious war to stem the tide of Revolution."[1]

It was not long before hostilities actually broke out. The war party refused to evacuate Manchuria, and the influential firm of Bezobrazov, which had been formed to develop the forests of Korea, was hoping to realize large profits. Among those associated with the firm were Hesse, the Governor of the Imperial Palaces, Count Ignatiev, Count Hendrikov, the Tsarina's Master of the Horse, and Prince Yussupov, but the prime mover was Bezobrazov, who enjoyed the direct protection of the Imperial Court. This precious crew by their intrigues soon made war inevitable.[2] Count Witte and Isvolsky have related how, despite all warnings, the Tsar appointed Bezobrazov Secretary of State—"a grotesque, half-mad individual". He became a kind of Minister without portfolio, and assumed the entire control of Russia's diplomatic relations with Japan, even arrogating to himself the right of corresponding direct with Russia's representatives in the Far East and of communicating the Tsar's instructions to them over the head of the Foreign Minister. In this way Nicholas II appointed Admiral Alexeyev as his viceroy in the Far East without the knowledge of his Ministers. Isvolsky was then (1903) in charge

[1] Witte, *Mémoires*, p. 222. André Cheradame had frequently been told by his friends in St. Petersburg: "We shall not get clear of this crisis unless we have a big war." (*Correspondant*, September 25, 1904.)

[2] Cf. *Revue de Paris*, July 15, 1905: "Les origines exactes de la guerre russo-japonaise". See also P. Marc, *Antécédents de la guerre russo-japonaise* ("Les menées de Bezobrazoff").

of the Russian Legation in Tokio, and was convinced that the attitude adopted by the Tsar under the influence of Bezobrazov and Alexeyev "was leading straight to war".[1]

On the very eve of the conflict Delcassé was saying that war was impossible, although all the French diplomatic agents in the Far East predicted it, especially Harmand, Minister at Tokio, and Crozier, who, while at Copenhagen, had received disquieting confidences from Isvolsky.[2] None the less, Delcassé had made no effort to dissuade the Tsar from his annexationist schemes in Manchuria. On the contrary, the agreement signed on March 19, 1902, had been an encouragement for the Russian partisans of an aggressive policy and had played into Bezobrazov's hands.

Clemenceau saw clearly that the French had helped only too effectively to persuade their allies to plunge into this foolish adventure. It was an inexcusable blunder, because France's most essential interest lay in retaining Russia's energies in Europe. What was French diplomacy thinking of, to allow the Alliance to be thus hampered in its efficiency by overbalancing towards Asia? "In our sheep-like docility", says Tardieu, "we had become accomplices in our ally's rashness, instead of requiring her to respect the fundamental claims of our pact."[3] It is true that, when Russia turned back to Europe again, her intrigues for Constantinople and the Straits became an even greater danger to the peace of the world.

Delcassé's most serious mistake, which, to be sure, was shared by the French General Staff, diplomatists, and public

---

[1] This shows how honest the Tsar was in his disarmament and peace proposals of 1898–9. Isvolsky, *Mémoires*, pp. 25, 289–91. Witte, *Mémoires*, pp. 100 sqq. See also Cheradame's article in the *Correspondant* of May 25, 1904, on the part played by the financiers in the Far East, and their hold on Manchuria. *Die Grosse Politik*, XIX (1).

[2] *Revue de France*, April 1, 1921.

[3] Tardieu, pp. 20–24. "To refuse to follow Russia in her Japanese policy", wrote Cheradame, "would have been to show perspicacity, to prevent her from weakening her position in Europe by diversion of energy, and thus to support and strengthen the Alliance, not to betray it." (*Correspondant*, September 25, 1904.)

opinion, was to be convinced that Russia would be victorious. The press, it need hardly be said, also fully shared this confidence.[1] Count Witte asserted on several occasions that, if Delcassé had intervened at St. Petersburg and represented that war would be contrary to the aims of the Alliance, peace would have been maintained.[2] The war was very unpopular in Russia from the beginning, not only among the industrial workers and peasants but with the factory owners, business men, and all the liberally minded. On February 23, 1904, a general meeting of the Institute of Mining Engineers in St. Petersburg passed a resolution declaring that the war with Japan had its origin in a policy conceived solely in the interests of a tiny minority of privileged people and detrimental to the vast majority of the Russian nation. Raymond Recouly, the *Temps* correspondent in St. Petersburg, wrote on January 15, 1905, that the people understood nothing of the war. Port Arthur, Manchuria, Japan were meaningless words to them.[3] Anatole Leroy-Beaulieu relates that, in Moscow in 1905, he was repeatedly assured by Russians: "Do not wish us victory. Victory would put back for fifty, perhaps a hundred, years the enfranchisement, the reforms, that we shall snatch from defeat."[4]

The war revealed the utter rottenness of the Tsarist organism. Everything that Leroy-Beaulieu had foreseen in 1888 was confirmed in an aggravated form. The state of the Russian army was what it had been in 1855; if anything, it had

---

[1] The *Temps* had not the slightest doubt as to the successful outcome of the struggle. (February 10th.) Colonel Marchand in the *Matin* asserted that "If the Japanese come away from Korea and attempt to march on Harbin they will be lost." (February 13th.) Even High Finance was entirely confident. Dorizon, Director of the *Société Générale*, was "sure that Russia would get through the war with Japan with less sacrifices than Great Britain had to undergo in the Boer War." (*Matin*, February 11th.)

[2] *Carnets de G. Louis*, I, p. 211; II, p. 70.

[3] See Recouly's messages, especially between August and December 1904.

[4] From an address delivered at the *École des Sciences Politiques*, May 13, 1907.

deteriorated rather than progressed. The corruption and inefficiency exceeded anything that could possibly be imagined. Funds sent out for the Red Cross failed to reach their destination. Cases of champagne and women's frocks were put on rail labelled "Munitions". During the retreat from Mukden, the kitchen and the harem of one of the Grand Dukes took up two complete trains, and the whole of one General's Staff had female travelling companions.[1] Agents demanded enormous tips for the delivery of ships, arms, or ammunition.

This venture, which was to end in such disaster and from which Delcassé had taken no steps to dissuade Russia, was all the more serious for France because the alliance of Great Britain with Japan might have given rise to complications which would have left Germany supreme on the Continent. What would have become of France supposing the Triple Alliance as a whole, or even Germany by herself, had declared war while she was engaged in a disastrous struggle with Britain? Delcassé's responsibility was overwhelming. Yet so utterly negligible is Parliamentary control over foreign policy in France that his position remained unshaken. Denys Cochin had given notice of a question in which he was going to ask the Foreign Minister what part France was to play in the dispute, and whether, under the terms of the Alliance, she might be bound to intervene, but he withdrew his question after a conversation with Delcassé, who explained that a debate on the subject would be "highly unfortunate at the present time".

At this juncture Jaurès displayed remarkable courage.[2] He

---

[1] Cf. the Margaine Report on the "Yellow Book", p. 80.

[2] Jaurès had at first intended to move in the Chamber of Deputies a resolution calling for the publication, in the form of a Yellow Book, of all the documents relating to the engagements undertaken by France towards Russia. But Combes, the Prime Minister, asserted definitely that he was resolved to assent to no measures, to allow no step to be taken, which might endanger directly or indirectly the liberty of France without the Chamber of Deputies and Parliament as a whole being invited, not only to state its views as to the line which ought to be taken, but also to examine in detail

alone revealed the dangers of the Alliance. He alone dared to put the question which every man in political life ought to have regarded it as his duty to put: "Is France committed to Russia by agreements of a positively binding nature?" On February 12th he wrote in the *Dépêche de Toulouse*:

It is really extraordinary that neither the text nor even any precise summary of the treaties concluded with Russia has been communicated to the nation which is bound by these treaties. If we should be led to the brink of war by secret conventions, the country would never forgive those who for the last ten years have always stifled with patriotic clamour the question which the Socialist Party has so often endeavoured to ask.

He pointed out that, even without written and formal engagements, a serious danger existed, created by the fanatical Russophilism which had been stirred up in the country. The Alliance had been represented to the French people as so vitally necessary that Ministers might have committed the gravest acts of imprudence to conciliate Russia. (Jaurès knew nothing of the 1899 modification in the Treaty.) It was in any case a blunder to allow Russia to get accustomed to relying on France so thoroughly that she had no scruples in overriding the rights of China and offending the susceptibilities of Japan. It was due to the fact that she had never met with any resistance or warning from France that Russia, after having solemnly promised the world to evacuate Manchuria, had now settled down there for good. The whole of this article is so closely applicable to the situation which existed in July 1914 that it might well be quoted almost *in extenso*:

The question arises, a poignant and tragic question: Will France be able to retain, in her dealings with Russia, sufficient liberty of action, or will she be gradually dragged, by the fatal logic of the Alliance, into committing herself to declare war in support of Russia? We do

---

all the events that had taken place. Thereupon Jaurès abandoned his idea. (*Matin* February 9, 1904.) This was a serious misfortune, for the opportunity did not occur again. If only France at that time had had at its head a politician of the time-serving or the jingo type, Jaurès' suspicions would not have been allayed, and he would have insisted on the whole truth.

not ask that France should cancel with undue haste *an alliance the dangers of which must be apparent to-day to the most wilfully blind.* We regard it as fit and proper that she should offer Russia her good offices in the final settlement of the conflict. But if France were so closely committed to Russia that she too joined in the war, if the Alliance, which has been represented to us as a safeguard for the peace of Europe, resulted in an Asiatic adventure, if France were destined suddenly to mobilize her navy, to pour out blood and treasure to help to victory the wild-cat schemes of Russian ambition, that would be one of the most flagitious scandals ever known in history. How often we have predicted this! How often we have tried to warn the community against it! In vain; we were shouted down with a few lines of some patriotic song. Now the spectre of war really appears, not war for justice, independence, territorial integrity, but war to serve the ends of Russian greed in a far-off land. It is high time that treaties which involve the whole of our national life should be revealed in the letter and the spirit. It is no longer a question of some distant uncertain contingency. The possibility of war is at our very doors, and the country has a right to know what engagements have been entered into in its name.

On the following day Jaurès delivered an important speech at the Socialist Congress at Saint-Etienne, in which he raised the question of the Alliance with still greater force:

Great Britain is allied to Japan and France to Russia. This situation creates a problem which means peace or war, according to whether we can succeed in forcing our working-class policy on the public and on our rulers, or, on the contrary, allow all the mischief-makers, all those who go about stirring up hatred between nations, to pursue their abominable task. . . . We have not yet brought this question up in Parliament, but this must assuredly be done.

He reminded his audience that the Socialists had been asking for the past twelve years what were the terms of the Alliance, what was the detailed wording of the contract which pledged France, and had received no reply but: "You are either very indiscreet or you are traitors, wishing to isolate France and leave her defenceless in face of the enemy."

They denounce us as unpatriotic, and then proceed to prolong the scandal of a Government standing for democracy, universal suffrage, and popular sovereignty, a French Government, being bound hand and foot by a secret treaty which the nation has never had a chance of ratifying because it has never had a chance of learning what its terms are. The question must be raised, we must be given an explanation, we must be told whether France is tied by a secret bond to the Russian army and whether we may be forced one of these days to go and pour out our treasure, our blood, our credit in a strange land.

In Jaurès' view, the Alliance had now lost its *raison d'être*, and the pressing arguments which had originally seemed to bear out the necessity of signing it no longer held good:

Let the two nations, in undiminished friendship, resume their independence, and let there be formed not another dual alliance, nor yet a triple alliance, but a general alliance of all the peoples of Europe. There is no attempt to do this now, because the nationalist forces of reactionary jingoism have taken charge of all questions of foreign policy, and because the nationalist forces of reactionary clericalism have taken fright at seeing the popular movement growing, seeing the working classes organizing, seeing the sun of Socialism rise above the horizon. Finally, Reaction has made up its mind that there is only one way left of holding these men back, only one way left of checkmating the proletariat, and that is to intoxicate them with the heady wine of jingo nationalism, to divert their attention from home problems, the social problem, to point constantly to the bogy of an enemy on the other side of the frontier, to sound constantly in their ears the trumpet call of coming wars. And in this endeavour to deafen the people with martial music, to reawaken old vibrations in the warlike soul of France, Reaction says not only "there is constant danger", but repeats incessantly, day after day, "See that friend across there —without him France will perish". And as you cannot have an ally without promising him something, the second act of the negotiations was opened by saying to Russia: "If need be, if difficulties arise in the Far East, we will discuss the situation together." That is how it has been possible for France to get involved in the Far East. . . .

We have often denounced the Franco-Russian Alliance for the inevitable dangers which it conceals and for the humbug it contains. No solemn protocol exchanged between the two Governments provides, to our mind, any guarantee of peace. And if ever a contingency arises which involves a threat of war, we have made up our minds to oppose it with all our strength by systematic obstruction of the most implacable, unyielding kind. . . .

When this scare has passed, we shall be able gradually to loosen the ties of an ill-advised, too exclusive alliance which has ceased to be a safeguard, if indeed it ever was, and has become a danger and a menace. . . . Imagine what risks we should be running if at the head of the Government to-day we had a man capable of entering into secret compromises with the clerical party and the Nationalists. They do not dare to admit openly that they desire war, but at the

bottom of their hearts war, for them, as always in history for parties
of reaction who feel insecure, is a welcome distraction. Let war but
break out, and you will see the General Staffs of the armies of forgery
and mendacity raise their heads unabashed. . . . Yes, for the clerical
party, for the "shoot-them-down", dictatorship-mad generals, for
all the partisans of reaction, oppression and darkness, war would be
a distraction, would be their salvation. That is why we loathe war
with a doubly deadly hatred, because it means barbarism and because
it means reaction.[1]

This speech reads like a vision of the future. Its elevated
tone might have been expected to command the assent, if only
tacit, of the overwhelming majority of public men. The question was a simple one: Could France run the risk of incurring,
through her secret treaty with Tsarism, war with Great
Britain and Japan over Manchuria? Yet for putting it Jaurès
was inundated by a flood of insult and calumny. He was
regarded as a traitor for having committed the crime of trying
to ascertain the truth—and this immediately after the Dreyfus
trial. The *Temps* held up to obloquy the Socialist leader's
conception of "national honour", affirming that the nation had
clearly shown its distaste for such "strange theories". "If he
wishes to cancel the Alliance or to relax its provisions, he will
find the nation opposed to him as one man. . . . M. Jaurès has
not changed; he was always a preacher of surrender and the
white feather." (February 16th and 20th.)[2] The *Journal des
Débats*, after declaring that Russia had been "subjected to

[1] *Tribune républicaine de Saint-Etienne*, February 14, 1904. Shortly
afterwards, Jaurès dotted the *i*'s and crossed the *t*'s: "Now that the power
of Reaction is threatened, what a triumph it would be if France were
plunged into war and obliged to suspend all her efforts at internal reform
and exhaust her energies in the inevitable struggle. . . . The Nationalists
will not shout openly for war, but they will drop their poison into all international incidents and stir up men's minds until war becomes inevitable. . . .
To inflame people's minds, to create tension in foreign relations, so that the
spectre of war shall obsess the nation and divert it from its work for
democracy—that is the scheme, that is the intrigue." (March 6th.)

[2] On February 10th the *Temps* had said: "France is Russia's ally. This
alliance is an intimate one and of general application. It connotes, besides
positive engagements, a moral co-operation which, under the pressure of
events, might well lead to further agreements. . . . This is our duty, and
we shall fulfil it."

provocation and wanton attack", that "nobody outside Japan desired war", and that it was too soon to say whether the war would remain localized, denounced the Socialist leader for his utter lack of judgment. "We looked in vain in M. Jaurès' speech for any sign of solicitude for his country's welfare." (February 10th, 16th, 17th, and 20th.) Pierre Baudin, in the *Journal*, referred in scathing terms to men who look for pretexts to "shirk the obligations of an Alliance entered into with our eyes open". It would be more fitting to devote oneself to perfecting our military organization. "Let us not cease to cherish peace, or to prepare for war." (February 21st.) The *République Française* published a number of very interesting letters from prominent politicians. J. Reinach, whose co-religionists in Russia were being mown down in organized pogroms, wrote that "the heart of France must needs beat with that of Russia, the barrier which protects old Europe against Asia". Barthou declared that Russia was the standard-bearer of European interests in this conflict, which she had not provoked, that the Alliance had increased France's security and moral authority, and that it had given birth to "unforgettable moments". Caillaux agreed with Barthou that the Alliance had increased the security and the moral authority of the country, and added, with reference to Jaurès' speech:

The most elementary sense of decency should have deterred any Frenchman from entering at the present moment on a discussion of the merits of an alliance from which we have all been glad to reap the benefits it has brought us. Our sense of duty and our solicitude for our country's honour coincide with her best interests. It is impossible for anyone not to realize what grave dangers would threaten the civilized world if the Japanese were victorious.

A. Deville, the Chairman of the Paris City Council, asserted that the Alliance was a safeguard for France and acted as a counter-weight to her home policy, which was inclined to be Socialistic.[1] Francis Charmes, a member of the Senate and

---

[1] *République Française*, February 13th to 22nd. See also the letters by Charles Dupuy and Poubelle.

director of the *Revue des Deux Mondes*, expressed the view that France was bound in any event to stand by her engagements, which were very general in their character.[1] Certain prominent members of the Radical Party took up a peculiar standpoint. Following Pierre Baudin, E. Lockroy, who seemed since the Dreyfus trial to have thrown in his lot with the Nationalists, wrote in the *Dépêche*: "Notwithstanding Russia's desire for peace, hostilities have broken out. . . . We are determinedly pacific, but the example of Russia shows us that we must not be guilty, in this direction, of wasteful and ridiculous excess." (February 14th and 27th.) And Méline, in a big public speech at Soissons on February 21st, displayed once more his customary gift of clear-sighted prophecy:

If there is anything certain in this world, it is that this war can only result in the complete victory of the great nation which has done everything possible to prevent it and has only drawn the sword from dire necessity. . . . Once France has pledged her word, she never retracts. This Alliance has become the keystone of our foreign policy. The contemptible campaign which certain individuals in our midst are trying to carry on will only have the effect of opening the people's eyes and showing them whither Collectivism can lead and what is in store for us if that doctrine is allowed to continue its ruinous propaganda.

At the same time as it heaped every imaginable insult on Jaurès, the French press was preparing the mind of the nation for the possibility of war. The *Matin* published an article by Charles Laurent, belabouring the "panic-mongers" who were proposing to let the Alliance lapse, suggesting to their fellow-countrymen that France should repudiate her debts instead of paying them, and, like Jaurès, were so immersed in their petty party outlook that they had lost touch with the feelings of the nation as a whole. "That is not the way to educate a race

---

[1] *Revue des Deux Mondes*, March 1st. Not long before this, Brunetière had stated, in the course of his address to Frédéric Masson on the latter's entry into the Académie Française: "At a time when the nations of the earth are aslumber on the feather-bed of peace, only dreaming of making profits out of buying and selling the produce of their colonies, you have had the courage to celebrate the glory of war. You have lifted up our national pride."

to fulfil its duty. . . . Do not let us shirk the danger before it is upon us." (February 21st.) The *Echo de Paris* maintained that Jaurès' anti-patriotic utterances and his attempt to poison the nation's conscience "would find no echo in any French heart". (February 16th, 17th, and 18th.) The *Figaro* stigmatized Jaurès as an enemy of the people and the Socialist Party as a body of Francophobes, and thence, by logical progression, called upon the country to form a movement of National Union, excluding the Socialists, and to suspend the policy of social reform for fear of creating divisions in the ranks. Latapie called for Combes' resignation, on the plea that he was unfitted to "marshal the forces of France, united, strong, and resolute in face of the enemy Powers, avid for conquest".[1] The *Gaulois*, after having denounced Jaurès' "abominable, criminal machinations", rejoiced that public opinion was reacting forcibly. "When all these apostles of flabbiness have been cleared out of France, the nation will become once more its old virile, warlike, and truly religious self." Aristide Briand was justified in writing: "It is now perfectly clear that a war party exists in France. This is now demonstrated beyond any shadow of doubt."[2]

We apologize for giving so many quotations, but it seemed necessary to furnish an accurate reflection of the outlook of the governing classes at that time, showing that they would have been glad to find some distraction abroad for the active Republican policy that was being pursued at home. The Alliance assumed more and more the aspect of a possible instrument for applying pressure on the course of internal politics. There is a striking analogy between all these expressions of opinion and those which we were to read and hear ten years later.

It was not long before Jaurès' predictions were confirmed. During the night of October 21–22, 1904, the Russian Baltic

---

[1] *République Française*, February 11th, 14th, and 16th.
[2] *Tribune de Saint-Etienne*, March 13, 1904.

I

Fleet under Admiral Rozhestvensky, which was on its way to
the Far East, opened fire on some British trawlers on the
Dogger Bank which they took for Japanese torpedo boats.
The British Channel Fleet, Mediterranean Fleet, and Reserve
Fleet joined forces and took up a position which threatened
the Russians' advance. If the French statesmen had not moved
heaven and earth to mollify Great Britain, there is no doubt
that she would have intervened against Russia, with the result
that France would have been dragged into the conflict. It
should be noted that the French authorities later on feigned
ignorance of the glaring violation of neutrality committed on
two successive occasions by the Russian Fleet in making
lengthy calls at Nossi-Be (Madagascar) and Kamranh Bay
(Cochin-China) for the purpose of taking in replenishments
and carrying out an intensive training programme. The
Japanese Government protested in vain, but there is no doubt
that if Rozhestvensky's tragic cruise had not ended in the
disaster of Tsushima, Japan would have attributed her defeat
to France.

Combes gave no countenance to any criminal attempts to
lead France astray. In any case the odds were too great. France
could not possibly cope with Britain and Germany at once,
with no assistance from Russia. The fire-eaters had to defer
the realization of their warlike aims until later.

Jaurès continued his opposition to the Alliance. At the
Amsterdam Congress of the Second International, on August 17,
1904, he again suggested that an understanding with Great
Britain and Italy would be the best means of "slackening the
bonds of the Alliance by which France is chained to Russia".
The Russo-Japanese War had, he said, been planned and made
inevitable by the intrigues of financiers, of dissolute, bullying
Grand Dukes, of a whole band of wolves with sharp teeth
and hungry bellies who sought in Korea a new field for profit
and plunder. The evil counsellors of Tsarism had provoked
this conflict in order to revive the waning strength of abso-

lutism by the prestige of victory, to swamp in war-fever the claims of the workers, the demands of the *zemstvos*, the scruples of the Liberals, the resentment of the Jews, and the bitter complaints of the peasants. The Tsar had only been the wretched dupe of a gang of mercenary and filibustering adventurers. Giving vent to his sense of shame at the lethargy of the people of all nations, Jaurès affirmed that the present generation was dishonoured by its failure, in face of this atrocious spectacle, to "take one step or say one word in advocacy of peace or preparation for it". Ten years before 1914, Jaurès was already pointing out that French public opinion was "so prejudiced and warped that to say one word about pity, humanity, mediation, peace, was to run the risk of being accused of high treason". He urged that it was "absolutely essential to work constantly for peace, to build up a sense of moral compulsion to peace, by powerful and unceasing international demonstrations inspired by humanity, wisdom, and pity".[1]

[1] *Humanité*, August 19, October 8, and October 16, 1904.

# CHAPTER VIII

## THE 1905 REVOLUTION

FAR from acting as a diversion, as Tsarism had hoped, the Russo-Japanese War only inflamed the revolutionary passions still more. It is necessary to give a brief summary of the chief events of this period in Russia in order to show, on the one hand, the attitude towards them which was adopted in France, and, on the other, how the Tsar's Government was upheld in its struggle against the Revolution by French financial support, and how the Alliance thus played a part of the first importance in Russian domestic politics.

It must not be forgotten that the Revolution of 1905 was the culmination of a series of efforts extending over many years in a nation consisting essentially of a tiny minority of rulers—the Imperial House, the higher bureaucracy, and the land-owning aristocracy—a small class of business men and members of the learned professions, and an enormous mass of peasants, who have always regarded themselves as the sole true proprietors of the land, since the soil should belong to those who till it. That is their fundamental claim, which gave to every revolutionary movement in Russia a primarily social tinge.

Apart from the peasants, a considerable part was played in the events now brewing by the Jewish population, which supplied the most active contingent in the revolutionary forces by reason of being the most harshly oppressed and reduced to the condition of helots. In addition, the Government and the ruling classes did their best to stir up the hatred of the people against the Jews, and anti-Semitism had become for Tsarism a regular instrument of government, especially as a means of staving off demands for social reform. Massacres, or pogroms, were organized, which had the result of diverting popular discontent and at the same time ridding the Government of its most dangerous adversaries. The pogrom developed into quite an institution under Tsarism. In 1903, at Kishinev, all previous records for horror were broken.[1] The massacre went on for twenty-four hours, and the atrocities remained unpunished. The chief organizer, a man named Krushevan, was left entirely undisturbed, and in 1906 was elected to the Duma as a Government candidate. Such facts are the strongest condemnation of the régime. And while the whole of the civilized world rang with protests, the chief organs of public opinion in France maintained complete equanimity, and even asserted that this was a question of Russian domestic politics of no concern to foreigners.

On July 28, 1904, the Russian Prime Minister, Plehve, the embodiment of autocracy in its most uncompromising form, was assassinated in St. Petersburg. Some of the French newspapers at once represented the deed as the act of a traitor and foreign agent.[2] Plehve's death actually marked the beginning of the Revolution, as if giving the signal. Prince Sviatopolk-Mirsky, a man of liberal tendencies, was called to power, and inaugurated the policy of "mutual confidence". In November the first congress of Zemstvos (County Councils) took place in St. Petersburg despite the Government's ban, the authorities not daring to dissolve it. It was composed chiefly of aristocratic Liberals and landed proprietors, forming in effect a sort of Assembly of Notables. By a majority the meeting adopted a number of classic resolutions relating to: legal equality of all

[1] Prince Yurussov, the Governor of Bessarabia, brings invaluable evidence on the subject: "In my opinion, it is impossible to acquit the Central Government of moral responsibility for the massacre and pillage that took place at Kishinev. . . . It is a proven fact that the Government sanctioned the pogrom. . . . The events of 1905 and 1906 and the inquiries that were held led me to attribute certain mysterious facts that had been left in obscurity to the indirect action of persons in high places. It is possible that the instigators and chief supporters of the pogroms are to be found in even more exalted spheres."—*Mémoires*, pp. 81 sqq., 128 sqq. Cf. the report of the inquiry in the *Siècle*.

[2] The English press, on the other hand, was not unduly astonished (cf. *The Times*). The *Daily Graphic* spoke of the coming of a Russian Revolution, compared with which the French Terror would be mere child's-play.

citizens, sanctity of the person and the home, freedom of conscience, speech, press, public meeting and association, and an amnesty for political offenders. Finally, it was asserted that "to ensure a normal development of public and social life in Russia, it is absolutely necessary that a national representative body should participate regularly in the exercise of legislative powers, in the preparation of the Budget, and in the supervision of the actions of the executive". In an Imperial rescript dated December 12th, Nicholas II refused to make any of these concessions and announced point-blank his intention to "adhere without any modification to the unshakable principles on which the Empire was founded".

All the leading newspapers in France took their stand against the Liberal movement, maintaining that the war ought to be the Russian people's sole concern. There were, however, some writers, more familiar with Russian conditions, who urged the need for peace. Anatole Leroy-Beaulieu blamed the Russian Government for declining to agree either to a conference or to outside intervention or mediation. "In their obstinate determination to continue the war in Manchuria", he wrote, "the Tsar's advisers have in mind not only the task of beating back the Japanese, but also, and perhaps chiefly, the need for damming the menacing flood of revolution and beating the enemy of autocracy on Russian soil." Not only the fate of Manchuria was at stake, in fact, but, above all, the home Government of Russia, the Tsarist régime. For the people of Russia, the cause of peace and the cause of freedom were closely linked. Among the more enlightened, those who longed to rescue Russia from the horrors of this disastrous war felt that political freedom was the one road along which peace could be attained. A general consultation of the people would have been the preface to peace, and Leroy-Beaulieu advised the Tsar to convene either a representative assembly or a congress of the Zemstvos, and thus to ascertain what views were held in regard to the war and to peace. "If, on the contrary, he persists, on the plea of raising the national prestige, in continuing the war indefinitely, against the wishes of the nation, then he will be multiplying present difficulties and endangering the future, both for the country and for the dynasty."[1] But the French bourgeoisie, led by Delcassé, would not hear of it. Instead of urging the Tsar to make peace, the leading organs of opinion (having, it must be remembered, certain reasons for doing so) preached the gospel of war to the bitter end for national honour and condemned every demand for reforms.[2]

Then came the tragedy of Sunday, January 22, 1905, when an unarmed crowd of workers, led by the "pope" Gapon, coming to beg the Tsar to convene a national Constituent Assembly elected by universal suffrage, was shot down at short range in front of the Winter Palace. The *Temps* correspondent wrote next day:

Yesterday was a day of terror. The troops fired on a crowd which included, along with the workers, women, children, and ordinary inquisitive passers-by. . . . The main burden of responsibility for what took place must rest with the Russian Government.

This massacre represents a definite milestone in the history of the Russian people. Thenceforward the idea of the "Little Father" was gone. "It has struck a blow," said Leroy-Beaulieu, "perhaps a mortal blow, at the Tsar's moral authority and the traditional prestige of Tsarism. Something has snapped in Russia;—it is the link, consecrated by agelong tradition, between the people and their sovereign." The common people had definitely lost their former trust in the Tsar. The events of "Bloody Sunday" had killed in them that hereditary faith.

"Whatever happens, this cannot be the end, but rather a beginning. They must be blind who can imagine that a few volleys of musketry and a few hundred dead are enough to keep a whole nation in servitude. For my part, I hold to the

---

[1] *La Revue*, January 15, 1905.
[2] See the *Temps*, January 21, 1905.

belief that ideas cannot be killed by gunfire."[1] Notwithstanding this testimony from a distinguished Frenchman, who was particularly well informed on Russian affairs, the attitude of the ruling class in France, as reflected in the comments of the popular press on the news of the massacre, was entirely callous, and Delcassé went so far as to defend the shooting in the Chamber of Deputies. In contrast to even the most reactionary journals in Great Britain and Germany, which expressed strong disapproval, the *Journal des Débats*, the *République Française*, the *Liberté*, the *Presse* represented the firing as simply the repression of an anarchist rising, a seditious, lawless riot. The *Matin* described it as the sanguinary onset of a mad revolt rather than the dawn of a revolution making for freedom. The *Revue des Deux Mondes* professed to recognize the work of international pan-German intrigue. The comment of the *Temps* was that Russia was not ripe for Parliamentary government and ought to devote her whole attention to the war. In the *Libre Parole*, Edouard Drumont asserted that the revolt was inspired from abroad and by the Jews, and that the Russian peasant was totally uninterested in it. The *Autorité* and the *Patrie* denounced the petitioners as traitors, who were quite rightly dispersed by force.[2] Maurice Barrès refused to sign a petition asking for the release of Maxim Gorky, who had just been arrested.[3] Practically the whole of the French press took up a standpoint of brutal opposition, not only to the revolutionary movement, but also to any sort of thorough-going reform. Like the *Temps*, Saint-Brice in the *Journal* wrote that, "in common with many enlightened observers", he considered that the Russians were not ripe for constitutional government (January 22nd), while the *Eclair* condemned "this mania for Parliamentarism". (January 24th.)

[1] *Courrier Européen*, January 27, 1905.
[2] It is noteworthy that the same papers were all filled with horror at the news of the assassination of the Grand Duke Sergius in the following month.
[3] *Figaro*, February 3, 1905.

On the whole, these extracts give a fairly accurate idea of what the French bourgeoisie really thought about political and social movements in general. The most striking feature is the similarity of the language then used with that which was current in 1917 and later. It was in vain that Leroy-Beaulieu pointed out that "while attention here is chiefly focused on Manchuria and Port Arthur, public opinion in Russia itself is concerned first and foremost with domestic affairs, and only refers to the war to criticize the Government for having entered into it, for mismanaging it, and for not putting an end to it".[1] History was to repeat itself with remarkable accuracy in 1916–17. In 1905 the *Temps* declared dogmatically that:

To talk of peace now would be tantamount to an admission of defeat, an impossibility for a Great Power with any concern not only for honour but for its vital interests. Russia cannot think of it. . . . In war, even more than in other games of chance, the gambler must never know when he is beaten. (February 24th.)

Fortunately for France's good name, Leroy-Beaulieu was supported by others in his defence of the Russian people. Jaurès wrote in *Humanité*:

A river of blood flows henceforth between the Tsar and his people. From this time forth, the Tsar and the régime he represents are the outlaws of human society. . . . No Republican statesman can in future hold any communication, even the most formal, without a feeling of painful shame, with this sanguinary autocracy, which meets the most justifiable demands of its freedom-loving subjects by wholesale murder. (January 23rd.)

But Jaurès was mistaken. A French Minister stood up in the Chamber of Deputies and defended the massacre. Five days after the event, Delcassé expressed his "vehement and indignant protest against the disgraceful language" used by two Socialist members in criticizing the action taken at the Winter Palace. "You are not judges", he said, "and even if you were, there are not sufficient data to arrive at an impartial judgment." At

---

[1] Letter to the *République Française*, January 25, 1905.

this Jaurès exclaimed: "For the sake of France's honour, it is to be hoped that the Foreign Minister will not constitute himself the advocate of a Government which has steeped its hands in the blood of a nation", to which Delcassé retorted: "I am the advocate of the interests of my country, which you, M. Jaurès, are serving very ill at present." Such was the part a Minister of the Republic was forced by the Alliance to play. Not only that, but he sank so low as to shower the most ignoble insults on Jaurès—insults which, handed round and repeated for the next decade by Nationalists and Moderates alike, had their inevitable result in his assassination.

Could any unprejudiced mind fail to protest against such language as Delcassé's? Clemenceau wrote in the *Aurore*: "Nothing can excuse M. Delcassé for having attempted to justify the massacre in face of humanity's world-wide condemnation. This misguided man is still beglamoured by his visits to St. Petersburg." He was grossly insulting the whole country in daring to call upon it for any other sentiments but those proper to a democracy.

Warm-hearted sympathy, instinctive pity for the oppressed, humanitarianism—these are part of the legacy we Frenchmen have received from our forefathers—such a precious trust that denial of it would spell decadence. M. Delcassé has forgotten this. That is regrettable if only for his own sake. (January 31, 1905.)

Francis de Pressensé reminded the Government that France was pre-eminently the land of Revolution. The Republic could not be false to its glorious origins without dishonour, without national suicide.[1] It is a melancholy reflection that almost all the Governments of the Third Republic have been at pains to gloss over the fact that modern France was conceived, born, and reborn in insurrection, on July 14, 1789, on August 10, 1792, in 1848, in 1870. Did not the Third Republic owe its existence to revolt in the face of the enemy, just as the First

---

[1] *Humanité*, January 29, 1905.

did?[1] Anatole France spoke witheringly of "this monstrous Alliance of a despot with a Republic". Octave Mirbeau predicted that the Tsar, now under sentence of death from his people, would not long escape his fate. The revolutionary movement might have its set-backs, but it would inevitably gather weight and momentum and manifest itself with "greater and greater violence, more and more powerful weapons".[2]

It was a critical time for the Alliance. Coming so soon after the Dreyfus trial, when men's minds were unwontedly stirred by the battle for civil liberty, the Russo-Japanese War, and more especially the revolutionary movement in Russia, could not fail to give rise to hostile comment on the French association with Tsarism.

The massacre of January 22, 1905, sharpened the edge of the revolutionary struggle. Strike followed strike without intermission. Demands for political and social reform grew more and more insistent, and the Tsar was constrained to announce his intention of summoning a new *zemski sobor*, a kind of Assembly of Notables, for the preparation of legislative proposals. The *Temps* was alarmed at the news and deplored the step as a sign of weakness. (February 22nd.) The leading organs of the French press were more reactionary than the Tsar himself!

After the Tsushima disaster, revolutionary agitation was intensified. First the Peasants' Union, then the All-Russian Peasants' Congress, demanded a Constituent Assembly elected

[1] Edouard Drumont pointed out with considerable force that the events in St. Petersburg had left public opinion in France on the whole comparatively cold, whereas in the previous century Paris would have been roused to a frenzy of excitement by such news. He instanced the serious rioting in 1830 under Louis Philippe, caused by the news of the massacres at Warsaw, and added: "Republicans who have remained faithful to the traditions of the Republic, if any such there be, cannot but be amazed at the inertia of the country, once so ready to thrill with sympathy with every liberal movement and every protest against brute force." (*Libre Parole*, February 1.)

[2] *Humanité*, January 28th. Mirbeau added: "He who fails to recognize that similar dangers threaten us is either blind or a fool. Our army leadership and the Russians' are as alike as two peas."

by universal suffrage, the nationalization of the land and the big industries, peace, and a system of Soviets. (June–July, 1905.) The *Bund* (the Jewish Workers' Union) put forward the same demands. The Revolution was seen to be a deep-seated movement, supported by all sections of the nation. In August, Sviatopolk-Mirsky having meanwhile been supplanted by Bulygin and Trepov, the Tsar promulgated a decree setting up a consultative Duma, elected on a very narrow franchise, whose legislative proposals could only be submitted to the Emperor through the Imperial Council.

This was hardly even the shadow of a Constitution,[1] and the decree aroused universal protests. Reforms without any change in the régime, with autocracy unimpaired, and with the same arbitrary power wielded by the bureaucracy, were acceptable to nobody. The revolutionary movement was only fanned to fiercer flame, and soon reached its furious culmination in the form of a general strike, which broke out in St. Petersburg on October 8th. This was the occasion of the birth of the first *Soviet*, or Council of Workers' Delegates. An appeal was issued to the workers of the capital, urging them to rise and give voice to their demands. Almost the whole of the working-class population obeyed the call of the Soviet with perfect discipline, and followed its directions during the following days. By the 22nd the strike had spread to every large town in the Empire and to all the railways. In St. Petersburg supplies of meat and milk were cut off, the lighting failed, the postal services came to a standstill, and the banks and shops closed.[2] The Court was inclined to take repressive measures, but the temper of the army was uncertain. Under the pressure of the insurrection, lacking sufficient resources in

[1] "It is all too evident", wrote Leroy-Beaulieu in the *République Française*, "that the new Constitution is the offspring of defeat, and that Russia owes it to Marshal Oyama and Admiral Togo rather than to the Tsar's advisers." When the first Duma met, some of the peasant members pointed to the representative of Japan in the gallery and said: "There is the real liberator of Russia, the man who gave us our Constitution!"

[2] Cf. Trotzky's account of the revolutionary events of this period.

men and money, the Tsar issued his historic manifesto of October 17th–30th, granting freedom of conscience, speech, public meeting and association, promising the widest possible franchise for all classes, and assigning legislative supremacy to a National Duma.[1] This document, which had been extracted by the threat of a rising, contained nothing but promises, and all depended on the way in which they would be kept—how the Duma would be elected, and to what extent the Government would respect the principles enunciated in the manifesto. The Government's first and chief concern was to evade them. As Gauvain has put it, "this phantom Constitution was almost immediately flouted by its very authors".[2] The sovereign remained an absolute monarch, the bureaucracy clung to its privileges. The Liberals supported the programme outlined in the manifesto, the "Cadets" (Constitutional Democrats) took their stand against insurrection, and only the Socialists persisted in their violent opposition. The *Temps*, which had condemned the general strike in strong terms, criticized the Tsar's capitulation in the face of the Revolution. (November 1, 1905.)

The strikes continued. In December the workers demanded a Constituent Assembly and the cessation of martial law. A fresh attempt to call a general strike was unsuccessful. A rising broke out in Moscow, but was crushed, and a pitiless campaign of repression followed. Up to the end of 1905 the victims of Governmental repression numbered 35,000 dead and 70,000 imprisoned or exiled. Autocracy seemed to take on a new lease of life, and on December 23rd the Tsar announced solemnly: "I will bear alone the burden of power which has been laid upon me, rendering account to no one but God."

[1] "The Tsar did not grant these reforms", wrote Recouly; "they were taken by force. He gave his sanction to the setting up of a Duma in a moment of panic caused by the triumphant general strike. The Duma represents a conquest over autocracy, and all other liberties will have to be won in the same way." (*Revue de Paris*, October 15, 1906.)
[2] *Revue de Paris*, May 1, 1917.

Was France content to remain the ally of a despotism such as this, which violated in the most outrageous way the very principles on which the Republic was based? Francis de Pressensé averred that something essential had snapped in the Franco-Tsarist Alliance,[1] and Jaurès summed up the situation in unambiguous terms in an article entitled "The End of an Alliance":

It is becoming more and more clear every day that the Russian Alliance represents for France a loss in security, strength, and self-respect. It is weakening, endangering, and degrading her. The French people have no knowledge of its terms, and are equally unaware of the precise guarantees it affords them and of the precise duties it imposes on them. The Alliance has become, as the result of the domestic policy of the Russian administration, a disgrace to France and a crime. The longer this struggle between Tsarism and the Russian nation goes on and the fiercer it grows, the more the Franco-Russian Alliance, which operates to the advantage of Tsarism, will constitute a flagrant intervention on the part of France in favour of the blood-stained autocrat and against his people. It is a horrible, wicked complicity which the conscience of the nation will surely refuse to assume, for France would be attainted in her very soul by the terrible remorse that such complicity would bring, a complicity of official sympathy and financial backing for oppressors and butchers.[2]

Several writers joined with Jaurès in denouncing the sorry part France was compelled by the Alliance to play in this connection. Anatole France wrote that it was both hateful and senseless that democratic France should be linked by means of a secret treaty with this murderous autocrat. "It is not an Alliance with Russia, but the very opposite; it is an Alliance with the Tsar that has been foisted on us by this Government of ours, with its monarchic traditions." And what had been the results hitherto of this Alliance, which combined noisy demonstrativeness with secrecy? A terrible war in the Far East, engineered with mad rashness in conjunction with Russia, and an infection with Tsarism which had taken in France the form of rabid Nationalism.[3] Gustave Geffroy described the Alliance

[1] *Humanité*, January 28 and February 5, 1906.    [2] *Ibid.*, February 3rd.
[3] From a speech delivered on February 3, 1905. (*Vers les temps meilleurs*, III, pp. 23–25.)

as a "monstrosity", while Séverine stigmatized it as a "monstrous heresy, something entirely illogical, incoherent, and scandalous". Elysée Reclus, Lucien Descaves, and Gabriel Mourey expressed similar views.[1]

These writers were even better justified than they could know at the time. When the French ruling class had testified to its hostility to Revolution and its devotion to Tsarism, even contemplating the possibility of armed intervention in Asia, one would have thought that France could at least count on the Tsar's remaining loyal to the Alliance. But at that very moment, without the knowledge of the French Government, an incident of the gravest importance was taking place. On July 24, 1905, Nicholas II met the Kaiser at Björkö in the Gulf of Finland, and, without consulting even his own Ministers, signed with him a treaty of defensive alliance, undertaking to induce France to adhere to it also. This treaty, under which, as the French ambassador Bompard has said, France would have been "suddenly confronted with the alternative of either accepting the virtual suzerainty of the two Empires or of breaking off her Alliance with Russia", and which is not even mentioned in the Yellow Book, was not made public until December 29, 1917, when it was published by *Izvestia*, the official Soviet organ.[2] The terms of the agreement were as follows:

(i) In the event of one of the Empires being attacked by a European Power, the other will assist it in Europe with all the naval and military forces at its disposal.

(ii) The high contracting parties undertake not to conclude a separate peace with any common enemy.

(iii) This treaty will come into force immediately peace has been signed between Russia and Japan, and will remain valid

---

[1] *L'assiette au Beurre*, July 1, 1905.

[2] Count Witte had, however, revealed its existence towards the end of 1914 in a conversation with the director of the *Istorichesky Vyestnik*, reported in May 1917 by the Moscow paper *Russkoye Slovo* and reproduced in the *Matin*, May 18, 1917.

until one of the parties withdraws from it, a year's notice being necessary.

(iv) The Emperor of All the Russias will, as soon as this treaty has come into force, take steps to communicate it to France and to persuade that country to associate herself with it as a third ally.[1]

This treaty was obviously directed against Great Britain. It may be that the Tsar imagined he was still loyal to the Franco-Russian Alliance, for, as Bompard has said, "he did not understand, and was indeed incapable of understanding, the feelings and interests of the French nation".

Count Lamsdorff, the Tsar's Foreign Minister, heard nothing of the treaty until after it had been signed, and Count Witte only heard of it after his return from Portsmouth, New Hampshire, U.S.A., where he had been negotiating the peace treaty with Japan. Both Ministers at once recognized that the difficulties then existing between France and Germany over Morocco made the Treaty of Björkö a dead letter, and were able to persuade the Tsar of this. Accordingly, at their suggestion, the latter wrote to Wilhelm II explaining that at the moment it was impossible to give effect to the treaty. At the same time, Count Lamsdorff informed the Russian ambassador in Berlin that, as the obligations imposed by the Franco-Russian Alliance could not at present be reconciled with the terms of the Björkö agreement, it would be well to notify the German Government that, until the situation changed in this respect, Article (i) could not hold good in the event of war between Germany and France. The Treaty accordingly remained inoperative.[2] Isvolsky, writing in 1919, maintained that—

The treaty of Björkö was not an act of disloyalty to France. It was quite clearly aimed exclusively at Great Britain, Russia's hereditary enemy, with whom she was constantly coming into conflict, both in

---

[1] *Die Grosse Politik*, XIX (2), p. 465.
[2] *Revue de Paris*, May 15, 1918. Cf. Nekhludov's article in the *Revue des Deux Mondes*, March 1, 1918. *Die Grosse Politik*, XIX (2), pp. 433 sqq.

Europe and Asia. . . . As the influence of Great Britain was everywhere felt, and always to Russia's detriment, was it not natural and even justifiable on the part of the Emperor Nicholas to seek guarantees against Britain in the shape of a continental coalition?[1]

Nicholas II had evidently got as far as believing that, in her desire to curry favour with Russia, France was prepared to join with Germany in a coalition against Great Britain!

Throughout the Russo-Japanese War, Wilhelm II maintained a very friendly attitude towards the Russian Government, endeavouring always to turn to account the Russian hatred of Britain. The war, says Bülow, made the relations between Germany and Russia distinctly warmer. Germany's object was to blunt the point of the Dual Alliance, in so far as it was directed against her, by "clearing up her relations with Russia", and she seemed to have succeeded in this, thanks to the personal touch maintained by the two Emperors, who met nearly every year.[2] In any case, the Treaty of Björkö is evidence of the Germanophile tendencies of the Russian Court and of the Tsar's peculiar conception of the Franco-Russian Alliance. It also explains how it was possible for the Russian Government to come to an agreement both with Austria and Germany in 1908 and 1910, at Buchlau and Potsdam respectively, without the knowledge of France.

[1] *Revue des Deux Mondes*, November 1, 1919.
[2] Cf. Bülow, *Deutsche Politik*, pp. 83–84.

K

# CHAPTER IX

# RUSSIAN LOANS AND THE 1905 REVOLUTION

IN 1913 the total face value of the Russian bonds held by
France amounted approximately to 17,000,000,000 francs,[1]
made up as follows:—

|  | Million francs |
|---|---|
| External State loans .. .. .. | 10,616 |
| Internal loans .. .. .. .. | 1,344 |
| Provincial and municipal loans .. .. | 310 |
| Industrial loans .. .. .. .. | 4,753 |

And in that year the French Government agreed to the floating
of a Russian railway loan of 500 million francs a year spread
over five years, making a total of 2,500 millions.

For more than a quarter of a century the finances of Russia
had been entirely dependent on the constant influx of French
capital. Yet warnings of all kinds, official and unofficial, had
never been lacking. In the earliest years, the French representatives in Russia had sounded a note of caution; at the
very beginning, in 1886, the French Consul-General in Warsaw
reported that the financial position of Russia was not good.
In 1893 de Vauvineux, the *chargé d'affaires* in St. Petersburg,
drew attention to the fact that an internal loan had become
necessary in order to meet the deficit on the budget and to
pay arrears of interest on the National Debt.[2] In 1894 and 1895
both the ambassador himself and the *chargé d'affaires* made
special reports on the expedients which the Russian Finance

---

[1] The amounts of the new issues from 1888 onwards were as follows: In
1888, 500 millions; in 1889, 467 and 1,200 millions; in 1890, 300, 600, and
350 millions; in 1891, 612 millions; in 1893, 173 millions; in 1894, 432, 378,
and 3,000 millions; in 1896, 400 millions; in 1901, 424 millions; in 1904,
800 millions; in 1906, 1,365 millions; in 1909, 1,220 millions. Some of these
loans were subscribed eight times over! (Tardieu, *La France et les Alliances*,
p. 11. C. Skalkovsky, *Les Ministres des Finances de la Russie. Correspondant*,
December 25, 1913.)

[2] General Bogdanovich mentions in his "Diary," in 1889, in regard to
the first loan issued in France, that "the money was certainly spent, but
neither our military equipment nor our railways showed any improvement".

Minister had had to adopt, and suggested that French investors, who already held such large quantities of Russian bonds, should not be allowed to remain in ignorance of the real financial situation of the allied country. In spite of this, Burdeau, the French Minister of Finance, gave an entirely reassuring account, in April 1894, to his colleague the Foreign Minister, who had expressed uneasiness as to the state of the Russian finances. All the big conversion loans issued between 1889 and 1894 had a huge success in France, and the proceeds duly went to repay the original German investors.

The French money market was ready and eager to meet all the Russian Government's demands. So much so, indeed, that in 1897, Cochery, the French Finance Minister, felt obliged to deprecate the attempts then being made to import Russian securities into France without Government sanction through the Crédit Lyonnais and the Committee of the Bourse. In six months the value of the bonds introduced in this way amounted to 2,700,000,000 francs, bringing the total holdings of French investors up to over 9,500,000,000, or one-third of the whole French National Debt. "It is important", said Cochery, "that the idea should not grow up that our money market is permanently open for all and every species of loan that Russia may think fit to launch without letting us know. . . . We must be kept in touch; we must know where we are going and when the process is likely to stop." In April and May 1899, Cochery's successor, Peytral, protested against the circulation in France of bonds of the Russian internal 4 per cent loan of 1894. Wishing to have authoritative information as to the actual position of the Russian finances, he had sent to Russia a special emissary named Verstraete, who, in his first report, in January 1899, had emphasized the Russian Government's urgent need of funds. They were anxious to find a way of unloading their internal loans on the French investor in addition to getting the foreign loans issued in France. "The Russian authorities", wrote Verstraete, "are not offering these

bonds for direct public subscription, but are arranging for the
Savings Banks to take them up. Thence they will be distributed,
either to the Russian public *via* the Imperial Bank or to the
French public *via* the Crédit Lyonnais." The latter organization had actually been offering its services direct to the Russian
Finance Minister for placing guaranteed Russian bonds in
France. In July 1899 and January 1900, Caillaux in his turn
had to draw attention to certain cases of unauthorized dealings
in Russian bonds on the French market, and deprecated "these
indirect methods which would lay our market open to the
wholesale introduction of Russian securities without any limit.
If Russia desires to appeal for capital in France, she must do
it openly by means of public issues."

The financial and economic situation in Russia showed no
signs of improving—it had, indeed, become acutely critical by
this time—and financial dodgery became the rule. On June 13,
1901, Verstraete reported that the position was so bad as to be
almost alarming. Of the last loan of 400 million francs, not a
sou had found its way into Russia, the whole amount having
been used to pay the interest on the National Debt for one
year. On October 27, 1902, he reported that, notwithstanding
the published figures, there was actually a deficit on the
Russian budget. Shortly after this Verstraete returned to
France, and his place was not filled. No more reports on the
financial situation were included in the diplomatic despatches
from Russia after this, and even comments were few and far
between. "Our representatives", says Margaine, "ceased to
send home any detailed memoranda on the subject because
they found their advice was ignored by Ministers. They no
longer even reported on the Bourse quotations of new loan
issues."[1]

---

[1] Cf. the Margaine Report on the *Livre Jaune*—evidence by the Foreign
Minister, pp. 106 sqq. No steps were even taken, despite the French
ambassador's advice, to negotiate for preferential treatment for French
imports into Russia, particularly wine, which was hard hit by the new
Russian tariff.

This was the period when the fate of the Revolution and the reforms, the future of constitutional government, the whole question of whether the despotism should be transformed into a self-govering parliamentary régime, actually rested with France. Tsarism was ruined, its credit gone, at France's mercy. She had only to say that no more loans would be granted until a modern régime had been definitely set up in Russia, and the thing was done. Moreover, by securing the guarantee of a representative body to any subsequent loans, France would have obtained the best of security for her investors. The plight of the Russian Treasury at that time was pitiful, and the most dubious practices went on. The position was indeed going from bad to worse. There were three distinct budgets: first, the "ordinary" budget, a mere blind to delude foreign investors; secondly, the "extraordinary" budget, showing a substantial deficit; and, lastly, the "administrative" budget, comprising the Tsar's Privy Purse and the expenses of maintaining order. The *Correspondant* revealed in 1905 that the Russian State expenditure was double the income as shown by the budget, and that the National Debt amounted to a sum equivalent to seven and a half times the revenue.[1] Barefaced jugglery went on in the national book-keeping in order to hoodwink the French public. The issues of railway debentures were only State loans in disguise.

The *Revue*, directed by Jean Finot, carried on for several years a vigorous campaign on behalf of the French savings which had been swallowed up in Russia.[2] It was proved that, out of the 12,000,000,000 francs lent to that country up to 1905, more than 4,000,000,000 had been used to meet budget deficits caused by Government extravagance and lack of foresight, about 6,000,000,000 had been thrown away in all sorts of dubious enterprises and in military equipment which had

[1] April 25 and May 10, 1905.
[2] Cf. more especially the issues for March 15, 1905, February, 1, 1906 and May 1, 1906.

been destroyed by the Japanese, leaving barely 2,000,000,000 which had been applied to more or less productive development. The 1906 budget showed a deficit of over £60,000,000. It was clear that, unless some four-fifths of her indebtedness were wiped out, Russia would have to go on borrowing afresh every year merely to pay the interest on earlier loans. Each new loan thus undermined the security of the millions already borrowed.

Kokovtsov, the Russian Finance Minister, in an interview granted to the representatives of the *Vie Financière* on September 21 and 22, 1906, stated that the financial situation was then satisfactory, and affirmed that there was no secret expenditure and that the Russian budget was an entirely honest one, whereas in actual fact the Treasury was at that moment more than £16,000,000 short.[1]

In a series of articles in the *Grande Revue* during the year 1910,[2] Lysis, who had previously waged an energetic campaign against the Russian loans in 1906–1907 in the pages of *Humanité* and *La Revue*,[3] demonstrated that:

(i) Russia had borrowed 16,000,000,000 francs over a period of fifteen years without ever having been in a position to pay the interest from her own resources.

(ii) The budgetary expenditure had increased by leaps and bounds, and strictly productive expenditure now only represented about 12 per cent of a total of £280,000,000.

(iii) The revenue had reached its maximum capacity, 88 per cent coming from indirect taxation.

(iv) To meet the interest on her loans, Russia would have to

---

[1] Cf. *La Vie Financière*, October 23rd to November 21st. All the leading industrialists in Russia opposed the loans.

[2] January 25th, February 10th and 25th, March 10th and 25th.

[3] November 1 and December 15, 1906, and February 1, 1907. Cf. *La Revue Bleue*, April 7, 14, and 28, and May 5, 1906. "We are getting to the position", wrote Clemenceau, "of having to put up with everything to avoid a rupture with Russia which might result in a financial catastrophe of incalculable gravity." (*Le Bloc*, September 29, 1901.)

find between 700,000,000 and 800,000,000 gold francs
each year, which she could only obtain by exporting
her wheat.

Thus the whole of Russia's financial system was rotten and
anti-social. To balance the budget, it was necessary to expand
to the maximum both the consumption of alcohol and the
export of grain. Drunkenness and starvation were the twin
sources of budgetary prosperity. Lysis, in *Humanité*, proved
that the Russian Government was on the verge of bankruptcy.
To allow the present practices to continue, to saddle the
budget with fresh burdens in the shape of new loans without
opening up new sources of revenue and cutting down expenditure, would be to plunge into chaos and ruin with open eyes.

Leroy-Beaulieu made it clear that Russian bonds could no
longer be regarded as a trustee security, and that investors
would be wise not to overload themselves with such stock.
There was only one way for Russia to avoid bankruptcy, and
that was by carrying out a drastic reform of all her institutions.
It was obvious that nothing short of the regeneration of Russia
could reassure her creditors as to the safety of their capital,
which, under the existing anarchic régime of Tsarism, ran the
gravest risks of utter extinction. If a fresh loan were agreed
to, the Tsar would be free to reject all demands for reform.
The Russian constitutional issue was thus closely bound up
with the security of French investments. The best guarantee
would be to see the Russian nation in effective control of the
budget. Writing, be it remembered, in July 1905, he maintained that to go on lending millions of money to the Imperial
Government without obtaining a pledge that the legitimate
claims of the Russian people would be met would be to
endanger French capital and the savings of the French people.
The signature of the Tsar's Ministers was not sufficient
security:

If there are any Frenchmen still left who have any confidence in the
Tsarist régime, we regard it as our duty to warn them that Russia

is on the brink of a revolution. What the future may have in store for
her it is not possible to say; but her creditors have a right to inquire,
before making any fresh advances, whether loans issued in future by
the Imperial Government are or are not likely to be repudiated by the
nation some day. If only from motives of self-interest, therefore, it
is imperative that France should see that any fresh loan is sanctioned
and guaranteed by a National Assembly.[1]

Jaurès argued that, if the French bankers had had sufficient
regard for the future, they would have insisted on the Tsar's
granting a Constitution, and mentioned as an interesting
historical precedent that the Rothschilds, as creditors of the
King of Prussia, had forced him, in 1848, to improve the
security of their loans by surrendering to the Landtag the control of the budget and by granting a charter of constitutional
Government.[2]

Thus the interests of French investors and of the Russian
people were equally at stake. From every part of Russia, from
every class in the nation, voices were raised to beg and implore
France not to lend any more money to Russia, at all events
until peace had been established and a constitution set up.
Leroy-Beaulieu carried out a thorough investigation to ascertain the actual feeling of the nation, and found that that was
the unanimous desire of the best minds and the most prominent
men in all the towns he visited.

The Cadet party, in a proclamation issued immediately
after the massacre of January 22nd, announced that a popular
Government would only recognize loans contracted prior to
that date, while a manifesto published in the following October
by the St. Petersburg *Soviet*, the executive of the Peasants'
Union, and the Social Democratic Party laid it down in the
most explicit terms that "the Russian people would on no
account repay the loans contracted by the Tsarist Government
during the period of its struggle with the nation".

Anatole France, in an appeal to the thrifty middle classes,
the small capitalists who were indefatigable in taking up

[1] *Courrier Européen*, July 28, 1905.    [2] *Humanité*, January 25, 1905.

Russian loans, pointed out that their money had "only been used to finance a policy of greed and stupidity", to pay the cost of the Japanese War and of the massacres organized by Tsarism throughout Russia.

You did not know this. But now that you do know, now that your eyes are opened, do not be led astray any longer. The Russian Government is negotiating a fresh loan. To subscribe to this would mean giving your support to crime and madness. It would be a criminal act. Do not forget that.[1]

None the less, the new loan was approved in principle by France towards the end of 1905. Charles Seignobos reported having heard from an authoritative source that the bankers had only agreed to the issue "to oblige the Prime Minister", who had a personal interview with them. "To induce them to consent, M. Rouvier did not appeal to their pockets, but dwelt on the political aspect, urging that it was France's duty to help the Russian Government to restore order."[2]

The Tsar could not avoid summoning the Duma. Notwithstanding shameless coercion and the imprisonment of the chief opponents of the Government, the new assembly, which met for the first time on April 27–May 10, 1906, showed a large majority for the Opposition Parties, who pressed for the strict fulfilment of the principles enunciated in the Imperial manifesto of October 1905, while the Tsar had no intention of forgoing any of the privileges of autocracy.[3] The Duma demanded that Ministers should be responsible to Parliament, and this put an end to all collaboration between the Government and the Assembly. The Goremykin Cabinet ignored the Duma's resolutions entirely, having indeed only intended to convoke Parliament so as to create the impression abroad that Russia now had a constitution, to get credits voted, and then to have an immediate dissolution. The new loan was duly

[1] At a meeting held on March 18, 1905. (*Vers les temps meilleurs*, III, pp. 34–38.)  [2] *Européen*, January 20, 1906.
[3] Cf. Leroy-Beaulieu in the *Revue Bleue*, June 18, 1906.

floated, thanks to the encouraging reports the Tsar's Government had received from Paris, and the Liberal and Socialist Parties of Russia again issued warnings to the French public. Maxim Gorky wrote to Anatole France:

The struggle will be neither a long nor a painful one if Europe ceases to give the Russian Government money to enable it to perpetrate these massacres and executions. . . . If the state of tension in which the nation is living goes on much longer, there will be such an accumulation of hatred and cruelty in the Russian soul that, when the inevitable explosion comes, the outpouring of these pent-up forces will horrify the whole world.

In an article entitled "Not a Penny for the Russian Government", Gorky implored the French nation not to subscribe to the loan, which would enable Tsarism not only to dissolve the Duma but to abolish the few liberties that had been secured and to adopt the most atrocious measures of repression. "Do not give a single penny to the butchers of the Russian people. The money will only help them to carry out more massacres. . . . Do not commit this crime in the eyes of history, this unprecedented crime, which would be not only dastardly but insane."[1] On April 26th, the Union of Russian Unions solemnly declared that the loan was a "crime against the nation", and that, as it had been contracted illegally, without the consent or control of the people, it could not be "regarded as binding on any future popular Government".[2] The Cadet Party took similar action, calling the attention of intending subscribers to the fact that they would be endangering the elementary rights of the Russian people. In France, the Socialist Party, in a manifesto issued in the 1906 election, affirmed that the sole object of the loan was to place the Tsar in a position to execute an arbitrary *coup d'état*, that it was illegal, and that it would only lead to a colossal *Krach*. "Inves-

---

[1] *Humanité*, April 9, 1906.
[2] *Russkoi Tribun*, May 3, 1906. "This loan", the statement continued, "will allow the Government to go on meeting our demands with bullets, bayonets, imprisonment, exile. . . . Our sons will be paying for our downfall."

tors, beware! Whatever happens, we predict that Tsarism will go bankrupt. We predict that the Russian people will hate as their enemies all who are responsible for putting additional weapons in the hands of a Government of thieves and murderers." Jaurès called the loan a "*coup d'état* reserve", and added: "Any Frenchman who subscribes to the loan will make himself an accomplice of the organized assassination of a whole people."[1]

But French investors were not in the habit of reading *Humanité*. They abominated it, and as for Jaurès, their hatred of him was so violent that they would instinctively have done the exact opposite of what he advised. That is the small capitalists' mentality. They preferred to listen to what the banks and the popular press told them, and these mentors issued no warnings. And so, instead of insisting, by way of security for the bondholders, on publicity and proper financial control, which could only have been exercised through a representative assembly, Poincaré, then Finance Minister, authorized the loan, to the tune of 2,250,000,000 francs, without any conditions. This loan, the largest that had ever been issued in the history of modern nations, enabled the Imperial Government, in Count Witte's words, to "surmount all the vicissitudes of the period from 1906 to 1910" by furnishing the funds which, together with the troops brought back from Transbaikalia, reintroduced a note of vigour and self-confidence into the actions of the Government.[2] The loan enabled Tsarism to crush the Revolution, to dissolve the Duma, and to avoid conceding any real reform. Prince Dolgoruki and Maklakov, the leaders of the Cadet Party, had tried in vain to persuade the French Government that the issue was illegal, having been arranged without the sanction of the Duma.[3] "What right has a Republic like France", asked one Russian paper, "to intervene in this fashion in our domestic

[1] *Humanité*, April 8 and 15, 1906.
[2] Witte, pp. 254–275.   [3] Ibid., p. 262.

concerns? Why is she so sedulous in persecuting the Russian people, who have never done her any harm?"

Jean Finot also protested against this tragic intervention in the internal affairs of the Russian Empire in favour of a régime which was at its last gasp. He blamed Poincaré for authorizing the loan, saying that he had

been guilty of unpardonable imprudence . . . If he had made his consent conditional on the Duma's functioning as a regular Parliament and setting up a proper budgetary control, we should have seen these desiderata taking shape within a very few months, to the greater happiness of the Russian people and the greater security of our loans, past, present, and future.[1]

It is noteworthy in this connection that Poincaré took this grave decision at a time when a general election was only a few weeks ahead. His colleagues, Bourgeois, Clemenceau, and Briand, made no protest.

At the same time the leading French newspapers kept up a running fire of attack on the Duma, to prepare public opinion for its dissolution. The *Temps* criticized the Cadet programme as "extravagant and premature", scoffed at the Assembly's demagogic excesses, and advised it to "avoid the pitfalls of popular sentimentality". The *Temps* had expected the representatives of the peasants to take a stand against the revolutionary spirit of the intellectuals, but as soon as they began to demand "land and liberty", it altered its tactics, denounced the spokesmen of the party, and maintained that the nation was not yet ripe for any drastic reforms. (May 1906.)

At this stage, when all the leading organs of the French press, far from expressing any adverse criticism of Tsarism, reserved all their severity for the movement for emancipation, a frightful massacre of Jews took place in the Polish town of Byelostok, filling the whole of the civilized world with horror. The massacre was stated by Prince Yurussov, assistant to Witte at the Ministry of the Interior, to have been instigated

[1] *La Revue*, May 1, 1906.

by the Government.[1] Leroy-Beaulieu was even more precise in his charges:

Organized by the police, who take care to disarm their victims in advance, these pogroms are carried out under the benevolent eyes of the Administration and very often with the complicity, either spontaneous or compulsory, of the troops called in to maintain order. . . . These anarchical conditions are encouraged, even engineered, by certain mysterious persons of influence who lurk in the corridors of the Imperial Palaces. They look to such conditions as a means of diverting what the Russians are already calling their Revolution.[2]

But this, according to the French press, which still went on running down the Duma, was only an incident in Russian domestic affairs. The French bourgeoisie had in any case never taken any particular interest in the fate of the Russian Jews. The Faculty of Law in the Paris University, that perfect embodiment of bourgeois political and social ideals, had just rejected, in a judgment delivered by the Dean of the Faculty, M. Renault, on March 27, 1906, a thesis by a M. Allemand on the "Sufferings of the Jews in Russia", on the plea that it

[1] Having received instructions from Witte to carry out an investigation of the facts, Yurussov discovered in the Imperial Printing Office certain proof-sheets of proclamations inciting the populace to massacre, and bearing the endorsement: "Approved for printing, (signed) Trepov". A printing works had been opened in St. Petersburg, at No. 16, Fontanskaya, in the autumn of 1905, which had been purchased secretly by the Department of Police with Crown funds. An officer of gendarmes named Komissarov was in charge there, and stated, in reply to questions: "We are in a position to organize a pogrom of any description you like, from a dozen up to ten thousand persons." "A pogrom", Prince Yurussov explained in his report, "is always preluded by rumours that one is being planned, and proclamations inciting the populace to violence are distributed among the inhabitants. These appeals, couched in the most disgusting language, are broadcast by tens of thousands. It is clear that there is a closely-knit organization of very wide scope at work." He came to the conclusion that the chief organizers of these massacres were persons outside the jurisdiction of the Minister of the Interior. "This menace will not disappear so long as the direction of the affairs of the State and the destinies of the nation remain under the influence of men who, policemen born and bred, are instigators of pogroms by conviction." (*Petit Temps*, June 28, 1906.)

[2] Letter to the *Temps*, June 24, 1906. He added that this had been, for the past quarter of a century, the "recognized procedure of the opponents of any liberal reform. To divert the masses from revolutionary propaganda they are stirred up to acts of violence against the Jews."

contained criticisms of the Tsarist administration, though other theses, with anti-Semitic tendencies, had been accepted.[1]

This massacre might have been expected not only to make the Russian Government an outlaw among the nations of the world, but also to compel the French Government, for very self-interest, to insist on guarantees that reforms would be carried out, as essential to future security. But nothing of the kind took place. Jaurès' voice was almost the only one raised in protest against Franco-Tsarist collaboration:

What a spectacle it is! That Republican France should subsidize an abominable régime like this! Jewish and Christian High Finance combined have thrown out a life-line to Tsarism and enabled it to go on with its cut-throat persecution of the Russian Jews. When shall we see the end of this sinister co-operation on the part of France? . . . After what has just happened at Byelostok, any Minister who could authorize a new financial operation in aid of these murderers would have innocent blood on his own hands. But no! that is all over! France will never again sacrifice her honour and her best interests by supplying funds to a Government of tyranny and massacre.[2]

But Jaurès was under a misapprehension. The French Radical Ministry not only placed no obstacles in the way of the loan of over 2,000 million francs, which meant salvation for Tsarism, but also adopted a Parliamentary manœuvre to which insufficient attention has hitherto been drawn, and which speedily led to the dissolution of the Duma. Most of the Parliaments in Europe had already sent messages of greeting to the Duma as the first popular assembly in Russia, but the French Chamber of Deputies, notwithstanding the large majority acquired by the Parties of the Left in the elections of May 1906, had not yet mustered up sufficient courage to follow this example. At the beginning of the new session, the Socialists and Radicals had jointly prepared a draft message to be sent in the name of the Chamber, and Steeg, the leader of the Radical group, had

[1] E.g. one by M. Comnène, on the Jews of Roumania, May 26, 1905.
[2] *Humanité*, June 25, 1906.

notified Léon Bourgeois, the Foreign Minister, of his intention
of moving a resolution in the following terms:

The members of the French Chamber of Deputies send warm fraternal greetings to the first Russian National Assembly, and earnestly
hope that the labours of the Duma may play an important part in
promoting the peace of the world, the progress of humanity and the
freedom and prosperity of the great nation which is France's friend
and ally.

Léon Bourgeois had, however, requested him to defer moving
the resolution, saying that "the passing of a motion of this
description at this particular moment might prejudice certain
diplomatic action now in progress". Steeg returned to the
charge after the Byelostok massacre, but the Minister again
asked him to wait. Finally it was agreed that the resolution
should be moved on the last day of the session, but suddenly
Bourgeois and his colleagues intimated that "they were very
doubtful as to the wisdom of passing the resolution as drafted",
and Steeg did not feel able to press the point.[1] On July 13th
the Socialists, realizing that the Radical leader was not going
to take the initiative as arranged, decided to propose a resolution of their own, but Clemenceau forestalled them by hastily
reading the decree of prorogation. It was a piece of trickery
hard to match in the annals of Parliament. Thus, whereas for
the past fifteen years a flood of congratulatory telegrams and
addresses had been sent to the Tsar, the Russian General
Staff, regiments, and fleet, even to the municipal Dumas, no
gesture of recognition was allowed to be made to the National
Assembly of the representatives of the Russian people! Officially, France knew nothing of the Duma, which had been
convened by the Tsar himself. The liberation of the Russian
people, the establishment of a constitution, the limitation of
the most terrible despotism known to history—all this was
merely embarrassing, and France, Revolutionary France,
turned her head away. The result of the loan and the snub

[1] This account of the facts is taken from a letter written by Steeg to
*Humanité* on July 16th.

combined was soon apparent. On July 19th the Duma was dissolved. Jaurès, commenting in despair on the fatal blindness with which French statesmen were afflicted, Bourgeois no less than Delcassé, spoke prophetically of the

dark abysses into which the life of Russia would be plunged by despotism—a terrible cataclysm from which freedom would emerge victorious, but rabid and bloodstained. The whole vast horizon is shrouded in mystery and apprehension. The first flashes of lightning have revealed fantastic shapes, the forerunners of the awful tempest which may shake the whole of Europe, the entire world. . . . May the storm be violent enough to sweep away this accursed régime for ever.[1]

The Clemenceau Cabinet explained the authorization of the loan by saying that the Tsar had insisted on it as a condition of Russia's support at the Algeciras Conference. The sacrifice of the rights of the Russian people was thus the price paid for the Tsar's backing of French colonial ambitions. This was tantamount to an admission that the *coup d'état* against the Duma had been carried out with the active complicity of the French Government. Meanwhile the French popular press sang pæans of praise to Stolypin and Nicholas II.

It is not to be wondered at that France completely forfeited the sympathy of the Russian Liberals and Democrats. In fact, a storm of indignation against the French swept the country, the whole nation being well aware that the loan was the real cause of the postponement of the reforms and the dismissal of the Duma. The violence of the emotions aroused by the loan was quite unsuspected in France. Georges Bourdon mentions that, in the course of a conversation he had at that time with a Russian writer, the latter suddenly exclaimed: "I hate France. . . . For the past ten years we have seen her giving support and guarantees to this vile régime which is devastating our country. Thanks to French capital, the autoc-

---

[1] *Humanité*, July 22nd and 23rd. Jaurès denounced the Tsar as a "hypo-critical scoundrel"; and Marcel Sembat wrote: "Next time the rifles of Tsardom shoot down the Russian people, France will have provided the powder and shot". (*Ibid.*, July 24th.)

racy has been able still to hold up its head in the world, and this has only increased its villainy. France is no longer the country we loved and revered in our youth. You must forgive my saying again, I hate France." And Bourdon added: "These are the sentiments, perhaps less harshly expressed, which one hears everywhere from the lips of liberally minded men."[1] Paléologue also testifies that the Russian *intelligentsia* never forgave the French for having given support to Tsarism and thus bolstered it up. Even in 1916 the majority of the Cadet Party had not yet abandoned their old deep-seated rancour against the French Alliance. Maxim Gorky wrote in 1906:

See, this is what thou hast done, France, Mother of Liberty! Thy hand, stretched out in greed, has closed the path of independence for a whole nation! The hour of our deliverance will not strike any the later, but more blood will be shed to gain our freedom, and the guilt will be thine. May the blood mantle in thy treacherous, false cheeks! I spit my hatred in thy face, oh thou once beloved![2]

A. Staal, a Moscow lawyer who was a member of the executive of the All-Russian Peasants' Union, warned the French that any new régime in Russia would make a clean sweep of old diplomatic traditions and would have other things to do than to worry about paying its debts or safeguarding French interests. It would be compelled to cut the Gordian knot by measures improvised on the spur of the moment. He predicted that the Alliance would be the ruin, not of the bankers but of the French and the Russian peoples, the former being the dupes and the latter the victims.[3] E. Semenov wrote that the great mass of the Russian people cursed France as synonymous with usury, and that a free Russia would never forget that the French Republic had allowed her to be stabbed in the back at the most critical stage of her struggle against the barbarous régime of the past. "The downfall of the Tsarist Government is inevitable, but if France continues to supply it with money,

[1] *La Russie libre*, pp. 484–486.
[2] Paléologue, I, pp. 234–235; II, pp. 241–242.
[3] *Courrier Européen*, December 14, 1906.

L

there will be such a *krach* that the failure of the Panama Canal Company will be nothing in comparison."[1]

The French bourgeoisie, who pride themselves on being wide-awake and well-informed, showed in this matter a degree of ignorance and credulity which is almost beyond belief. They had two alternatives: either to meet the Tsar's demands for money and head straight for bankruptcy and disaster, or to decline to lend to any but a national representative régime, and thus save their millions. They chose the first course, that being the instinctive preference of their reactionary souls. They obstinately refused to believe in the success of the Revolution or to recognize its real character, although Leroy-Beaulieu had assured them that, owing to the land question, the Russian Revolution was just as much a social revolution as a political one.[2] They had not even the excuse of doing good business with Russia. The figures for Franco-Russian trade at that time were so poor that Doumergue had had to ask the Prime Minister on February 6, 1906, to appeal to the Russian Government on the subject. France reaped the hatred of the Russian people, while the value of the loan stock fell and fell. Warnings from the most unexceptionable sources were disregarded, and French gold continued to find its way into the Tsar's coffers. Russian industrialists called upon the French Government to stop any further supplies of credit, which could only perpetuate the waste and the state of anarchy and make bankruptcy inevitable.[3] The *Revue* blamed the financial

---

[1] *Revue*, December 1, 1906: "The Russian Loan a National Danger". Leroy-Beaulieu wrote a letter to the *Temps* on August 27th, *à propos* of the attempt on Stolypin's life, containing the following sentences which the paper saw fit to delete: "By dissolving the Duma, suppressing the opposition press and outlawing all who oppose the Tsarist régime, the Russian Government has made it impossible to carry on a legal constitutional struggle, and has forced the nation into paths of conspiracy and violence. As we have pointed out again and again, bombs are the natural product of a country and a régime in which the Government will not tolerate any open opposition." Cf. *Courrier Européen*, August 31st.

[2] Lecture to the *Alliance Française, Revue Bleue*, June 18, 1906.

[3] *Vie Financière*, October 23 and November 21, 1906.

houses for inviting the public to throw their savings into the bottomless pit of Russian extravagance. "The public is entitled to ask the Crédit Lyonnais, the Comptoir d'Escompte and the Société Générale to explain this betrayal."[1]

The question was raised in Parliament by the Socialist Party. On February 7, 1907, Rouanet drew attention to the power of suction exercised by the big financial houses on French savings, which were being diverted from home funds and industrial stock into the abyss of foreign bonds. He also strongly criticized the system of secret issues. Delcassé, who had been forced by Rouvier to resign in 1905 in consequence of the attitude he had adopted in Moroccan affairs, had the audacity to affirm that he could not understand how anyone could call the financial position of Russia shaky. Meslier deplored the fact that France was not taking any steps to safeguard the security of her invested capital, not even any of the elementary guarantees which a creditor was accustomed to require from a debtor. This brought Pichon, the Foreign Minister, to his feet with the declaration that "there is nothing in the state of Russia's credit or in her commercial position to justify such attacks as these". The Russian Government was adding to all the guarantees already offered to French investors constitutional safeguards which it had shown itself determined to maintain. He praised the Alliance, to which, he said, "we are more firmly attached than ever".

When the debate was resumed on the following day, Willm asserted that the economic situation in Russia was such as to offer no guarantee to investors, who would never see their money back. When he referred to the responsibility of the police and the Government generally for the pogroms, there were interruptions from the Centre and Right, "That is not our business!" and Pichon felt called upon to remark: "I cannot refrain from protesting against these constant attempts to interfere in the domestic affairs of another nation." Jaurès

[1] *Revue*, May 1, 1906, and April 1, 1907.

asked why the will of the nation should be frustrated at a critical moment by the manœuvres of financial oligarchies, which tended more and more to become monopolies:

> If the French bondholders, to say nothing of Russia herself, are not given the guarantee of a responsible Government which will set the budget on a sounder basis and put a stop to the orgy of waste . . . Russia will sink beneath the burden of despotism without having the strength to shake it off. And when, by sanctioning fresh loans, you put additional weapons into the hands of that despotism, which it uses against the nation, then you yourselves are working for the *débâcle* to which Russian credit is doomed.

After drawing attention to some of the indirect and underhand methods employed in floating the loans, he went on to denounce the "real intervention, the real interference in other people's affairs", involved in handing over to the Tsarist bureaucracy the hundreds of millions of francs which it needed in order to be able to dissolve the Duma.

> When these men who are struggling and dying and trying to build up institutions based on freedom and justice, following in our footsteps, looking to us as models—when they see that, on the eve of the decisive battle, we step in to assist those who are oppressing and torturing them, they conclude that we are a nation of money-lenders unworthy of our traditions. I for one do not wish that said of France!

Caillaux, the Finance Minister, admitted that certain of the allegations made were not unfounded, and agreed that it was well to draw the attention of the country to them. He condemned the secret issues of bonds, and undertook to insist on all possible guarantees, both legal and constitutional, for all future appeals made from abroad to the French investor.

Despite the Viborg manifesto, in which the great majority of the Russian Duma, meeting after the dissolution, announced that all fresh loans contracted without the consent of the people's representatives would be "regarded as invalid by the nation and would never be repaid", the loan of 1906 was not the last to be issued. In 1908, the *Information* suggested that, as it would be difficult to ensure regular interest payments on any new loans of any magnitude, some further guarantee should be secured, and proposed the abolition of the "extraordinary" budget.[1] But, notwithstanding all warnings, a new loan issued in 1909 was fully subscribed, and only the Socialists raised any protest. Lysis, in a series of articles in *Humanité*, had warned investors that the Russian Government was heading straight for bankruptcy. Jaurès was justified in saying that the Socialist Party alone had made a stand in defence of the nation's savings, "to attempt to protect the small investors from the fatal consequences of their credulity and from the machinations of High Finance, which was leading them to ruin". On January 21, 1909, Rouanet, moving a resolution against the proposed new loan, pointed out the preposterous nature of the financial operation on which the Russian Government was embarking. To meet Treasury Bills amounting to 800 million francs which were coming to maturity, a loan of 1,200 millions was being floated at an issue price which, after allowing for brokers' fees and commissions of all sorts, represented a loss of roughly 17 per cent of the capital, or about 150 millions, so that the 800 millions about to be paid off would be swollen by another 150 millions. "Events will surely justify our protests", he said, "and in tragic fashion. We repudiate our share of the responsibility." He protested against any further loans to Tsarism, which was on its last legs, and reproached the French Government for intervening in the domestic politics of Russia by supplying the Tsar with the funds he needed to organize the "black hundreds" and to pay those who organized the massacres of Jews. Pichon, the Foreign Minister, declared that the proceeds of the loan would be utilized in accordance with the national interests of the

[1] *Information*, January 20, 1908. The reply of Geo Gérald was typical of the attitude of most politicians: "To attempt to dictate to a Government what its duty should be is to confuse the spheres of responsibility in a way which cannot be too strongly deprecated and condemned. A Government is not a Party organ; it is carrying on the work of the nation as a whole." (January 28th.) Cf. *Pages Libres*, January–February, 1909.

two countries, which had never been more closely in agreement than now. Caillaux, the Finance Minister, explained that there were only two cases in which France could refuse a foreign State the privilege of issuing loans in the French market: firstly, if it should appear that the French investor would be prejudiced by the issue—"and I am here to-day", he said, "to assure you on my responsibility as a Minister that that is not so in the case of this loan, which is open to small investors"— and, secondly, if reasons of State were against it, and the Foreign Minister had just stated that State policy was all in favour of permission being granted to issue the loan which had been prepared by the friendly and allied nation. Rouanet's resolution, that unconditional authorization should be refused, was rejected by 381 votes to 95.

These frequent new issues naturally added progressively to the difficulty of elucidating the real position, while the hatred of the Russian democrats for France grew steadily year by year, seeing that the money provided by the loans enabled Tsardom to maintain itself in autocratic power and to get Dumy elected which were subservient to it. France had become in their eyes merely a bank kept by a rapacious bourgeoisie, profoundly reactionary, hand in glove with Tsarism, the oppressor. A professor in the Moscow University said to R. Labry, while he was showing him over the site of the Battle of Borodino: "Napoleon did a great deal of harm to Russia, but your Republic has done still more." Many Russians thought that all the French loans had gone into the Tsar's Privy Purse, and propagandists of all parties spread this idea among the masses. "Make no mistake", wrote Labry, after the war,

the Bolshevik decree repudiating the foreign loans was among those which were received with the greatest unanimity. The masses welcomed it as a just reprisal against the capitalists who, after having exploited their misery and engineered the war, were now trying to prevent the spread of World Revolution. . . . At the present day, even more perhaps than just after 1905, the French financial claims are regarded by the average Russian, if not with open hostility, at least with profound indifference.[1]

Was it the Russians' fault if the French bourgeoisie, in their ignorance and obscurantism, had remained blind and obtuse in spite of all warnings?

The Tsar, having promised to convene a second Duma when the first was dissolved, was obliged to keep his word. In the succeeding elections, the measures of coercion adopted were unprecedented,[2] but in spite of this and of the fact that 25 per cent of the peasants had been disfranchised and the number of working-class voters reduced by 10 per cent, the reactionaries and moderates only numbered 127 in a Duma of 448 members. "Russia is divided more than ever into two irreconcilable camps", wrote the correspondent of the *Journal des Débats*, "the Right growing more and more uncompromising and the Left more and more extreme. The Revolution may be postponed, but it cannot be postponed indefinitely."[3]

The second Duma, which met on March 6, 1907, started its work in an accommodating, chastened mood. Guided by the Cadet minority, the majority refrained from demanding the expropriation of the landlords, for which the peasants were pressing so warmly, turned down many indiscreet resolutions, and allowed the army vote to go through. On the most controversial subjects they contented themselves with appointing Committees to report to the Duma after investigation.[4] These signs of ordered progress were all the more alarming to Stolypin, the Prime Minister. He confronted the Duma one day, amid universal amazement, with a demand for the arrest

---

[1] *Dépêche de Toulouse*, October 9, 1924.

[2] Some idea of the coercion may be gleaned from the following extract from a circular addressed to Provincial Governors by the Minister of the Interior: "A further measure to which the Government would not be averse in principle is the deportation of all members of the Parties of the Left. The Minister desires that the new Duma shall consist of men who will represent the real feelings of the country." (Quoted by Gauvain in the *Revue de Paris*, May 1, 1917.)

[3] *Journal des Débats*, March 6, 1907.     [4] *Ibid.*, June 28, 1907.

of sixteen of its members and the exclusion of thirty-nine others on the ground that they were implicated in a plot against the security of the State. He gave the Assembly twenty-four hours to decide, with the alternative of dissolution.[1]

It might be thought that, in face of such a blow at the principle of popular representation, the French press would have protested or, at the very least, maintained a disapproving silence. On the contrary, the *Temps* wrote solemnly that Stolypin had "justice and common sense" on his side and was giving a proof of his desire to act by and with the consent of the Duma in asking it to agree to this act of self-mutilation—a sacrifice that was justified "beyond the shadow of a doubt" (although the Duma was actually dissolved before the action against the incriminated members had even started). Both the *Temps* and the *Journal des Débats*, differing in this instance from the opinions of their correspondents in Russia, approved whole-heartedly of the decision to dissolve the Duma.[2] The stock argument used by the press and by the French governing class generally was that the Russian people were not yet ripe for a régime of free Parliamentary institutions. Leroy-Beaulieu pointed out unanswerably that "no nation is entirely ripe when it begins to make use of constitutional institutions. It only reaches full maturity gradually, by the very fact of its developing such free institutions."[3]

---

[1] "An imaginary plot", according to Gauvain. (*Revue de Paris*, May 1, 1917.)

[2] June 16th, 17th, and 18th. Cf. the Financial Notes of the Week, by G. Manchez, in the *Temps*, June 17th.

[3] Lecture at Rouen, June 12, 1907. Jaurès himself had replied, two years before, in words which lost none of their force when the Revolution broke out in 1917: "In 1788, when no representative institutions of any kind existed in France, a superficial observer might have wondered how this country, with no traditions of free self-government, could have given birth to a Republican democracy, and how a Revolution could spring forth like Athene, fully armed, only a year later. It is true that the ground had been prepared by the philosophers. But look at Russia! They may have a briefer classic tradition than ours, but their intellectuals are in closer touch than ours were with the suffering masses. Their bourgeoisie is not the same as the French bourgeoisie of 1789, but the Russian proletariat, nurtured and

The Tsar followed up the dissolution by abolishing the electoral law and promulgating a revised law by ukase without consulting the Imperial Council as required by the October manifesto. This was a flagrant violation of the very Constitution which the Tsar himself had granted. The new law disfranchised 19 towns entirely, cut down the number of seats allotted to Poland from 37 to 14, and reduced the representatives of the Caucasus by 19 and those of Siberia by 26. In the electoral assemblies (containing voters of the second degree), there was one elector to every 230 landed proprietors, to every 1,000 to 15,000 citizens according to their taxable wealth, to every 60,000 peasants, and to every 125,000 urban workers. Two hundred thousand political prisoners were also disfranchised. By these means the Government secured for its third Duma a Conservative body in which 130,000 nobles had more representatives than 130,000,000 peasants.[1] The result was that this Assembly, which met on November 15, 1907, was without any moral authority and might have been an organ of the Government. The *Correspondant* described it later as having helped to postpone all reforms of any importance and having relinquished one by one almost all the concessions obtained in 1905.[2] In fact, the Duma allowed its powers of control and initiative to lapse to such an extent that the Minister Kokovtsov exclaimed in the middle of a sitting, on May 8, 1908, "Thank God, we have no Parliament!" much to the discomfiture of

educated in revolutionary lore by propagandists and theorists from Kropotkin down to the latest disciples of Marx, is more class-conscious, more self-reliant, more keenly aware of the mission of liberation which it is destined to accomplish. And when you consider the varying circumstances to which democratic representative principles have been applied with success, you will be confident that Russia, too, will succeed in discovering methods of popular representation in harmony with her national genius and with her racial and mental characteristics." (From a speech delivered at the Tivoli-Vauxhall, January 30, 1905.)

[1] The correspondent of the *Journal des Débats* wrote: "It must be frankly admitted that the present allocation of seats is the result of wholesale electoral trickery, and by no means reflects the nation's real opinions." (November 17, 1907.)   [2] December 25, 1912.

French journalists.[1] The French press did not realize, either, that the Russian masses would have no respect for laws passed by an unrepresentative Duma. Professor Kovalevsky sounded a note of warning here. "It would be a great mistake", he wrote, "to imagine that the concurrence of a body of pseudo-representatives implies any pledge on the part of the Russian people in regard to foreign debts."[2]

In these circumstances, Stolypin was able to devote himself undisturbed to his favourite sport of repression. His firmness can best be expressed statistically:

| | | |
|---|---|---|
| Shot or hanged | .. | Several thousands. |
| Imprisoned | .. | 170,000, rising by about 3,000 a month on an average. |

This useful score led to the necessity of a supplementary estimate of 7,000,000 roubles for the erection of additional prison accommodation—the same sum, curiously enough, as was included in the Education Vote for the elementary schooling of the nation.

Again the French Socialist Party was alone in its protests. On June 29, 1908, on a vote of credit for the visit of the President of the Republic to Russia, Edouard Vaillant referred in turn to the massacre of January 22, 1905, the dissolution of the First and Second Dumy, and the pogroms, but was interrupted after every few words by shouts from the Centre and Right: "That is not our business! Leave off; that is nothing to do with us!" And Pichon, the Foreign Minister in the Clemenceau Cabinet, intervened to express an "indignant protest" against the remarks of the Socialist spokesman. They were "contrary to the truth, to patriotic feeling, and to the

---

[1] Khomiakov, the President of the Duma, called this an "unfortunate remark", but was forced by Stolypin to apologize. The latter had himself said, on the very first day of the session: "The historic power of Autocracy and the unfettered will of the Monarch are the valued heritage of the Russian State."   [2] *Revue Bleue*, June 29, 1907.

best interests of France". The Tsar was a "constitutional monarch". Pichon repeated this phrase on January 21, 1909. These reiterated statements on the part of Radical Ministers, who at every public dinner would pose as sons of the Revolution and at the same time went on asserting the "constitutional" character of the Tsarist rule, when Kokovtsov had just been congratulating himself and Russia on having no Parliament, create a mixed impression of unconscious humour and nauseating cant.

In 1909 two sensational scandals were disclosed, one after the other, which threw a sinister light on the disintegration of the Tsarist régime: the Azev case and the Harting case. They were exposed by Burtzev, who laid bare the organization of the Russian secret police in Paris and revealed that the Russian Government had placed in charge of the branch an *agent provocateur* named Harting, a former Nihilist who had made an attempt on the Tsar's life in 1890, and had also been convicted in the French courts for crimes of violence. The popular press in France, led by the *Temps*, was, needless to say, against the abolition of the Paris branch of the Tsarist police.[1]

In August 1909 the Tsar visited the King of England and the President of the French Republic at Cowes and Cherbourg. A chorus of reprobation arose from the intellectual *élite* of Europe. Branting spoke in denunciation of "Tsardom, that scourge of modern civilization". In England, seventy-five Members of Parliament and twenty-seven university professors declared their detestation of a régime which, between October 1905 and December 1908, had put 4,000 people to death, sent 74,000 to Siberia, and imprisoned 180,000. In France, the Socialist Party issued a manifesto of protest in which they asserted that, "but for the funds supplied, with the connivance of the French ruling class, to the torturers of the Russian nation, it would be free by now". Jaurès inveighed with all

[1] *Temps*, July 17, 1909.

his eloquence against the decision to receive on French soil the man primarily responsible for such a régime. He had previously expressed the acute mortification they all felt at the President's visit to Russia "at a time when there was a gallows in every town, when firing parties were busy day and night, when all the sons of Russia who had been fighting for freedom, invoking the Rights of Man proclaimed by France, were being strung up, shot, or tortured. It meant that France was assuming a share of moral responsibility for these outrages, this reign of terror." Referring to the execration aroused by the Tsar's visit to England, Jaurès said that was why he had not dared to land either at Cowes or at Cherbourg, and that his ship was "doomed to sail round for ever", like the Flying Dutchman. (July 2nd.) "It is France's misfortune that the men who have governed in her name have not been sufficiently jealous of her dignity. In the Alliance with Russia they have not acted as partners, but as flunkeys." (August 4th.) The Duma, he concluded regretfully, was now only a screen to hide the gallows, a scanty covering for the nakedness of Tsardom.

And, indeed, every feeble attempt made by the Duma to exercise any real control over the finances of the country had failed. Suggestions had been made for the prevention of unauthorized transfers between votes, the prohibition of supplementary estimates, the scaling down of salaries in the higher ranks of the Civil Service, the supervision of State monopolies, and the submission of the budget to the Duma for investigation, but all in vain. The Government even compelled the Duma to pass a number of bills by threatening it with dissolution. In spite of this, the *Temps* wrote in all seriousness: "There is no country in the world where the transition from absolutism to constitutionalism has been accomplished with so little friction as in Russia. . . . She has now planted her feet firmly on the path of constitutional government and liberal institutions." And the moral was pointed in the approved style by a denunciation of the Socialist Party, a "real national menace, ready to betray the interests of their own country".[1]

Stolypin pursued with redoubled vigour his dual task of repression, directed against the advanced parties and the Jews, and of the russification of the subject nationalities. In defiance of the solemn pledges given by Alexander I in 1809, the Duma was forced, under the threat of dissolution, to enact on June 3, 1910, the abrogation of the right of self-government in Finland,[2] and, shortly afterwards, an Act providing for the extension of the *zemstvo* system in the Western provinces intensified the process of russification in Poland. Anti-Semitism, too, fully maintained its position as a governmental institution, as was evidenced by the Beylis scandal in Kiev in 1911.

Stolypin himself, the man who had boasted that he had "taken Revolution by the throat and strangled it",[3] perished at the hand of the assassin in September 1911. The *Temps* averred that he had adapted Russia to representative institutions (September 16, 1911), but, as a matter of fact, the old autocratic Russia had not changed. French capital had enabled it to dispense with self-government, and this very fact constituted the gravest possible peril for the future, both from the financial and the military point of view. Meanwhile the financial situation in Russia went from bad to worse. By 1914, the amount of French investments in Russia was equivalent to nearly 17,000,000,000 francs. The *Journal de Genève* admitted openly that it had been a serious blunder for France to tie her hands with such frequent issues and such large amounts:

[1] July 9, August 1, August 2, 1909.

[2] The action of Nicholas II in 1899 in arrogating to himself the right of legislating for Poland without the advice and consent of the Diet had been the first infringement of the charter which he himself, as well as his predecessors, had sworn to maintain inviolate. Cf. J. Deck, *Pour la Finlande*, in *Cahiers de la Quinzaine*, August 1902; A. Leroy-Beaulieu in the *Européen*, Nos. 59 and 75, January and May 1903; Kaspar, *Finlande et Russie*, in the *Correspondant*, January 25, 1918.

[3] Interview with G. Dru (Preface to Poleyayev's *La Russie de 1906 à 1912*).

This was an error of judgment for which a heavy penalty may have to be paid some day. . . . The unfortunate aspect of the matter is that the longer one goes on and the more one is induced to agree to fresh financial sacrifices the more one enhances the difficulty of elucidating the exact position when it becomes necessary to do so.

Russia had never been in a position to pay the annual interest on her bonds from her own resources. On February 25, 1912, the *rapporteur* of the budget in the Duma declared that every budget for the past twenty-two years had shown a deficit. The direct taxes only produced 12 per cent of the total revenue, indirect taxation accounting for 80 per cent. One-third of the total receipts came from intoxicating liquor, and alcoholism had made frightful ravages among the people. To meet interest payments on bonds held abroad, between 700,000,000 and 800,000,000 gold francs were required each year, and Russia could only secure this sum by fresh loans and by the exportation of grain. As regards the latter expedient, during the previous nine years the excess of exports over imports had been only one-fifth of the total sum due in interest payments for 1912.

Between 1902 and 1911, the National Debt rose from 6,430,650,000 roubles to 9,014,141,000 roubles, an increase of nearly 2,600,000,000 in ten years.[1] The large sums placed at Russia's disposal by French investors had not even ensured any commercial advantages to French traders. On the contrary, the Germans had benefited. Their exports to Russia increased in value from 224,714,000 roubles in 1904 to 440,951,000 roubles in 1910, and Russian exports to Germany also rose from 234,741,000 roubles to 390,600,000 roubles. Imports from Great Britain during the same period increased from 101,832,000 to 153,547,000 roubles, and exports to that country from 230,400,000 to 314,000,000 roubles. Trade with France, on the other hand, remained comparatively negligible, imports rising from 26,213,000 to 59,368,000 roubles, and exports from 61,782,000 to 93,700,000 roubles.[2]

---

[1] Cf. the *Correspondant*, September 25, 1912, and H. Ganz, *La débâcle russe*.    [2] From the *Revue de commerce étranger pour la Russie*.

# CHAPTER X

# RUSSIA'S FOREIGN POLICY, 1907–1911

## STAGE I. BUCHLAU

HAVING met with nothing but disaster in the Far East, Russia might have been expected to welcome a breathing-space for convalescence, for reorganization and recuperation in an atmosphere of seclusion and self-restraint. But, on the contrary, she at once turned her eyes elsewhere with unabated cupidity, and not only took up again the old, far-reaching designs of Tsardom on Constantinople and the Straits, but also stretched out a greedy hand at Persia and part of Asia Minor. The traditional Pan-Slav policy tenaciously pursued ever since the time of Peter the Great was revived and continued right up to the Great War, when, of course, it was displayed in its fullest florescence. Tsarism had succeeded, with the aid of the French loan, in checking the Revolution for a time, and the tottering autocracy was now looking round for an opportunity to crush it completely by bringing off some successful national *coup* abroad, or at least some diplomatic victory. A quarrel with Turkey promised to be more popular than the war with Japan and would thus provide an excellent lightning-conductor for revolutionary fanaticism. This calculation was the normal expedient of a reactionary government. But besides this, certain economic interests were pressing for satisfaction, especially the industrialists of the Donetz basin, who, backed by a substantial participation of French capital, were keen partisans of a forward policy, not so much to conquer the markets of the Levant as to set the seal on their hegemony over the Balkan States. But this grandiose Slav policy, besides having no deep roots in the heart of the nation, was without any solid justification. During times of peace, the system already in force for the regulation of traffic in the Straits provided ample safeguards for all legitimate Russian interests, while in war the Dardanelles, whether under Russian suzerainty or not, would be bound to be blockaded, and hence closed to the Russian Fleet, by any enemy commanding superior naval forces.

The revival of this policy synchronized with the début as Foreign Minister of Alexander Isvolsky. He had always been opposed to the war with Japan—in fact, averse to Asiatic gambles in general—and took steps without delay to clarify the situation in the Far East by signing a convention with Japan. Russia was then free to make her re-entry on the European stage, and Isvolsky set himself the task of bringing to fruition her old-standing designs on the Straits. What Russia aimed at securing was not the privilege of free navigation, to be shared with all other nations alike, but an exclusive right for the warships of countries with a seaboard on the Black Sea to pass through the Bosphorus and the Dardanelles. This would have been a threefold gain to Russia, in that she could dominate Roumania, who had no outlet to the sea elsewhere, turn the Straits into a base from which she could command the Aegean and the whole of the Levant, and also prevent enemy fleets from threatening the Russian ports on the Black Sea. This claim quite naturally expanded, in 1914, into a demand for the annexation not only of the Straits and Constantinople, but also of the adjacent territories and even the islands of Imbros and Tenedos.[1]

In 1907, with Russia still bleeding from her wounds, there could be no question of her realizing such predatory aims with her own unaided resources, while France, with her preoccupations in Morocco, had no intention at that time of going to war to secure Constantinople and the Straits for her ally. Consequently Isvolsky was constrained to consider pacific means of arriving at the same end, and he conceived the ingenious plan of securing the support of his possible opponents one by one by offering them ample compensation at the

---

[1] Cf. Rosen, *Forty Years of Diplomacy*, II, and his confidential memorandum (*Correspondant*, September 10, 1913.)

expense of third parties. He began by negotiating a convention with Great Britain, Russia's traditional enemy in Asia, which was signed on August 31, 1907. This Entente, cemented in the following year by a meeting between King Edward VII and Nicholas II at Reval, gave Isvolsky grounds for hoping that Britain might be induced to look favourably on his Balkan aims. She was showing conciliatory tendencies towards Russia, both because the Tsar was giving up his dreams of expansion in Asia and because Germany was fast becoming a much more formidable adversary.[1] Next, Isvolsky made great efforts to arrange an agreement with Austria, Italy, and Germany, all without consulting France, without even notifying the ally who, by continuing to pour her gold into the coffers of Tsardom, had enabled it to master the Revolution. France was kept in ignorance of these negotiations, and it was a long time before she even became aware of the main features of the pacts concluded at Buchlau, Racconigi, and Potsdam with the three members of the Triple Alliance. This aspect of the foreign policy of Russia will throw some light on her attitude, both theoretical and practical, towards the Alliance with France at that time. Exclusively concerned with her own interests and without the slightest regard for those of France, she came to agreements with the Triple Alliance Powers on the most serious matters without making any attempt at concerted action with France, whose statesmen were thus precluded from even drawing the necessary lessons from the negotiations.

It will be remembered how, with a view to securing Austria's neutrality in the Turkish War and the projected march on Constantinople, Russia had concluded with the Dual Monarchy the convention of Reichstadt, signed on July 8, 1876, and confirmed by the further agreement of January 15, 1877, which recognized Austria's claims on Bosnia-Herzegovina and thus abandoned to their fate an appreciable section of the Slav family which Russia had always proclaimed her intention of

[1] Cf. *Die Grosse Politik*, XXV (2), pp. 439 sqq.

M

delivering from the Turkish yoke. It was this convention
between the two Emperors, Alexander and Francis Joseph,
much more than the Congress of Berlin, which secured Austria
in her hold on the two provinces.[1] A further agreement concluded in St. Petersburg in February 1897, and renewed in
1902 and 1907, even recognized Austria's zone of influence
in the Balkans as including Serbia, while Russia allotted to
herself the control of Bulgaria and of Turkey east of Salonica.
In 1903 the "Mürzsteg programme" confirmed these spheres
of influence and provided for reforms in Macedonia, while
each party undertook not to pursue a policy of separate self-
interest in the Balkan Peninsula. This was aptly termed a
protocol of altruism by Isvolsky.

Austria, being an essentially Continental Power, without
colonies, and with a very limited seaboard at the head of the
Adriatic, always regarded the Balkans as a field of action
specially marked out for her activities and as the natural
market for her industries. To give effect to these views, railway
communication was essential, but as it happened, the Turkish
line from Salonica, through Usküb, came to an end at Mitro-
vitza, in the Sandjak of Novibazar, some seventy miles from
the Bosnian frontier. It was necessary, therefore, to extend
the Austrian system as far as the Turkish terminus. This
railway policy was defined by Baron von Aehrenthal, the
Austrian Foreign Minister, in a speech to the Austro-Hungarian
Delegations on January 27, 1908, when, announcing his project
for a line running through the Sandjak, he declared that their
mission in the Balkans was purely economic. His plans for the
annexation of Bosnia-Herzegovina were by then, it may be
mentioned, already cut and dried. Having been unable to
prevent the Austrian concession, Isvolsky then conceived the
idea of supporting the plans for railway construction put
forward by the Balkan States, in particular the Serbian proposal

[1] See *Die Grosse Politik*, II, pp. 111 sqq., and Max Hoschiller, *La Russie
devant Constantinople*.

for a line from the Danube to the Adriatic, which would have intersected the Austrian line. Italy was in favour of these branch lines, especially that from Salonica to Avlona, which would have opened up the Balkan market for her trade.

Not that Isvolsky had given up his scheme for an agreement with Austria on the subject of the Straits. He decided to turn to account Baron von Aehrenthal's designs on Bosnia-Herzegovina, and a series of conferences took place. In fact, "quite a stream of negotiations and confidential communications" began to flow between St. Petersburg and Vienna, and agreement seemed to have been reached.[1] On June 19, 1908, the *Times* published a memorandum by Isvolsky which had fallen into its hands, showing that he had offered Bosnia-Herzegovina to Austria in exchange for the right of navigation through the Straits for Russian men-of-war. On September 4th, at Karlsbad, the Russian Minister advised the Serbian Foreign Minister to resign himself to the inevitable and merely to claim "compensations" for Serbia. Then, on September 15th and 16th, he had a meeting with Aehrenthal at Buchlau in Moravia, in Count Berchtold's *château*, and gave his consent to the annexation of the two provinces, asking in return for the support of Austria in securing a free passage through the Straits. In an official communiqué, issued after the interview, it was stated that "perfect harmony existed in regard to the respective interests of the two countries".

Isvolsky subsequently maintained that, when Aehrenthal announced his decision to annex Bosnia-Herzegovina, he (Isvolsky) endeavoured, although the position of Russia was weakened by the existence of certain earlier secret agreements, to persuade him to submit the question to a general conference of the European Powers, which would also have revised (of course in a direction favourable to Russian interests) the terms of the Treaty of Berlin in regard to the Straits. Thus Austria

[1] V. Bérard, *Les raisons de St. Pétersbourg*, in the *Revue de Paris*, May 1, 1911.

would not have been able to realize her aims in respect of Bosnia-Herzegovina without Russia also realizing hers in the matter of the Bosphorus and the Dardanelles. Aehrenthal, according to this account, had made up his mind to hasten matters in view of the Young Turk Revolution, but undertook to notify his Russian colleague in advance, and also to refer the whole question to an international conference, for which Isvolsky promised to prepare the ground in Paris and London. On October 3rd, however, on the latter's return from Italy, the news reached him in Paris that the annexation had been carried out. Aehrenthal claimed to have received *carte blanche* from Russia and Italy, and had discreetly forgotten all about the *quid pro quo* he had promised Isvolsky. The latter realized that he had been tricked, but did not give up the game as lost. He still rested his hopes on a European conference for the revision of the conditions governing the use of the Straits, and proceeded to London. There, on October 12th, he saw Sir Edward Grey, who made it clear that public opinion in Great Britain would be unlikely to regard any unilateral agreement as acceptable, and said that the recent overthrow of the constitutional régime in Persia, due to the action of certain Russian officers, had created a very bad impression in England. Isvolsky maintained that Russia's intention was to give support to Turkey as a barrier to further advance by Austria, and declared that the French press was entirely in favour of the opening of the Straits. The British Foreign Minister finally handed Isvolsky an *aide-mémoire* in which he stated that, if an agreement were contemplated which would give the Black Sea Powers the advantage of maintaining this great lake in war-time as a kind of impregnable fortress, from which their cruisers and destroyers could sally out at will and waylay merchant ships, without being themselves open to pursuit within the Black Sea, then he must make it clear that public opinion in Great Britain was not favourable to any such arrangement and would not be prepared to sanction it. Any agreement made must contain an element of reciprocity, placing all belligerents on an equal footing in carrying on hostilities.

On the other hand, Turkey, with the support of Germany and Austria, declined to consider any modification in the *status quo*.[1] Thus Isvolsky's plans fell through. But it still did not occur to him to enter into France's view of the matter and realize the impropriety of his having opened up secret negotiations with an Austrian Cabinet Minister—negotiations which involved shameless bartering at the expense of a Slav community. On December 25th, Isvolsky had to admit in the Duma that Austria's action was in conformity with agreements that had been in force between her and Russia for the past thirty years. None the less, he continued to raise loud protests against the *démarche* in the name of international law, demanding that Bosnia-Herzegovina should be allowed self-government. He even appeared to favour Serbia's claims, without, however, losing touch with Austria, until the German ambassador in St. Petersburg presented his ultimatum. (March 23, 1909.)

As a matter of fact, in view of all the conventions by which Russia was bound, and particularly after the Buchlau interview, any protest on her part was "particularly inacceptable". As Philippe Crozier, formerly French ambassador in Vienna, has pointed out, "the annexation was virtually the regularization

---

[1] Cf. V. Bérard, *Revue de Paris*, November 15, 1908, and August 15, 1910. R. Pinon, *Revue des Deux Mondes*, May 1, 1908. Wickham Steed, *The Hapsburg Monarchy*, pp. 261–262, *Through Thirty Years*, pp. 290–295, and *Fortnightly Review*, September–November 1909. Letters from Isvolsky to Gauvain, *Journal des Débats*, October 3 and 9, 1918. *Livre Noir*, II, p. 458. Sir Edward Grey, *Twenty-five Years*, I, pp. 183 sqq. *Die Grosse Politik*, XXVI (1) and (2). In letters to the Serbian Ministers in Paris, M. Vesnich, and London, M. Gruich, Isvolsky counselled acquiescence, pointing out that Bosnia and Herzegovina had long ago ceased to be possible acquisitions for Serbia, since Austria would never have given them up without a war, and also that the evacuation of the Sandjak would cut off Austria permanently from Salonica. (Bogitshevich, *Causes of the War*, pp. 18–26. Cf. Choublier, *La Question d'Orient depuis le traité de Berlin*, pp. 97–98, and Gauvain, *Revue de Paris*, December 15, 1912.)

of a state of things that had existed for thirty years". The
Russian Minister's hands were tied by no less than five previous
treaties or other agreements which had been signed in Russia's
name, under which she had repeatedly conceded to Austria
the right of annexing Bosnia-Herzegovina. Furthermore, these
Austro-Russian pacts had been accepted and ratified by the
whole of Europe. The Congress of Berlin had handed over to
the Dual Monarchy the absolute right of administering Bosnia
and Herzegovina without let or hindrance. "By giving up their
privileges of extra-territoriality in Bosnia-Herzegovina, the
Great Powers had afforded clearer evidence than any formal
declaration could have done that in their eyes the two provinces
had definitely passed from Turkish rule to that of Austria-
Hungary."[1] This opinion was shared by René Pinon. In his
view, the annexation of Bosnia-Herzegovina was merely the
"regularization of a *de facto* situation" which had been in
existence, by virtue of the Treaty of Berlin, ever since 1878.
None of the parties to the Congress of Berlin, no one in Europe
in fact, had been under any illusion as to the protectorate
being anything but an annexation. "In the minds of all the
plenipotentiaries, the provisional arrangement which they were
setting up was clearly, in actual fact, a definitive one."[2]
Hanotaux expressed the opinion that, as the occupation of the
two provinces during the past thirty years had been a serious
burden for Austria-Hungary and had entailed an expenditure
of zeal, attention, and money which well deserved some reward,
it was quite natural that "she should be contemplating the
more or less complete absorption of these two 'liberated'
provinces in the main structure of the Monarchy in the more
or less early future". It was only, in short, a "matter of form".[3]
Moreover, the extension to the Bosnians and Herzegovinians
of the liability to military service in the Austrian army without

---

[1] *Revue de France*, April 15, 1921. Cf. Grey, *Twenty-five Years*, p. 175.
[2] *Revue des Deux Mondes*, December 15, 1908, June 1, 1912.
[3] *La politique de l'équilibre*, pp. 161–162.

question by any other Power had already set the seal on the definite union of the two provinces with the Dual Monarchy.

Isvolsky, who had gained nothing, not even the convening of a Conference of the Powers, as a reward for the sorry part he had played in the negotiations with Austria, was seized with violent resentment and determined to get his revenge. Jaurès stigmatized his state of mind at the time as that of a criminal played false by his accomplices who was now seeking an opportunity of getting even with them:

What right has M. Isvolsky, who was informed of Baron von Aehrenthal's plans in confidence and encouraged them in the hope of participating in the ill-gotten gains, to protest now against his colleague's handiwork, which he knew of all along, but concealed from his country's friend and ally France? An individual like this, who, after having aided and abetted his accomplice to perpetrate the crime, is dissatisfied with the proceeds and raises cries of indignation at the risk of starting a conflagration in Europe, is deserving only of universal public contempt. . . . We are not going to be led into warlike measures for the sake of solacing M. Isvolsky's wounded pride.

Two years later, Jaurès reminded the Chamber of Deputies again that Isvolsky, in his secret interview with Aehrenthal, had taken action which compromised France's whole future without informing her and without any of France's diplomatic representatives being able to warn the Government. "What do our allies take us for?" asked the Socialist orator.

The great danger is not so much that certain nations may declare war deliberately and with their eyes open. It is that every nation may be taken unawares by sudden manœuvres, by lying machinations, by disloyal intrigues hatched in the parlours of secret diplomacy, which may at any moment give rise to panics and misunderstandings.[1]

At all events, on this particular occasion the French Foreign Minister, Pichon, did make it clear to Russia that she must do everything possible to "avoid the risk of a conflict in such a matter, where her vital interests were not at stake, seeing

---

[1] December 27, 1908, and January 13, 1911. In Jaurès' view, Isvolsky with his "inveterate habit of mischief-making", was "grossly and shamelessly disloyal".

that public opinion in France would certainly not regard a war on such an issue as a *casus foederis* involving joint action by the armies of France and Russia". As Crozier has put it, "the French Government stood out for a European policy in the interests of France", as against a Balkan policy in the interests of Serbia.[1]

Apart from this, Russia would in any case have been absolutely incapable of carrying on a war, and even if France had taken a different line, the Tsarist Government would have been bound to give way to Germany. And barely a year later, by a sudden *volte-face*, Russian diplomacy began to take steps to come to an understanding with the latter Power.

### Stage II. Racconigi

Meanwhile Isvolsky, outwitted by Austria, made a bid for the support of Italy. The ground had been prepared by Count Muraviev, the Russian ambassador in Rome, who had projected a tripartite Balkan agreement between Russia, Italy, and Austria. Isvolsky had already been cultivating intimate relations with Tittoni, and had suggested to him, at Desio in 1907, the outlines of a treaty. This was now developed, and signed by the Tsar at Racconigi[2] on October 24, 1909, in the following terms:—

(i) Russia and Italy undertake to make it their chief aim to maintain the *status quo* in the Balkan peninsula.

(ii) In any eventuality whatever that may arise in the Balkans, they undertake to apply and support the principle of nationality, working for the development of the Balkan States free from all foreign domination.

(iii) They agree to take joint action to resist any attempts to frustrate the above-mentioned aims, "joint action"

---

[1] *Revue de France*, April 15, 1921.
[2] The Tsar was careful not to touch Austrian soil on his way to Italy.

in this connection meaning diplomatic action, since any steps of a wider nature would naturally be reserved and form the subject of a further separate agreement.

(iv) If either Russia or Italy should desire to enter into any fresh agreements with a third party in regard to the Balkans apart from those now existing, each would seek the co-operation of the other before doing so.

(v) Italy and Russia undertake to give sympathetic consideration, the former to Russian interests in the question of the Straits and the latter to Italian interests in Tripoli and Cyrenaica.[1]

This agreement makes it clear that Russia was contemplating in 1909 the break up of the *status quo* in the Balkans and a consequential change in the arrangements governing the Straits. The two parties to this treaty only made a parade of their intentions to maintain the *status quo* because they were planning to destroy it. The same formula was a feature in the secret treaty between Serbia and Bulgaria which was drafted shortly afterwards under Russian auspices. Reading between the lines, one can see the beginning of the Balkan League and of the Balkan Wars of 1912–1913, already adumbrated in the mind of the Russian Government.

The text of the Racconigi Agreement was not communicated to France until 1912. Even then Poincaré had great difficulty in obtaining the precise wording of the treaty, and when he pressed for this in November of that year the Russian Foreign Minister, Sazonov, stipulated that he should not even discuss it with his colleagues in the French Cabinet.[2] Thus Russia continued to enter into agreements with the Triple Alliance Powers on the most important subjects without consulting France.

[1] *Livre Noir*, I, pp. 357–358. *Die Grosse Politik*, XXVII, pp. 397 sqq., and letter from Isvolsky to Count Osten-Sacken (October 22nd), in which he gives vent to his bitterness against Austria, pp. 423–425.

[2] Poincaré, *Au service de la France*, I, p. 32; II, p. 364.

## STAGE III. POTSDAM

In 1910 a regular Entente came into being between Russia and Germany, again behind France's back. Nicholas II, quite oblivious of his "capitulation" in the previous year, met Wilhelm II on November 4th at Potsdam, where the two Emperors, accompanied by their Foreign Ministers, signed an agreement in which each undertook not to join any combination of Powers that might be formed against the other. In addition, Germany was given a free hand in the pursuit of her economic ambitions in Persia and Asia Minor, especially in regard to the Bagdad Railway, Russia pledging herself to link up the projected Russian system with the great Bagdad line. In exchange, Germany recognized Russia's political interests in Persia, where Tsardom was preparing a *coup de main*.[1] As a result of this agreement, the Russian army corps previously stationed on the Polish frontier were withdrawn a considerable distance into the interior.

These negotiations were of exceptional gravity in that they obviously constituted a challenge to the Entente Cordiale. According to Hanotaux, Russia seemed to be altering her aim and falling into line with German policy. The ex-Foreign Minister, in an article published early in 1911, asked what France stood to gain for all the risks she was taking, what advantages her mysterious pact with Russia brought her in exchange for her friendship. In his view, it was essential that France should choose between a Russophil and an Anglophil policy.[2]

In French official quarters, when the first shock of surprise was over, it was maintained that the Russian Government had kept France fully in touch with the negotiations, and that this agreement in no way modified the relations between the two

[1] Cf. *Die Grosse Politik*, XXXVII (2), pp. 827 sqq. Russia also undertook not to countenance an aggressive policy on the part of the Balkan States.
[2] *Revue Hebdomadaire*, February 25, 1911.

allies. As a matter of fact, however, France had been left in complete ignorance of what it was proposed to discuss at the Emperors' interview. Neither the Government nor even the French ambassador in St. Petersburg had been apprised of the important agenda proposed. Pichon, the Foreign Minister, complained to Isvolsky, asking why Sazonov, before setting out for Berlin, had not notified the French ambassador in greater detail of the programme of the discussion on Persian affairs, and, more especially, mentioned that the question of the Bagdad Railway was going to be raised.[1] The actual information obtained in Paris made a strange circuit, namely, *via* Vienna. Crozier relates that Baron von Aehrenthal disclosed to him, two days afterwards, the substance of part of the conversations that had taken place at Potsdam.[2]

The Potsdam Agreement was referred to in a series of important speeches in the Chamber of Deputies in the course of the debate on the Foreign Office vote. Denys Cochin did not hesitate to affirm that the *rapprochement* was all to the advantage of Germany and all to the disadvantage of France. Jaurès pointed out that, for some years past, France had been "tacitly opposing the Bagdad scheme" out of consideration for Russia, who had fancied that her interests might be prejudiced by the construction of the railway, and this had now led to a Gilbertian dénouement. "You introduced an element of tension into Franco-German relations by opposing the Bagdad Railway merely to please Russia, and now Russia herself, without telling you, has gained moral *kudos* with Germany by seeming to persuade you, who were only standing out on her account, to agree to the Bagdad Railway." Thus France was impairing her own relations with Germany by showing too great a zeal for Russian interests. Jaurès protested against such docility on the part of French diplomacy, and asked to what extent France was going to be associated with this latest twofold

---

[1] *Livre Noir*, Letter from Isvolsky, January 18th, I, p. 27.
[2] *Revue de France*, June 1, 1921.

menace, this blow aimed against Persia and Turkey in the sole interests of Russia and German expansion. Pichon's reply seemed strangely halting. It was a question of harmonizing rivalries which were rather of an economic than of a political nature. The agreement was in no sense prejudicial to France. The Franco-Russian Alliance remained as stable and as potent as ever. But Jaurès pressed him again to say definitely whether he had been notified in advance that Russia was going to abandon her opposition to the Bagdad Railway, and he had to admit that it was

possible, even though the Russian Government may not have had time to notify us in advance, that the conversations in question touched on the possible linking up of the Russian projected railway system in Persia with the Bagdad line, and that Germany asked Russia not to place obstacles in the way of such eventual linking up. But (he added) in what way is France concerned with such a project and why should she raise any objections?

André Tardieu, in the *Temps*, wrote in warm support of Pichon, asserting that there was nothing in the Potsdam agreement to which France could take exception or which could have come as a surprise to French diplomacy. In exchanging views in a friendly way on Turkish and Persian affairs, Russia and Germany had only been following the example set by France and Great Britain in 1904, at the time of the Russo-Japanese War. He maintained that, as regards the Bagdad Railway, Russia had been perfectly justified in saying to Germany: "Here is my railway system; there is yours. Shall we not link them together and so add a link to international concord?" Why could not France, with equal justification, follow the same course? Statecraft would be all the better for paying a little more attention to economic policy.[1]

In a debate in the Senate on April 6, 1911, grave misgivings were expressed by Gaudin de Vilaine and de Lamarzelle, who complained of the inertia and lethargy into which the Franco-

[1] *Temps*, December 14, 1910.

Russian Alliance seemed to have fallen. Ribot, in a considered reply, defended the Alliance, and explained wherein its real character lay. We shall return to this explanation in a later chapter.

Many critics considered that the particular feature which constituted the gravest threat to French interests was the withdrawal of the Russian army corps from the Polish frontier a considerable distance into the interior, as this step, which had been taken as a direct result of the Russo-German agreement, obviously weakened the offensive power of the Russian army. Nevertheless, Joseph Reinach, Vice-Chairman of the Army Committee in the Chamber of Deputies, coolly asserted that the withdrawal was, on the contrary, to France's advantage. Any doubts raised in the mind of the French public as to the sterling quality of Russia's friendship were, he said, suggested by German agents. In the same strain, the periodical *La France Militaire* declared that, as the result of this measure, the Russian army had improved its power of concentration and its speed of mobilization. And as late as 1914, Stephane Lauzanne, in the *Matin*, was still attacking Jaurès as the only Frenchman who had adversely criticized the withdrawal of the Russian troops from Poland. Russia, he maintained, had taken this step with a view to "speedier mobilization", and the French General Staff, far from being uneasy, had "welcomed it with delight, had favoured it, had practically asked for it".[1]

Other results of the Russo-German agreement were soon in evidence. Russia sent an ultimatum to China, followed by movements of troops, and China had to give way. In flagrant defiance of the Anglo-Russian Agreement of August 31, 1907, the Russian Government, which had never really ceased to disregard the independence and integrity of Persia, now assumed a provocative attitude and sent fresh troops across

[1] *Temps*, March 8, 1911. *France Militaire*, February 7 and 15, 1911. *Matin*, January 4, 1914. Lauzanne asserted that the German General Staff had received the news of the withdrawal with mortification, uneasiness, and anger.

the frontier.[1] On all sides Tsarism developed its schemes of aggrandizement.

There is little doubt that the *rapprochement* between Russia and Germany which Isvolsky had engineered was the outcome of the attitude adopted by France immediately after the annexation of Bosnia-Herzegovina and by Great Britain in opposing the Russian aims with regard to the Straits. Russia had felt threatened. Now, fortified by having come to an understanding behind France's back with the Triple Alliance Powers, she seemed to be hinting that her ally had only two alternatives: either to support her designs on the Straits even at the risk of war, or to see her combine with Germany. This was the crowning reward for France's untiring financial support and for the way she had assisted Russia to crush the Revolution! But, in point of fact, Russia could not have formed any really intimate combination with Germany and Austria unless she had been prepared to sacrifice her fellow-Slavs in the Balkans and to give up her grandiose schemes in regard to the Straits; while, on the other hand, no other country would have dreamed of taking France's place as Tsardom's banker. Thus everything conduced to a firm stand being made by the Republic; instead of which, Russia proceeded to drag France in the wake of her designs in the Balkans.

[1] Cf. the *Correspondant*, December 10, 1911.

# CHAPTER XI

## THE RESHAPING OF THE ALLIANCE

WE have seen how ineffectual the Franco-Russian Alliance had become during the period just dealt with. It was like a machine that has broken down, no longer equal to the demands made upon it—if indeed it ever had been. Events had all gone to prove how essentially at variance the real interests of the two countries were, both at home and abroad.[1] It would surely have been wise for France to take advantage of the questionable attitude of the Russian Government at Buchlau, Racconigi, and Potsdam to loosen the ties which linked her with Tsarism and to direct her diplomacy towards forming a new grouping, with its centre of gravity in Western Europe, or, better still, towards maintaining an unfettered isolation, which would at all events have obviated the danger of a war for causes foreign to France's vital interests and in company with an ally in the last stages of decrepitude. This was a course dictated both by self-respect and by enlightened self-interest.

But, on the contrary, instead of making a thorough investigation of the situation in Russia, which was still bleeding from the wounds of the Japanese War and needed not only plenty of time to recover but also drastic internal reorganization, France's votaries of *Realpolitik* fitted the facts into the strait-jacket of their pet theories, encouraged by the whole-hearted support of the governing class. Alarmed at the prospect of a definite Russo-German Entente, they thought it simplest to tighten up the bonds which united them to Russia. The Alliance was "too free and easy", and must be given a more aggressive turn if French interests were to be properly safeguarded. Instead of attempting to remould the vast resources of Russia, which

[1] Delcassé once confessed to André Mévil that he had become so nervous in regard to the Alliance that he opened his paper every morning with vague apprehension, fearing the day's news would contain some fresh cause for worry.

could only have been done gradually and systematically, they imagined that, after a hasty and superficial patching up, Tsardom, whose un-European polity was falling to pieces before their eyes, could be made to play the part of a powerful Western State on an equal footing with the major European nations, and that the Alliance would then attain its fullest effectiveness. Instead of advising their ally to seek the recuperation she so badly needed, they persisted in assuring her that she could rely on French support in her Balkan aims under any circumstances, offering her in effect a blank cheque for the realization of her ambitions. This was the only way French statesmen could discover of making sure of Russia's help in an emergency. But there was another reason for their attitude, a politicians' reason. The policy of "appeasement", as it was called, in domestic politics had brought to the front a mercenary nationalism which was eagerly in search of ways and means of staving off the growing menace of Socialism. "National unity" would favour the relegation of "internal squabbles" to the background and put a stop to "arid party strife"—all the patter of the demagogue tired of having to defend his booty—and to bolster up this new slogan a certain liveliness in foreign politics was called for, which would distract attention from demands for budgetary and social reform. As it happened, this tendency was greatly facilitated by undoubted blunders on Germany's part.

As early as 1909, André Tardieu, one of the rising hopes of the younger generation, had expressed the view that the joint activity of the two allied countries during the period 1893 to 1902 had been "lacking in intensity and cohesion". After the Potsdam agreement, he wrote that successive French Governments, having "operated the Alliance with a complaisance which savoured of servility", were left without a programme of their own and without initiative. Germany had always influenced Russia in the direction of a forward policy in the East, but the Franco-Russian Alliance had never won anything but Pyrrhic victories in Asia, for which it had then invariably had to pay dearly in Europe.[1] These views were sound enough, but the mistake arose in imagining that Russia could ever play a sufficiently active part in Europe to cope with Germany and Austria. Not long afterwards, André Mévil declared that the chief object of the Alliance ought to be to combat Germany.[2] To base such expectations on Russia was actually as futile as to hope to stop a bull with the horse of a picador. It must not be forgotten, moreover, that the illusion was shared by such men as Méline, Ribot and Poincaré, the three chief leaders of the moderate progressive Party. On April 6, 1911, in the course of a debate in the Senate on the Potsdam interview, Ribot, with all the prestige of one of the authors of the Franco-Russian Treaty, offered his interpretation of the Alliance:

When two great nations enter into a permanent bond of friendship, they join forces in foreign policy, not merely with the object of maintaining the peace of the world, but also of dealing jointly with all sorts of eventualities which cannot at the moment be foreseen and which they themselves may be powerless to prevent. They accordingly keep a watchful eye on events with a view to framing a suitable joint policy which will secure the greatest advantages for themselves from any concatenation of circumstances that may arise. This is the kind of pact which we have concluded with Russia.

He added, with reference to the statement that had just been made by Pichon to the effect that France was not directly concerned with the Bagdad Railway:

This is perhaps somewhat short-sighted. For the statesman there are no degrees of importance in world affairs. He is concerned with them all, and must keep a watch on them all. We must maintain closer touch with Russia. For the last few months we have been neglecting our interests in the Balkans.

This interpretation was in line with the principles underlying the modification introduced into the Alliance by Delcassé in

[1] *La France et les alliances*, p. 19. *Temps*, February 18–23, 1911.
[2] *La Paix est malade*, p. 101.

N

pretexts for his country to avoid her obligations under the Alliance", and that de Selves and G. Louis had been perfectly right in declining to admit that Russia could take up the attitude of a mediator between Germany and France, and insisting on her carrying out her duty as an ally.[1] But the fact remains that Russia did definitely advise France to avoid a war over Morocco.

We shall see how Poincaré's conception of the Alliance was to gain the ascendancy between 1912 and 1914, in connection with the Balkan disputes.

[1] Telegrams from G. Louis, Nos. 313, 316, 318, 428, and 432. Poincaré, I, pp. 297–303. Caillaux, *Agadir*, pp. 141–144.

# CHAPTER XII

# THE BALKAN WAR OF 1912

THE Balkan war resulted from Italy's aggression in Tripoli, which was itself a direct outcome of the Moroccan affair.[1] Italy, finding it difficult to impose her will on Turkey in Africa, schemed to assail her in the Balkans, with Russia's connivance, by creating a situation of such difficulty that she would be compelled to make peace. Isvolsky took a hand in this, in intimate association with Tittoni.

The Balkan States, impatient to realize their national ambitions, were determined for their part to profit by Turkey's embarrassment in her struggle with Italy.[2] This war set appetites on edge, and all the more since "Italy's aggression could find no justification in any precedent of equal flagrancy".[3] Had not Italy given the most glaring example of a country violating her most solemn engagement to respect the integrity of the Ottoman Empire, with the complicity of the other Powers? Panafieu himself, France's Minister at Sofia, declared

---

[1] "The launching of the Tripoli venture", wrote Gauvain, "is the result of the opening up of the Moroccan affair. The two events were like cogwheels. . . . It is only too probable that our responsible Ministers did not intend that their actions should produce this result. But that is no excuse whatever. The exercise of power involves responsibilities which in the end present their bill. . . . The occupation of Tripoli threatens to raise endless complications in the Near East. . . . We have crossed the threshold of confusion and of the unknown." (*L'Europe au jour le jour*, IX, p. 105.) The *Correspondant* wrote: "The secret agreements between France, Italy, Spain, and Britain, the Algeciras conference, and the events that followed are all wheels within wheels. To anyone aware of France's engagements towards Italy it was clear that the moment the beneficiaries made up their minds to profit by them the Balkan question would be reopened in one way or another. It is no secret that Signor Giolitti and the King still hesitated. The march on Fez decided their line for them, and from the very first day it was manifest that the Tripoli expedition had been determined on only after agreement with Russia, and with little regard for the observations of Berlin and Vienna." (October 25, 1912.)

[2] See Tittoni's statement to the *Matin*, October 10, 1912.

[3] René Pinon, *Revue des Deux Mondes*, June 1, 1912.

that the Italo-Turkish war was responsible for the Bulgar-Serb *rapprochement* under Russia's auspices.[1]

The Balkan war of 1912 thus takes its place in history as a phase of Russia's struggle for the conquest of Constantinople and the Straits. Until then Russia had sought to attain her ends through peaceful bargains with Austria, Italy, and Germany. Faced with Britain's attitude in 1908, expressed in the advice to seek a direct agreement with Turkey, the Russian Government considered the idea of a Balkan federation including Turkey and aimed primarily against Austria. With this end in view, Russia entered into a military convention with Bulgaria (December 1909), though this did not prevent her from showing complaisance towards Italy's designs on Tripoli, a Turkish possession. Charykov, the Russian ambassador at Constantinople, soon received instructions to raise the question of the Straits in his conversations with the Turkish Ministers. But the negotiations came to nothing; the Turks claimed, as Isvolsky himself had done in 1908, that the *status quo* could only be modified by an international conference, of which Russia would no longer hear. The Tsarist Government was reduced to disavowing its ambassador, and finally to recalling him and beating an undignified retreat.[2]

Pacific methods having thus been exhausted, there remained to Russia only one expedient, so long as she was still unready for a European war—Balkan federation, which she proceeded to promote, encourage, and arm; a federation directed at first against Turkey, later against Austria, and engineered in order to take advantage of the efforts of the small States to attempt

---

[1] French Yellow Book, *Affaires Balcaniques*, No. 24.

[2] In a note dated December 4th, Charykov had brusquely demanded a right of passage for Russian ships of war in exchange for a guarantee against any sort of hostile move on the part of the Balkan States. Sazonov, who was on his way to Paris at the time, did not hesitate to declare to the *Temps* that there had not been "any official *démarche*—only conversations arising out of the fear that in laying submarine mines Turkey might do injury to Russian commerce. . . . I do not know why Russia has been credited with taking steps which she is not dreaming at present of taking and has no motive for taking." (*Temps*, December 9, 1911.)

to seize the Straits. In 1912 she was very near success, but the discord between the allies, together with Austria's attitude, prevented her from attaining her end. After that there remained no way of realizing her purpose save through the destruction of her rival when the opportunity should be provided by a European war. This conviction was reached in the course of 1913.

Nothing was farther from the intentions of the French Government than to put obstacles in the way of its ally's schemes. After the annexation of Bosnia and Herzegovina, Russia received the "most precise assurances" that in the question of the Straits she could count on France's sympathy. André Tardieu declared that the régime of the Straits was "vexatious and intolerable for Russia".[1] But sympathy was not enough; Russia needed tangible and efficacious assistance. Isvolsky set to work to secure it at the source when he took up his post in Paris at the end of 1910.

In 1911 French progress in Morocco had the result of exciting Russian ambitions. At the beginning of September the Tsar's Government requested Isvolsky to let the French Government know that in consideration of the Russian support which it was receiving it was hoped that France would consider herself "morally bound to make repayment in like coin". It was desired to obtain from France the promise not to offer opposition to Russia's "point of view or to any possible intervention" at any moment when the Russian Government might consider it "necessary to enter into pourparlers and perhaps even take definite action" in the Straits. It was considered by the Russian Government that an agreement to this effect might be registered in the form of an exchange of letters between the two Foreign Ministers, as had been done with Italy at Racconigi.

France, in fact, had had to give compensation to Italy and Germany, and now Russia was taking advantage of the fact to

[1] *Temps*, October 12, 1908.

put forward claims of her own. But the compensation offered
to Germany cost decidedly less; it consisted of colonial
territory in France's own possession. What her ally was
demanding was support in seizing, at the risk of war, a position
of capital importance in world politics.

On October 11th Isvolsky pointed out to de Selves, the
French Foreign Minister, how the radical changes produced
in the Mediterranean basin (French hegemony over Morocco,
Italy's acquisition of Tripoli, and the consolidation of Britain's
position in Egypt) made it incumbent upon Russia to aspire
to the formal acknowledgment of her rights and interests in
the Near East. He hoped that France would look with favour
on the "actions" on which the Russian Government might
"think fit to enter, sooner or later, with regard to the Straits
and the adjacent territory". Isvolsky wrote to St. Petersburg
that he would choose the moment for stating Russia's desires
in more concrete terms "in connection with the course of the
Franco-German pourparlers and the development of the
Tripoli conflict". He also agitated for the means of procuring
"a good press" on the question by means of subsidies.

On November 4th, the day of the signature of the Franco-
German treaty, Isvolsky officially acquainted de Selves with
Russia's desires in the Near East and in Manchuria. He
claimed that Russia's "freedom of action" in the sphere of
the Straits should be recognized and French assent given to
the measures which Russia might find herself in a position to
adopt to safeguard her interests and establish her position
there. The whole Balkan question was thus opened up. Georges
Louis, however, who was then temporarily at the Quai d'Orsay,
was disturbed at the indefiniteness of the formula "freedom
of action". He raised objections and asked for definite information as to the Russian Government's intentions. Isvolsky
declared that "Russia cannot allow the Straits to pass into
other than Russia's own hands", but he supposed the Caillaux
Ministry would "fight shy of committing itself unconditionally

to a recognition" of Russian freedom of action. De Selves,
however, in a letter dated January 4, 1912, confirmed the
assurances given in 1908 by the French Government with
regard to the satisfaction which Russia might find herself
called upon to demand in the Straits question. He was still
ready to exchange views on this question. Isvolsky, however,
wanted more than this.[1]

A few days later the Caillaux Ministry fell. Poincaré came
into power, and inaugurated the new policy of "national
union", which at once inspired Isvolsky with entire confidence.[2]

On February 10th the new Prime Minister made in the
Senate categorical declarations with regard to the Alliance,
which, with the Entente Cordiale, was an "inviolate article"
(*article intangible*) in France's foreign policy. He did not shrink
from affirming that if ever a Government were so blind as to
depart from these guiding lines, which had been traced by
the considered will of the country, *it would be smashed by an
indignant revolt of public opinion*. He added that French foreign
policy was being conducted more and more under the enlightened control of Parliament and the nation. A little later,
in reply to a protest from M. Piou against secret diplomacy,
Poincaré defended secret treaties, for, he said, "the thing that
gives force to diplomatic agreements is the fact of their con-
secration in the deepest feelings of peoples", and this was, of
course, the case with the Russian Alliance.

From the moment when he came into power M. Poincaré
worked for the conclusion of a naval convention between
France and Russia. It is a curious thing that no one thought
such an agreement worth while between 1892 and 1905, when
Russia's sea power was considerable, but that when her navy

---

[1] *Livre Noir*, I, pp. 145–146, 155–159, 164–166, 178, 179, and II,
pp. 464–466.

[2] Poincaré showed him "great cordiality", and told him that he was
"ready at all times to enter into conversation" with him "on Balkan questions", and to "discuss matters with me as frequently and as thoroughly as
possible". (*Livre Noir*, I, pp. 203–204.)

had been destroyed by Japan and was in the very first stages of recovery a naval agreement was suddenly thought to be of the utmost importance.

The documents which the "Yellow Book" includes on this subject begin with a letter to Poincaré from the French ambassador in St. Petersburg, Georges Louis, dated February 6, 1912. Louis writes:

The Minister of the Navy told me this evening that he was authorized to inform me officially that the Tsar would be glad to see direct relations established between the French and Russian naval staffs on similar lines to those which have existed since 1892 between the General Staffs of the two countries. The Admiral communicated this to me in very cordial terms. He added that M. Sazonov would confirm the communication officially to me.[1]

It is impossible to suppose that a question of such importance was raised for the first time in this way in a conversation. M. Georges Louis' letter was obviously the sequel to correspondence, conversations, or at the very least a preliminary note explaining the reasons which, in the view of the Governments, made a naval convention necessary; preliminaries which it was considered advisable not to include in the "Yellow Book". On the day of receipt of M. Louis' letter, the Prime Minister wrote to Delcassé, Minister of the Navy, and made a point of saying that he saw "nothing but advantage in the innovation proposed". Delcassé replied agreeing, and made use of the same language; he added that the matter had been raised with him some months before by the Russian naval attaché, and that he had then suggested that it would be well if the Russian Government took the initiative.[2] In the intervening period there must necessarily have been exchanges of views.

The French Government's acquiescence was conveyed to St. Petersburg. The two Chiefs of Staff, Vice-Admiral Aubert and Prince Lieven, met in Paris, and, "after having examined together the various hypotheses which might be presented in

[1] *Livre Jaune*, No. 96.    [2] *Ibid.*, Nos. 97, 98.

the event of war, and having determined the movements of the allied fleets", signed on July 16, 1912, a convention in the following terms:

Article One.—The naval forces of France and Russia will co-operate in all eventualities in which the Alliance envisages and stipulates combined action of the armies on land.

Article Two.—The co-operation of the naval forces will be prepared for in peace-time. To this end the Chiefs of Staff of the two navies are henceforth authorized to correspond direct with one another, to exchange all information, to study all war hypotheses, and to draw up in collaboration all necessary strategic programmes.

Article Three.—The Chiefs of the two Naval Staffs will confer personally once a year at least; they will keep minutes of their meetings.

Article Four.—In regard to duration, application, and secrecy, the present convention is to be on all fours with the military convention of August 17, 1892, and the subsequent agreements.

This convention was definitively approved during Poincaré's visit to Russia. Poincaré pointed out to Sazonov that the military convention had been incorporated in the diplomatic Alliance and ratified in 1899 through the exchange of letters between Count Muraviev and Delcassé, and suggested that the same procedure should be followed now, the naval convention being ratified by an exchange of letters recording that the Tsar and the Government of the Republic approved the convention.[1] This was done.

It should be borne in mind that at this time the Russian Baltic fleet was virtually non-existent, and that Russia's whole navy consisted only of a squadron in the Black Sea, mainly composed of old vessels. This convention was thus intended mainly to operate in the Mediterranean, where the bulk of the French naval forces were stationed, and apparently in order to assist Russian ambitions in regard to the Straits. It is perfectly clear that the main burden of the convention was in ended to fall on the French navy, of which the third squadron was shortly afterwards transferred from Brest to Toulon, on

[1] *Livre Jaune*, No. 102. Poincaré, II, p. 112.

the exclusive responsibility of the Government, at a time when Parliament was not in session.[1]

Prince Lieven told Isvolsky that the exchange of views with Admiral Aubert had had very advantageous results for Russia. The French Chief of Staff, wrote the Russian ambassador, had thoroughly realized "that it was necessary to help us to maintain our naval predominance in the Black Sea by putting pressure as required on the fleets of our conceivable enemies, especially, that is, Austria-Hungary, and possibly Germany and Italy". To this end France had declared her readiness to concentrate her naval forces in the Mediterranean even in time of peace more towards the East, that is, towards Bizerta. "This decision represents in Prince Lieven's view a great success for us, especially as it is not conditional upon any undertaking on our part."[2] By the Russians' own admission, the obligations entered into were not reciprocal: a strange circumstance, which would be worth investigating if the whole contents could be known of the files concerning the naval convention, of which all that has been made public is a few, all too few, documents.

This new eastward concentration risked diverting part of the French naval forces from their principal object, the maintenance of communication with Northern Africa for the transport of African troops to the capital.

But why have waited until 1912 to draw up this convention? It may be replied that the military convention provided for the mobilization and joint operation only of the land forces.

[1] See the article by Francis de Pressensé, signed "Diplomate", in *Information*, September 22nd and 23rd. "It has become", he wrote, "almost a commonplace during the last few years that the less Parliament concerns itself with questions of foreign policy the more cause there is for satisfaction. . . . A democracy is committing nothing less than suicide when it permits the penetration within its organism of a principle so directly opposed to the very basis of its existence."

[2] *Livre Noir*, pp. 297–298. In his report to the Tsar on Poincaré's visit, Sazonov wrote "France has undertaken the obligation to help us by diverting the Austrian fleet in the Mediterranean from us and preventing its penetration into the Black Sea". (*Livre Noir*, II, p. 339.)

That is no sufficient reply. Can a war be imagined in which the two armies were seriously engaged and the navies idle? During the Manchurian war, when the question arose of intervention in Russia's favour, no other than a naval activity was conceivable, and yet no naval convention had then been signed. What, then, was the meaning of the drawing up in 1912, twenty years after the treaty of Alliance, of a naval convention largely unilateral in scope, requiring France, for no agreed consideration, to put her fleet at Russia's disposal— a convention signed on the eve of the Balkan war, of which, in Poincaré's own phrase, the Russian Government had, by the conclusion under its auspices of the Serbo-Bulgar agreement, "started the motor"?[1]

At the moment when Poincaré was pronouncing in the French Chamber his justification of the existence of secret treaties, there was being concluded between Bulgaria and Serbia, under Russia's auspices, a treaty of which the clauses remained unknown in France until August 1912, and which the French Premier, when he learned its terms during his visit that month to St. Petersburg, described as "a war agreement".

Thanks to Russia's good offices, the mutual distrust between Belgrade and Sofia had been removed. The way had been paved for the alliance between Serbia and Bulgaria by Hartwig, the Russian Minister in Belgrade, who had been appointed in 1909 with this policy in view on the morrow of the annexation of Bosnia and Herzegovina. A Russo-Bulgar military convention was signed in December 1909 providing against the eventuality of war with Austria. Since April 1911 the Russian *chargé d'affaires* in Sofia had been urging on Gueshov, the Prime Minister, the importance to the Balkan States of the search for a basis of agreement between themselves and of the direction of their efforts towards a common goal. Gueshov had been unimpressed; an agreement of this nature would, in his judgment, be regarded as directed against Turkey

[1] See *Die Grosse Politik*, XXXI, pp. 457 sqq.

congratulated him on the conclusion of the treaty and had expressed his joy at the prospect of the early realization of Serbia's aspirations in Austria.

The Russian Minister in Sofia, Prince Yurussov, considered that the moment was a particularly favourable one for the Balkan States to settle the Macedonian question and to realize their national aspirations. If Italy were to attempt any *coup* against the Dardanelles or Salonica, he considered that Bulgaria and Serbia would not hesitate to cross the Turkish frontier. He did not conceal from the French representative, de Panafieu, that Russia could not abandon the Slav peoples to their fate and would offer opposition to Austria's views in regard to the Sandjak. He wanted "to see the opening of a new chapter in Balkan history, in which Russia should write some glorious pages".[1]

Finally, on March 12th, the very day before the signature of the treaty, Charykov, the Russian ambassador in Constantinople, who had been pursuing a policy of Balkan reconciliation with Turkey, was recalled.

Pourparlers, alliance, the quick sequel of an agreement with Greece—of none of these was France informed. Russia had achieved the Balkan entente, initiated and carried through the negotiations without France's knowledge; only much later was France indirectly brought face to face with the accomplished fact.

In February, Sazonov, who was then hoping for the arrival of the Italian fleet off Constantinople, had communicated to Georges Louis, the French ambassador in St. Petersburg, a questionnaire which "raised very big questions"; he wanted especially to know whether France would be prepared to follow Russia in her policy towards Turkey and Austria. Already he had in mind the Balkan war and its possible sequels.

---

[1] I. E. Guéchoff, *L'Alliance balkanique*, pp. 58–75, 196 sqq. Gauvain, *L'Europe avant la guerre*, pp. 239–240. *Livre Jaune*, Nos. 24, 57, 184. *Die Grosse Politik*, Vol. 33. Bogitshevich, *Causes of the War*, pp. 29–30. Francis Delaisi in the *Grande Revue*, July 10, 1913.

But he did not venture to go further with Georges Louis, and requested Isvolsky to discuss the matter in confidence with Poincaré. On March 30th he informed London and Paris that a Serbo-Bulgar alliance had been signed "for reciprocal defence and the protection of mutual interests in the event of any modification of the *status quo* in the Balkans or aggression on the part of a third Power". He added that the treaty contained a secret clause binding both contracting parties to consult Russia before proceeding to active measures. The Russian Foreign Minister thus concealed from his allies the essential character of the pact.[1] On April 1st, Isvolsky communicated the news to Poincaré in the same terms, in confidence, assuring him that the agreement aimed at the maintenance of the *status quo* and expressing gratification at a result which he represented as essentially pacific.

Later, when movements of troops took place in the Caucasus region, Poincaré requested Louis to represent to the Russian Government the necessity of prior consultation and agreement between the two Governments on any initiative taken by either outside the limits of the treaty of Alliance; he also reminded Isvolsky that Russia had no right of isolated action which might involve France without first consulting her. Isvolsky and Sazonov both promised that any Russian initiative should be preceded by consultation.[2]

This formal promise should be borne in mind. Sazonov repeatedly and shamelessly broke it at critical moments in the Balkan war, embarking on all sorts of enterprises without a word of warning to France. At this moment it was his most elementary duty to acquaint France with the details of the Serbo-Bulgar treaty, which was soon to set the Balkans aflame. The French Prime Minister asked for details several times, through Georges Louis, but was unable to obtain any summary

[1] *Livre Jaune*, Nos. 12, 13, 16, 26, 29. Siebert, *Diplomatische Aktenstücke*, pp. 153–154. E. Judet, *Georges Louis*, pp. 171, 185.
[2] *Livre Jaune*, Nos. 19, 21.

O

should occupy the principal islands in the Aegean; a little later the Italians landed in Rhodes.[1]

Though Sazonov had refused to communicate the text of the Serbo-Bulgar treaty to the French Premier, he requested Isvolsky to recommend to him a project for a Bulgarian loan, guaranteeing at the same time Bulgaria's pacific intentions. On May 11th the Russian ambassador went again to see Poincaré, and once more pressed the matter of a loan of 180,000,000 francs.[2]

De Saint-Aulaire, the French *chargé d'affaires* in Vienna, wrote at this time that the day when the Balkan agreements became known, Austria-Hungary would see in them something more than a Russian plan of revenge for the annexation of Bosnia and Herzegovina; the mystery which surrounded them would give them the character of a dark plot against the Vienna Cabinet. He regretted that these agreements had been concluded under the auspices only of Russia, for the association of Britain and France with them "would have assured a right of control and a guarantee against the *obscure and feverish policy of Sazonov*". The Russian Foreign Minister did not, apparently, very favourably impress France's leading diplomats.

De Saint-Aulaire ingenuously admitted that if France's interest in peace and her interest in "*feeding the Franco-Russian Alliance on Austro-Russian rivalry*" were to be reconciled, it was to be hoped that the relations between the Vienna and St. Petersburg Cabinets would "be kept equidistant between entente and crisis".[3]

Russia proceeded to play her self-allotted part of "protectress" of the Slavs, which made it impossible for her to view with unconcern the fate of the Balkan peoples. This attitude was merely a pretext for extending her influence in the Balkans. History shows how Tsarism followed an unceasing policy of

---

[1] Judet, pp. 185–186. See also *Die Grosse Politik*, XXX.
[2] *Livre Jaune*, No. 184.          [3] *Ibid.*, No. 37.

subjugation of Slav nationalities. Poland is the most striking example. In the Balkans in 1876, Russia had, by the Treaty of Reichstadt, authorized Austria to annex Bosnia and Herzegovina; later, on the morrow of Plevna, she had set up a Greater Bulgaria, hoping to dominate it and make of it a Russian province. General Kaulbars, by dint of interference in the internal affairs of Bulgaria and Serbia, brought them to the point of seeking protection and support from the other Powers, with the result that there developed within each of the two countries a strong Austrophile party. De Giers himself recognized how heavy a hand Russia had placed on her little Slav brothers. In 1885, after the Roumelian revolution, Tsarism had been hostile to the union of Roumelia and Bulgaria. In 1897, under the St. Petersburg agreement, she recognized an Austrian sphere of influence comprising Serbia and a large part of Macedonia. Finally, in 1908, she authorized Austria to annex Bosnia and Herzegovina in order herself to dominate the Straits; and she was careful to place her veto on the march of the conquering Bulgarians to Constantinople.

Poland's martyrdom and Russia's policy of drastic russification showed the lot meted out by Tsarism to the Slav nationalities within its frontiers. Russia as "protectress" of the Slavs was a fraud of which only French diplomacy was—perhaps willingly—the dupe. The truth was that Tsarism was making use of the Balkan peoples for the realization of her ambitions in the Straits and her revenge against Austria.

The financial and business leaders in Russia were against war for the Balkans. It was scandalous to see a Government working for external conquest under the guise of protection of nations beyond its frontiers, while itself owing far-reaching reforms to its own people. It was certainly a legitimate ambition of the Balkan peoples to seek to achieve union, but this was properly the task of the people themselves, and Tsarism had no qualifications to be their guide in the enterprise.

On June 10, 1912, Dumaine, French ambassador in Vienna, reported to the Quai d'Orsay the conclusion of a general understanding between Bulgaria, Serbia, Greece, and Montenegro. In his view, this was clearly an offensive alliance, since if any of the four "conspirators" found himself compelled to advance "in consequence of one of those frontier incidents which are always easy to provoke", the three others were at once to come to his aid; he considered, therefore, that the combination presented a "very disturbing" aspect from the point of view of the maintenance of peace.[1]

The question was then under discussion of a European conference to liquidate the Italo-Turkish conflict. Sazonov had said in the Duma on April 26th that it was hoped to end the war through the mediation of the Powers, but subsequently he opposed this plan, fearing that other questions might be brought up at the conference, and preferring to keep his hands free in anticipation of fresh events. The Balkan States had no desire for a rapid conclusion of the Italo-Turkish conflict; its prolongation would sensibly weaken two Powers which were both hostile to the Slav ambitions in the Balkans, and would thus be all to the advantage of the designs of the new allies, as Todorov, the Bulgarian Minister of Finance, said to Isvolsky while in Paris to negotiate a loan.

Not content with wrecking this proposal for a conference, Sazonov subsequently rejected the essential phrase in a formula on which Britain and France had agreed with a view to mediation, declaring the disinterestedness of the mediating Powers. He telegraphed to Isvolsky that Russia's acceptance of this formula would be read both by Russian and Balkan public opinion as a renunciation for the future of her traditional policy in the Balkans. Georges Louis wrote that Russia's attitude for seven months past showed that while affirming her desire for the maintenance of the *status quo*, she foresaw that it could not be maintained. "One finds the idea", he

[1] *Livre Jaune*, No. 40.

added, "never absent from her thoughts that big events are perhaps at hand."[1]

As a natural result of the Balkan agreements and of Russia's policy, activity was reported in July in military quarters in Bulgaria.[2] How could it be otherwise? Very soon the unrest spread to Serbia. At this moment there would, to all appearance, still have been time for acting, in close association with Britain, to arrest the preparations and prevent the war.

Poincaré had just declared in the Chamber of Deputies that the Franco-Russian Alliance, consecrated by definite agreements, was being put into application in every quarter of the globe. He now decided to go to Russia. For what purpose? An article in the *Temps* of August 7, 1912, gives the answer as accurately as it is possible to expect in these matters. The Prime Minister hoped to pave the way for "agreement as to the decisions which would have ultimately to be taken" on the subject of the Italo-Turkish war, the Ottoman crisis, and the negotiations between the Balkan States. Although it was hardly possible to imagine that definite decisions could be arrived at in regard to facts still in a state of flux, it was at least possible "to facilitate to-morrow's decisions by to-day's explanations". Poincaré was going to do this, for he was "concerned to keep

---

[1] *Livre Noir*, I, pp. 276–272. Judet, p. 185. Poincaré, I, pp. 311–312. Paul Cambon, the French Ambassador in London, is reported to have wanted the projected conference to deal with the Balkans; he thought that Britain and France ought to settle the question of the Straits in Russia's favour. This would be the only way of re-establishing the balance of power in the Mediterranean; this had been shifted by the Tripolitan war in favour of Italy, and so of the Triple Alliance. In arguing so, was Cambon unaware that France and Russia had definitely been in favour of the Italian occupation of Tripolitania? As to the Straits, was he aware of the British point of view? He submitted this idea to the French Premier, who agreed that it was very desirable that the Straits should be opened to the passage of Russian war vessels and promised his support towards the solution of the question. It is easy to understand how, in spite of Poincaré's apprehensions over the interview between the German and Russian Emperors at Baltic Port, Isvolsky was full of satisfaction at his presence at the head of the French Government. "It is important for us to have his energy and decision entirely on our side and to profit by this advantage." *Livre Noir*, I, pp. 270–282. Poincaré, I, pp. 310, 352.       [2] *Livre Jaune*, No. 42.

alive in its exact terms the technical convention signed in 1892 by General de Boisdeffre. . . . The Prime Minister's journey to Russia", added the well-informed *Temps*, "will be of quite special military importance. Its purpose is the improvement of the instruments of Franco-Russian solidarity which serve unchanging aims." This, it will be agreed, was a regular programme of action for the grave events of which the approach was sensed.

On August 5th Poincaré went on board the *Condé* and sailed for Russia. At the moment when the Russian *chargé d'affaires* in Paris was able to read in the papers that France attached "more value than ever" to the Franco-Russian Alliance, the French Premier received from the Russian people a decidedly cool welcome. He himself relates that he went about "everywhere almost unnoticed. There seemed to be much more indifference towards the Alliance among the population of St. Petersburg than in the most lethargic of our provincial towns."[1] This did not prevent him from declaring a few days later in Dunkirk that "the friendship of the two countries was infrangible, and far from cooling, had gained a fresh life with the passing of time".

To Kokovtsov, the Prime Minister, he complained that in Paris Isvolsky had done everything to stir up opinion against him. Kokovtsov replied that he did not believe Isvolsky to be inaccessible to financial influence. Sazonov communicated to Poincaré, for the first time, the text of the Serbo-Bulgar agreement. "But this", cried the French Prime Minister, "is a war treaty! Why have you been representing it to us as a pacific agreement, and asking us to give it the seal of our approval by allowing a Bulgarian loan to be issued in the French money market?" Sazonov admitted that the Russian Minister in Sofia, in transmitting the document, himself described it as a war agreement; as, however, Serbia and Bulgaria had undertaken not to declare war or even mobilize

---

[1] Poincaré, II, p. 106. *Livre Noir*, I, p. 312.

without Russia's approval, she had a right of veto which
would assure the maintenance of peace, and would not fail to
exercise it. Poincaré replied—and wrote later to Paul Cambon—
that "this agreement, arranged under Russia's auspices, gives
her an active and a preponderant part in present and possible
future events. . . . At the least it is certain that she has been
aware of everything, and that, far from protesting, she saw in this
diplomatic document a means of assuring her hegemony in the
Balkans. It is Russia", he added, "who has started the motor".[1]

It was at this moment that Poincaré, in spite of his insur-
mountable distrust of Isvolsky, who, as Jules Cambon declared,
was pursuing a personal vendetta against Austria and "was
doing all he could to upset everything",[2] and in spite of the
dubious attitude of Sazonov, who had left him for five months
in ignorance of the text of the Serbo-Bulgar treaty, gave to
both the assurance of French support in their Balkan policy.
It is true that in St. Petersburg he declared to Sazonov that
France would give Russia no military assistance in the Balkans
in the event of Austrian intervention; "but", he added, "we
have to lend you our armed support if you are attacked by
Germany or by Austria supported by Germany. In the event
prescribed we shall fulfil our duty, but do not ask more."

This was exactly what Russia wanted. The French Prime
Minister recognized that public opinion in France would not
allow the Government to take military action over questions
of a purely Balkan nature, *so long as Germany remained entirely
aloof*; but if Germany came in, the terms of the Alliance would
come into play, and Russia could certainly count on France's
precise and complete fulfilment of her obligations towards her.[3]

Similarly, in September, in conversation with Isvolsky,
Poincaré admitted at the outset that Austrian intervention in
the Balkans with German support would bring the treaty into

---

[1] *Livre Jaune*, Nos. 57, 184.
[2] Letter from Beyens to the Belgian Government, March 18, 1913.
[3] *Livre Noir*, II, p. 342. Poincaré, II, pp. 117–119.

play. In a conversation which he reports verbatim, he confirmed to the Russian ambassador that "if Germany came to Austria's assistance, the Alliance would make it our duty to march". He did not hesitate to affirm that opinion in France and the French Parliament would accept this obligation, and he adds in his book: "That is what I said on that day as on many another occasion, and how could I think or say anything else? Ought I to have said that the Alliance was a scrap of paper and that I considered France capable of tearing it up?"

There are several things that are worthy of note in these categorical declarations, made with so much conviction to the Tsarist Ministers with their concealed designs. To begin with, it is clear that as early as August, well in advance of the Bulgar-Serb mobilization, Russia was not only prepared to see war break out in the Balkans, but was also envisaging the possibility of taking an active part herself. Poincaré, for his part, promised her French military support, over a purely Balkan question, in the event of Austrian intervention supported by Germany, disregarding altogether the question of provocation. More than this, he refused to admit that Isvolsky had had any right to tell the French Government in 1911 that Russian public opinion would not tolerate a war over Morocco. That was merely looking for pretexts for his country to avoid her obligations under the Alliance. "I should not for a moment", writes Poincaré, "have accepted a declaration from M. Sazonov that Russia would take no part in a Franco-German war arising out of colonial matters. . . . When another crisis was approaching, in the Balkans, a crisis as grave for Russia as the Morocco crisis had been for us, how could France have forgotten on her side that she was Russia's ally? How could she with any justice have done what she had reproached M. Isvolsky with doing, and dissociated herself completely from Russia's interests, thus completely jettisoning the Alliance?" There were some who thought that the scope of the Alliance did not cover Near Eastern questions. Poincaré declares that the actual words of the pact make this restricted interpretation impossible. "We had concluded the Alliance in order to safeguard our eastern frontiers; Russia had signed it in order to protect herself against the Power whose rivalry she most feared."[1] This seems an entirely new conception of the Alliance, extraordinarily dangerous and contrary both to the spirit and the letter of the treaty.

Nowhere does Poincaré touch on the fundamental question of provocation; for him it had no existence. He recognized that Russia had "started the motor" in the Balkans, and that in consequence the primary responsibility for the war would rest on her shoulders; in spite of this he promised her French support if Germany should give military aid to Austria. He himself had drawn attention to the fact that the Serbo-Bulgar agreement, entered into under Russia's auspices, might be the starting-point of a war with Austria. In that case it would be impossible for Russia to allow her "little Slav brothers" to be crushed, and for Germany to allow her ally, at grips both with the Balkan nations and with Russia, to be crushed would be even more impossible. It was a vista leading straight to a European war.

We have seen, however, that the original negotiators of the Franco-Russian Treaty of Alliance attached cardinal importance to the question of provocation. This was the constant concern of the Russian Ministers, and especially of Alexander III, who up to the last moment wanted an article added stipulating that in the event of provocation on France's part the military convention would be null and void. The same consideration was in Ribot's mind; he had no desire to see France drawn into war over difficulties in the Balkans. A reference to the plain statements made on the subject by de Giers in 1891 shows clearly to what an alarming extent Russian policy in the Balkans had developed along imperialist lines.

---

[1] Poincaré, I, pp. 302–303, 333–335; II, pp. 126–127, 319. *Livre Noir*, I, pp. 323–326.

But this was no longer Poincaré's conception; as he read it, the military convention came into play in any event and in any quarter, whether in the Balkans or elsewhere, and wherever the primary responsibility might lie, as from the moment of Germany's intervention. It was no longer merely a question of self-preservation from aggression, but of using the Alliance to prevent Austria and Germany from intruding in private preserves where their presence was not wanted. As G. De- martial has said, the words were the words of a tempter, and amounted to this: "Bring Germany on the scene, and you may count on me."

Thus Russia, whatever part she might have played in the preliminaries to a conflict, was assured of French support in case of need. Instead of living in solitary fear of Austria, she could now look forward to the moment when she could destroy her. What influence could moderating counsel have over people with such an outlook, people who avowed their designs on the Straits and were only waiting for the chance of revenging themselves on Austria? They would pay no heed even to repeated requests to secure French concurrence before taking any action.

"No French Government", writes Poincaré, "had dreamed of excluding the Near East from the normal play of the Alliance." That is an admission that the question of provoca- tion counted for nothing. For where in the Balkans could the aggression against Russia envisaged in the treaty occur? Nowhere in the treaty was it laid down that an Austro-Serbian conflict would necessitate Russian intervention.

On the other hand, no French Government, and no Minister except perhaps Delcassé, had until then contemplated the possibility of war over a Balkan question. We have seen what Hanotaux replied in 1897 and Pichon in 1909. Why was Russia not recommended in 1912, as in 1909, to do everything possible to avert the risk of a conflict, and warned that French opinion was resolutely opposed to one? The truth is that in

1909 French official circles were against war over a Balkan question, but in 1912 they had come seriously to consider it.

According to the official communiqué issued with reference to Poincaré's journey, the two Governments had found that they were in entire agreement and that the bonds uniting the two countries had never been more closely knit. They had agreed on lines of action and had recognized that the Entente must be "progressively adapted to all the eventualities which every alliance is bound to have in view".

On his return, the Prime Minister declared at Dunkirk on August 21st that the Alliance enabled the two countries to combine their diplomatic action and vigilantly to follow events, protecting themselves by mutual agreement against the risks of the future. He spoke of the unity of national feeling which makes the greatness, the glory, and the immortality of a people, and added that France could only count on a continuance of the co-operation she at present enjoyed abroad if her material and moral strength remained unimpaired. The Alliance with Tsarism—with Rasputin—was becoming more costly every day.

The *Temps* undertook the duty of explaining that this new formula implied uninterrupted consultation, prior agreement in the choice of the measures to be adopted and the right moment for adopting them, the united development of military and naval strength, the resolution to put to use more actively than in the past the Alliance thus revived and braced. "It is good", wrote the great Paris paper, "to find France, who for so long has been deafened by her rulers with the base discords of party strife, hearing now from the lips of a Prime Minister this appeal to the ideals of patriotism couched in the sober accents of a loyal Frenchman." (August 23rd.) In the light of events, the whole significance of these words, written on the eve of the Balkan war, and of those of the Prime Minister, is revealed. They were a whole programme of home and foreign policy, preparing men's minds already for the *Union Sacrée* with its call to end the old quarrels—in other words, to shelve democratic reforms in view of an approaching war which there was no intention whatever to discountenance, and which even entered into the calculations of the men in power.

Jaurès, however, spoke out against the secrecy which had surrounded the journey to Russia. France, he said, should beware of those who were leading her astray "with soft words for her chauvinist passions, linking her vanity to their financial operations or ambitious calculations". He asked what were the measures concerted with Russia, the engagements entered into with her; what part was France going to play in Persia? Was she going to associate herself with Russia's permanent *coup d'état* against the Persian constitution—with Russia, who had, through her agents, twice dissolved the Persian Parliament and forbidden it to reassemble? "France has the right to know whither she is being led."[1] No answer was made to any of these questions. What would Jaurès have said if he had but known the conception which the men in power had of the Alliance? But he was not allowed to discuss the interpretation of a treaty of every clause of which the country was ignorant, though its very existence was soon to be hazarded by it.

Events moved rapidly from the end of August. Russia had started the motor, but she herself was unready for war. She made no serious effort to hold back the Balkan peoples, but felt bound, for the sake of appearances, to make a pacific gesture when it was too late. Hence the contradictions and inconsistencies which irritated Poincaré, without ever disturbing his sublime confidence in the pacific intentions of Russia's rulers.

Fleuriau telegraphed on August 22nd, with reference to a suggestion from Berchtold, that the Russian Government had rejected that part of the suggestion which proposed diplomatic action to restrain the Balkan States, accepting only the proposal for representations to Turkey. The result was not long in showing itself. Bulgaria secretly pressed Greece to mobilize; Panafieu wrote that Gueshov, the Bulgarian Premier, could no

[1] *Dépêche*, August 29th.

longer be trusted by the friends of peace; Serbia was in ferment and pushing on her preparations.[1]

Suddenly, on September 14th, when the Balkan allies were virtually ready for war, Sazonov informed Belgrade, Cettinje, and Athens that Russia would give Serbia, Montenegro, and Greece no support unless they refused to countenance hostile action on the part of Bulgaria; at the same time he informed Bulgaria that she could not count upon Russian good will. What did this attitude mean, after six months during which the Balkan States had been incessantly accumulating material of war? During the summer Greece had bought warships in England, and the general staffs had elaborated in consultation a plan of combined military action. Russia could not fail to know that these preparations would produce among the Balkan populations an irresistible current of warlike feeling. Gauvain, writing at the beginning of August, remarked that none of the local movements would produce war unless it were encouraged by an interested Great Power. "Bold and eaten up with greed as one or another small State may be, it will not venture on the great conflict without the assurance of support, or at least of protection in the event of defeat."[2]

Sazonov, however, was averse from the arranging of a conference, as Poincaré proposed; and when, on September 22nd, Britain and France agreed to take joint action to preserve the *status quo* and to secure reforms in Macedonia, adding a warning to the Balkan States that they would not be allowed any territorial expansion, Isvolsky raised objections, and Sazonov deleted the paragraph (No. 4) relating to reforms. Yet, ten days later, when the conflict had become inevitable, he demanded that these reforms should be effected. It is evident that these occasional pacific moves aimed at masking the Russian Government's real designs.

[1] *Livre Jaune*, Nos. 66, 101, 102. Poincaré, II, p. 190.
[2] Poincaré, II, p. 233. Gauvain, *L'Europe au jour le jour*, IV, pp. 150-152. (August 8th.)

Thus it is not surprising that when, at the end of September, Poincaré confined himself to advising the Balkan States to avoid all rash action, they did not listen to him. If great Powers had been coolly looking on at the preparations for the drama, how could they now offer opposition to its consummation? Powerful forces were working for the great liquidation in the Near East, and "the rulers made use of them to achieve their own ambitions". On September 30th general mobilization took place in the Balkan States. Poincaré considered that Europe could still hold them back if she acted promptly and with decision. He sent "friendly remonstrances" to the Ministers of the Balkan States in Paris, and asked them to appeal to their Governments not to pursue the adventure. "They promised me", he writes, "to do all that I wanted." Disarming candour! One cannot but share the surprise of the *Correspondant* that "since March, when all the signs of the coming storm had begun to show themselves plainly, Poincaré had nursed the comfortable faith that everything would be settled by soft words".[1]

Then, when Neratov, permanent secretary of the Russian Foreign Ministry, had become convinced that hostilities would begin within a week, and Hartwig considered that war could no longer be avoided, Sazonov agreed to join Austria in informing the Balkan States that the Great Powers would not allow the peace to be broken and were determined to maintain the *status quo*, to localize the conflict should it break out, and not to permit the States which had mobilized any hope of territorial gain.

On October 7th this Austro-Russian initiative was agreed to by all the Powers; but the Balkan States proceeded to demonstrate its futility. A week before, on September 30th, Gueshov had replied to a summons from Nekludov to suspend all movements of troops to the frontier that it was too late;

---

[1] Gauvain, IV, pp. 186–188. Poincaré, II, pp. 223–226. *Correspondant*, October 25, 1912. See also articles by Pressensé in *Information.*

now, on October 8th, he repeated, with good reason, to the
Austrian and Russian Ministers that the advice of the Concert
might have had useful results a fortnight earlier, but that now
it was too belated. Pashich gave the same answer. Venizelos
said that the promise of reforms had come too late. "The
Balkan States", writes Poincaré, "politely bowed us out." As
for Montenegro, she had not given the Austro-Russian *démarche*
time to arrive, but had already declared war on Turkey. Is it
to be believed that King Nicholas, father-in-law of the King
of Italy and a pensioner of the Tsar, had begun the campaign
—playing his allies' game—without the knowledge of the
Russian Government?[1]

In the face of this, is it possible to think with Poincaré that
Russia "put on the brake as soon as she realized the possibility
of a collision", when the collision was made possible by the
Serbo-Bulgar treaty and had become inevitable by May? Is it
possible to admit that the collision "was finally rendered
inevitable not by the Balkan States—apart from Montenegro—
but by Turkey"? The facts prove the exact contrary.

Every day Gauvain found evidence of Bulgaria's fixed intention to bring about war. "The present crisis", he wrote,

was deliberately provoked by the Balkan States, Bulgaria among
them; they were determined at all costs to throw themselves against
Turkey while she was at grips with Italy, although the Ottoman
Government had provided them with no serious ground of complaint.
One may even add that the Balkan States exercised their ingenuity in
lulling the Constantinople Cabinet into a false security with assurances
of goodwill and friendship while they were actually getting ready
for mobilization. In trying to throw on other shoulders the responsibility for events, M. Gueshov and his allies are showing a poor
opinion of our intelligence.

---

[1] *Livre Jaune*, Nos. 48, 118, 132, 140, 141, 157, 172. Poincaré, II,
pp. 249–254. Five weeks before the Montenegrin declaration of war the
*Daily Chronicle* correspondent saw a Russian general and four officers
supervising mobilization operations in Montenegro. According to Wickham
Steed, King Nicholas's precipitancy was due to his desire to make money
by bear operations in Vienna and elsewhere. (*Through Thirty Years*, I,
p. 362.)

P

And what is one to think of these four Balkan sovereigns who, on October 13, 1912, on the eve of marching, declared that their intentions were free of all personal ambition, and scorned all idea of territorial conquest, while they had in their pockets their secret treaties under which they had already shared out Turkey's territories?

It is evident, as Baron Beyens recognized, that the Balkan States only began their campaign when they were assured of the approval of the St. Petersburg Cabinet, which had no intention whatever of stopping their enterprise with the veto which it was entitled to pronounce under the Serb-Bulgar treaty. The Russian Government hastened in its turn to throw the responsibility for the hostilities on Turkey, and declared at once that if Austria should intervene Russia would be unable to view events with indifference. On October 12th Isvolsky published a note announcing that, although Russia was anxious not to be drawn into war, it would be difficult for her to resist the pressure of her public opinion if the Slav States should be driven into a critical situation. This showed that the Russian Government's efforts to localize the conflict had not at any time been sincere.[1]

Jaurès had been raising his voice in warning since the beginning of October, for he had immediately seen the possibilities of the extension of the conflict as the appetites of the rulers might dictate. "A terrible visitation for Europe is approaching", he said, and he dwelt on the sinister chain of events which he had unceasingly revealed and denounced for ten years past, and which was leading Europe to the supreme crisis: Morocco had produced the Tripolitan adventure, which in turn had created the state of disorder which had ended in the Balkan war, out of which might come the European war.

---

[1] Poincaré, II, p. 266. Gauvain, IV, pp. 209–213, October 12th–13th. Letter of Baron Beyens, Belgian Minister in Berlin, to his Government, March 18, 1913. *Livre Noir*, II, p. 556. Sazonov said to the *Nationalzeitung* on October 8th, when on a short visit to Berlin: "The Balkan States are aware that even if victorious they can hope for no territorial change".

The difficulty of giving counsel of wisdom and moderation to the Balkan States was increased by the example that had been set before them of the worst of greeds. "Those who started the fire in order to go looting have been trying in vain to put it out now that it threatens to destroy the whole city." He showed the consequences of the Alliance for France:

It appears that France and Russia have undertaken to come to one another's support in the event of either being attacked by two Powers. Consequently, should Russia be drawn into conflict with Austria and Germany come to Austria's assistance, France would be bound to support Russia. That engagements of so serious, so terrible a nature could be contained in secret treaties, that to-morrow millions of Frenchmen might be thrown into war by the operation of treaties of the clauses of which France herself is ignorant, will be a horrifying fact for any thinking man. One of the worst results (he added) of the Moroccan affair, with its inexhaustible store of mischief, an affair connected like the Tripolitan enterprise with the basest of financial intriguing, is that it has given Russia, by a sort of reciprocity, the right to make use of us for her most adventurous enterprises.

If Austria, in face of the threat to her ambitions, appeals to her German ally against this Russian inundation, at once the people of France will be drawn into the most sinister of wars by the chain, forged in the dark, of a secret treaty, and by Russian interests in the Balkans. The blind and megalomaniac statesmen who have sealed France's fate have set in motion a profound disturbance in Europe of which the terrible repercussion is advancing now towards us. From the poisoned seed of Morocco there has come a huge and fatal tree whose murderous shadow has hung over Tripoli, is spreading over the Balkans, and to-morrow may cover all Europe. It will be that cursed tree of which Dante wrote, the tree of which each bough lets fall drops of blood when it is broken. But will the peoples allow this monstrous development of the crisis? It is regarded as a crime even to make an effort to probe the mystery of the secret treaties, to ascertain whether to-morrow millions of Frenchmen will be compelled to rush into war at a signal from St. Petersburg.

Jaurès showed in detail the responsibility of Russian diplomacy, which, infuriated at having been outwitted by the Austrians, and at having failed to secure at once its own share of the booty, had engineered the Balkan agreement as a means of revenge against Austria. He would have no European war for the Balkans. "Such a war", he said, would be a monstrous crime of which the very idea sets reason in revolt. . . . Millions of men in arms, condemned to destroy one another for an insensate quarrel, would end by turning their weapons against a European régime of folly and murder.

He saw how the extension of the conflict would begin: Austria and Russia launching mutual charges of evil intentions, each taking precautions which the other would take as provocations. The two rivals would raise their arms simultaneously; each would be convinced that its movement was defensive and that the other's was aggressive. So, in accordance with an agelong recipe, brawls are started at will. And actually the rivals are duped each by his own cries, appalled at the peril of their own creation; war is born fatally of their reciprocal panic and their common stupidity.

On the morrow of the opening of hostilities, Jaurès wrote again:

If to-morrow the conflict which the base greeds of the European Governments have made possible should spread, if Austria and Russia should come to grips, if through the chain of alliances France and Germany were drawn into the war, every heart would be filled with immeasurable horror; the rulers would be unable to gloss over the criminality of the war; they would be unable to throw over it the thinnest veil of national honour. Never would war be exposed in such naked stupidity and wickedness. Democracy everywhere would realize at once that it was the dupe and victim of the most monstrous manœuvre in European counter-revolution attempted since 1849.[1]

The *Correspondant* shared all Jaurès' apprehensions:

Those who have been working for a Turco-Balkan war, those who had not the courage to intervene in time to prevent it, those who allowed themselves to become the tools, conscious or unconscious, of a criminal Machiavellianism, have gone fatally astray; the Near Eastern question is now opened up; it will resolve itself with all the dire consequences involved, and will one day, it is to be feared, end in producing the great European war which will be its logical and inescapable consequence.[2]

---

[1] *Dépêche de Toulouse*, October 23rd and 30th; *Humanité*, October 10th and 20th.

[2] The *Correspondant* also wrote: "The Moroccan agreement led to the Franco-Italian agreement over Tripoli, and the immediate consequences

Sazonov, during his visit to England at the end of September, carefully avoided any mention in his talks with Grey of the Serb-Bulgar treaty, which was so soon to let loose war in the Balkans. Poincaré also kept the secret—feeling that he was "not authorized to communicate all his impressions to the British Government"—between the time of his return from Russia and the outbreak of the Balkan war. Clearly the two had agreed that up to the opening of hostilities they would say nothing about a treaty which could not but inspire British disapproval both with regard to Russia and the Balkan States. If the efforts of the French and Russian Governments to avert war were sincere, why did they keep the text of the Serb-Bulgar treaty from the knowledge of the British Government until the beginning of November? The British Government would not have failed to take effective steps to maintain peace while it was still possible. This strange delay is fresh proof of Russian duplicity and French subservience. Not until October 15th did the French Prime Minister feel it necessary to clear his conscience by speaking of this treaty to the French ambassador in London in order that he might inform the British Government, adding that Russian diplomacy was endeavouring "to conjure away the evil which it had unloosed", and that he threw "no doubt on the sincerity of the pacific intentions of the Russian Government".

There followed a strange thing. Poincaré's dispatch to Cambon had hardly been sent when certain of his colleagues pointed out to him that "it was perhaps not altogether right to betray a secret which Russia had confided to us". It would be interesting to know the names of these friends of peace who thought it wise to continue to conceal such an instrument of war from Britain, with whom France unceasingly protested

---

were the annexation of Bosnia and Herzegovina and the Tripolitan war, out of which came the Turco-Balkan war, which had for its easily predictable sequel the war between the allies. To say that the next act will be the war of liquidation rendered necessary by this series of events is, perhaps, to draw no rash inference." (July 25 and September 10, 1913.)

her desire to act in concert. What a flood of light the incident throws on the state of mind of the leaders of the *Union Nationale* in 1912–1914! They advised the head of the Government "to put off the communication which Paul Cambon had been instructed to make, and first to tell Isvolsky that we wished M. Sazonov to make the communication himself". The Russian ambassador was requested to inform his Minister of the French desire, but he did not do so. Poincaré had to remind him several times, and was obliged in the end to write himself, on October 29th, to the Russian Foreign Minister, who made the required communication to the British Government on November 3rd through Benckendorff. "But what a business to get so far!"[1] By then Turkey was already crushed. It is impossible not to be astonished that Poincaré should have kept from British knowledge until the opening of hostilities the contents of a treaty which he himself regarded as an instrument of war.

Hostilities began on October 16th. After the Bulgarian victory at Kirk Kilissé, Poincaré discussed with Sazonov the idea of mediation suggested first of all by Germany. Sazonov considered that the situation had not yet cleared sufficiently, and felt that mediation could only be attempted after a decisive event such as the capture of Adrianople; in other words, when Turkey was crushed and the Bulgars began to be a danger to Constantinople. Suddenly, however, on October 30th, Sazonov asked Poincaré to take responsibility for a proposal of mediation, based on a declaration by the Great Powers of their disinterestedness and renunciation of any sort of compensation. This proposal was obviously directed against Austria, at the moment when the Tsarist Government began to see ahead, thanks to the efforts of the Balkan allies, the realization of its ambitions in the Straits. At the same time Sazonov abandoned the demand for the maintenance of the *status quo* and expressed approval of the Balkan States being allowed the fullest satisfaction.

[1] Poincaré, II, pp. 263–265. *Livre Jaune*, No. 184.

Thus, so long as Russia had doubts of Balkan victory, she demanded the maintenance of the *status quo*; but so soon as victory seemed certain she hastened to abandon the demand, at Turkey's expense. France followed suit.

Poincaré complaisantly undertook this mission, and agreed with Grey on a formula on the lines indicated by Sazonov. Yet at this moment Austria, against whom France had no subject of complaint, might have seemed entitled to some consideration on France's part, especially in view of her attitude at Algeciras, where she had made no demand for French disinterestedness. Three days before, moreover, the French Prime Minister had declared at Nantes that France remained faithful to her Alliance and her friendship, that is, to the Triple Entente, and he seemed to dismiss the idea of direct conversations with the other Powers. Already the French Government considered Austria as a potential adversary, though until then it had always regarded her as an essential element in the Balance of Power and in peace.[1]

On November 2nd Sazonov asked for prompt mediation, in order to prevent the Bulgars from entering Constantinople. He proposed that this city should remain in the Sultan's possession, with the adjacent territory up to the Maritza, that the Balkan peninsula should be partitioned between the allies in accordance with their agreements, and that Serbia should be given access to the sea. He made the same proposal to Berlin, without informing France. This delimitation of Constantinople, with its thin disguise of Russian designs, seemed premature to Poincaré. Three days later Isvolsky informed the French Government that the occupation of Constantinople by the Balkan allies might lead to the appearance of the Black Sea Fleet off Constantinople.[2]

Poincaré complains in his book of the shifting and dispersed

---

[1] Cf. speech of François Deloncle in the Chamber of Deputies, December 21, 1912.

[2] Poincaré, II, pp. 275, 295, 306. *Livre Jaune*, Nos. 211–234.

activities of Sazonov, of his "daily inconsistencies which are assuming alarming proportions"; but Sazonov had not changed for a year past. He continued along his settled course. The truth was that Russia was making use of the Balkan States to get the Straits. She had speculated on their victory, but now she was vetoing their entry into Constantinople. The possibility was even discussed at St. Petersburg of her occupying the city herself. It was quickly realized, however, that it would be impossible to transport in two months more than two army corps, and that the operation could not possibly be carried out as a surprise attack.[1]

As the men in power in Russia had foreseen, the success of the Balkan States had awakened in Russia an aggressive enthusiasm, an expansionist ambition which a well-organized press campaign had inflamed. They knew how to profit by this popular excitement both abroad and at home to consolidate Tsarism once more after the disasters of the Japanese war.

Everyone knows how this war was carried on against the Turks, and of what atrocities the Balkan allies, especially the Bulgarians, were guilty. This did not prevent the French middle class from enthusiastically taking their part. Was it not a struggle of Christianity against Islam? Loti and de Farrère were almost alone in espousing the Turkish cause.[2] But there was another reason for this enthusiasm. Much of the Bulgar and Serb artillery had been manufactured at Creusot; the Greek army had been instructed by the Eydoux mission; while the Turkish General Staff had been receiving the sinister advice of von der Goltz. The nationalists thus saw in the Bulgar-Serb victory the proof of French superiority over the German army. Already some saw on the horizon the dawning promise of *revanche*.

[1] Sazonov to the Tsar, November 23, 1913. *Livre Noir*, II, p. 368.
[2] "The Allies showed frightful ferocity, burned, pillaged, killed, violated as no savages would have done. Witnesses revolted by these scenes could find no channel through which they could make their protests heard." *Correspondant*, July 25, 1913.

As early as October 30th, Albert Malet, professor at the Lycée of Louis-le-Grand, and former tutor to King Alexander of Serbia, wrote to his colleague Albert Milhaud, of the *Rappel*, that Russian public opinion would not allow the Government to remain an idle spectator of an Austro-Serbian conflict, and that it would be able to compel it to go to war:

When that time comes! Germany will march; and we shall. . . . The war will have come. It is indispensable that the press should prepare the French people for this eventuality, especially by stimulating the feeling of self-confidence. After all, the victory of the Balkan States is a French victory over Germany.[1]

The situation became worse when Serbia occupied the Adriatic port of Durazzo, clearly exposing the economic causes of the war. Francis Delaisi, in an article "A war for railways", exposed the greedy ambitions of the men in power, and all the financial interests at the root of the struggle. Serbia, cut off from Salonica, was seeking an outlet into the Adriatic for the Danube-Adriatic railway, which had been planned to divert Austro-Hungarian traffic from the Salonica route and to favour Italian and French trade at the expense of Vienna. There was also the Salonica-Avlona line. These railways were to be built by Schneider and Vitali with the aid of the Banque Ottomane and the Banque de Paris et des Pays-Bas. French financiers, in collaboration with Russian diplomats, had pushed Serbia across Austria's path in order to block the famous *Drang nach Osten*, the German pressure towards Constantinople and Salonica.[2]

For all these reasons, French diplomacy was taking up a strong attitude at the very moment when Russia, feeling still unready for war, was telling Serbia that she was determined not to go to war for a Serbian port on the Adriatic, to which,

---

[1] Shortly afterwards M. Malet stated his views at length in a lecture reported in the *Revue du Foyer*.

[2] *Grande Revue*, July 10, 1913. See also a curious interview with a Serbian Secretary of Legation, by F. Delaisi, in the *Bataille Syndicaliste*, December 16, 1912.

moreover, Italy was as energetically opposed as Austria. Isvolsky was able to write to his Government on November 7th:

Hitherto France has merely declared to us that local happenings, virtually of purely Balkan interest, could only occasion diplomatic steps on her part and no sort of active intervention; now, however, she seems to realize that Austrian territorial conquests would affect the general balance of power in Europe, and so France's own interests.

Isvolsky had pointed out to Poincaré that in proposing the examination with Russia and Britain of the means of preventing such conquest, he had *ipso facto* raised the question of the practical consequences of this agreement; Poincaré so expressed himself in his reply that the Russian ambassador wrote to St. Petersburg that the French Prime Minister "entirely realizes that France may be drawn into military operations".

Sazonov asked for more definite statements, though he refused himself to join in any too positive declaration, such as that no annexation of Ottoman territory could be permitted; that formula could have been held to cover Russian action in the question of the Straits. Isvolsky replied that in Poincaré's view it was

for Russia to take the initiative in a matter in which she is the most closely interested party. France's task is to accord to Russia her most effective support. . . . "Broadly", added M. Poincaré, "it all comes to this: if Russia goes into the war, France will do the same, as we know that in this matter Germany would stand at Austria's back."[1]

Poincaré protests energetically against the words which Isvolsky puts into his mouth:

I repeated to M. Isvolsky what I had said to M. Sazonov at St. Petersburg, that in the event of the terms of the Alliance coming into play we should loyally perform our duty [and he had a correction telegraphed to Georges Louis]. I drew attention to the terms of the treaty of Alliance: "If Russia is attacked by Germany, or by Austria with Germany's support, France will throw her whole strength against Germany." I had neither the desire nor the right to say anything else.

---

[1] *Livre Noir*, I, pp. 342–346.

But in all this there is still no mention of the question of the initial provocation. Russia had "started the motor", but the fact was persistently ignored. There was readiness to bring the treaty of Alliance into play on any occasion in Russia's favour, although the treaty plainly laid down that its terms *could only come into operation if Russia had not provoked Austria into an attack.* In order to emphasize his readiness to support Russia, Poincaré wrote to Isvolsky on November 16th:

> The Government of the Republic cannot define its line of action until the Imperial Government has revealed its own views. It is Russia's primary responsibility to decide on the steps to be taken and the proposals to be made. . . . Meanwhile the Government of the Republic has neither said nor hinted anything which might imply that it is not giving its wholehearted support to Russia.

Were these not unequivocal assurances of French support in a purely Balkan question? What Poincaré agreed to do was to plunge France into a war over a conflict of interests between Austria and Serbia in the Balkans. He declared that France had a direct interest in Balkan questions. This reading of the terms of the Alliance was, in 1912, an absolutely new departure, unanticipated even by the Russians. Isvolsky was delighted and astonished.

Poincaré assures us that if France had exposed herself to the reproach from Russia, as in 1909, of failing to come to her support, she would herself have been in danger of the Alliance being denounced.[1] But in 1909, when Pichon had said that public opinion in France would not have tolerated a question of this nature involving her in war, the Alliance was not brought to an end. Rather than run the risk of this breach, it was preferred in 1912 to give Russia an assurance of French support in any circumstances; there was even surprise that she was not inclined to go to war for a Serbian port.[2]

---

[1] Poincaré, II, pp. 336–340.

[2] On July 6, 1922, Léon Blum maintained in the Chamber of Deputies that there could have been no question of bringing the treaty into play when one of the allies had deliberately kept his partner in ignorance of moves which

It is easy to understand the praise which Isvolsky, who had not expected to get so much, showered on Poincaré:

At the critical minute a great many things will depend on him . . . if the crisis comes, the decision will be made by Poincaré, Millerand, and Delcassé. It is a piece of good fortune for us that we shall have to deal with these personalities and not with one or another of the opportunist politicians.[1]

This conception of the Franco-Russian Alliance was not Poincaré's alone, but was shared by Delcassé, Paléologue, and also by Paul Cambon, for whom the Prime Minister expressed great admiration. Poincaré has made public a telegram which he received from Paul Cambon on November 12th. In connection with the proposal to work out a scheme for a railway from the Danube to the Adriatic with a free port at St. Juan de Medua, Russia had asked whether in case of need she might count on French support, and Cambon telegraphed:

As to the question of our intentions in the event of a conflict coming, I take the liberty to express the opinion that we cannot make any other reply than an assurance of our support. Hesitation on this point might sooner or later bring the rupture of the Franco-Russian Alliance.

Poincaré also prints a letter of December 4th from Cambon, denouncing Austria's warlike intentions, but carefully avoiding mention of Russia's responsibilities. Saying nothing of the Tsarist ambitions in the Straits, the Serb-Bulgar treaty, and the part played in it by Russia, though all this had been quite clearly explained to him on October 15th by the Foreign

were the actual origin of such a war as the Balkan war, and had sought to commit his partner through acts for which the partner had no responsibility whatever. Poincaré replied: "It was a totally different thing to say generally to Russia that the treaty of Alliance would be abandoned when she asked us what we should do if she were attacked by Austria and Germany came to Austria's support. I was unwilling to say that I should abandon it, because I know what would have happened. The Alliance would have been denounced once for all. The day would have come when Germany would have attacked Russia and then have attacked France, and from the outset we should have been alone." Léon Blum replied: "The Alliance would not have been broken. Russia would have put the needed pressure on Serbia to prevent friction between her and Austria."    [1] *Livre Noir*, I, pp. 351, 364.

Minister, Paul Cambon was blind to all but Austria, and, after
declaring that she still preserved her old ambitions, added:

> To these expansionist designs for the future in the direction of the
> Aegean, to these ambitions France, Britain, and Russia are bound to
> offer opposition . . . and if the Vienna Cabinet, by its attitude,
> obliges us openly to oppose its views, the French Republic will be
> drawn into a renewal of the struggle carried on by the French Monarchy
> against the house of Austria!

Poincaré comments admiringly: "What a magnificent history
lesson!"[1] Such was the background of ideas in the mind of
one of the principal ambassadors of the Republic in 1912–1914!

At this juncture Grey advised the neutralization and inter-
nationalization of the Straits. Sazonov, in a letter to Isvolsky
on November 28th, defined the attitude which Russia at once
took up on the question. In the evident intention of avoiding
conflict with the British view and postponing the revelation
of Russian intentions, as to which he was, indeed, possibly not
yet entirely certain himself, since Russian designs would be
liable to develop as events developed, he said as little as could
be helped; but he declared that Russia's fundamental interests
in the Straits could not be protected by guarantees or the
clauses of agreements, since the terms of these could always
be eluded. "No guarantee of any sort" must be given, he said,
"which might tie our hands or be capable of standing at a
future date in the way of a solution of the question of the
Straits in accordance with our interests." He considered it
inopportune, moreover, for the time being to put forward
independent proposals. If circumstances changed, however, it
would be important to learn the French point of view. Thus
the Russian Government, not venturing to reveal its whole
mind, took up a waiting attitude; but it made no secret of its
opposition to a neutralization of the Straits, which would have
been, from its point of view, the worst of solutions.

On December 3rd Isvolsky sent to Poincaré a résumé of

---

[1] Poincaré, II, pp. 326, 359, 363.

Sazonov's and his own views. It seemed that the question could be put in the terms formulated in 1908: "Right of the riparian Powers of the Black Sea to bring their ships of war in and out during peace-time, on certain conditions safeguarding the security of Constantinople." Without desiring to take any steps in the matter, since it was not to Russia's interest to raise the question of compensations, the Imperial Government felt justified in relying on French support should the question arise. Russia, it is clear, was anxious above all to prevent the neutralization of the Straits, which would have been the end of her dreams. So long as the Bosphorus and the Dardanelles remained in Turkish hands, she could still hope to realize her great ambition. This was not moderation but calculation.

Poincaré found all this very sensible, and replied that should the question arise, France would give Russia such support as she could. In other words, France, too, was waiting to see what happened.[1] But so far as military aid in the event of complications arising was concerned, the French Government remained perfectly definite. On December 5th, Isvolsky wrote to Sazonov that Poincaré did not for one moment deny France's obligation to give Russia armed support under the treaty the moment Germany intervened militarily. Even before that moment, besides the most active diplomatic support, the possibility of naval demonstrations was not excluded. Thus Russia had every guarantee. But she was not ready for a general war. Sazonov declared to Georges Louis that Russia must not go to war except for her supreme interests; that was why she had not intervened over the question of a Serbian port on the Adriatic.

Once again there was disappointment in military and diplomatic quarters in France over Russia's attitude. "It is still only a short time", wrote Isvolsky to Sazonov on December 18th, "since the French Government and press were inclined to

---

[1] Siebert, p. 687. Poincaré, II, pp. 367, 369.

suspect us of egging Serbia on, and one was constantly hearing
people say that France had no desire to go to war about a
Serbian port. Now, however, there is astonishment and uncon-
cealed dismay at our indifference to Austria's mobilization."
Poincaré and his Ministers had, in fact, been very astonished
to learn that a Russian staff officer had told the French military
attaché in St. Petersburg, General de la Guiche, that if Austria
attacked Serbia Russia would not strike. So lively were the
apprehensions of the French General Staff that Millerand, the
Minister of War, had felt it necessary to inform Poincaré of
this. The French Government, Isvolsky added, viewed the
possibility of first Germany and then France being dragged
into the war

with perfect calmness, aware of its obligations under the Alliance and
firmly resolved to act up to them. It has taken all necessary steps:
plans for mobilization on the Eastern frontier have been overhauled,
war material is in readiness. . . . I have no longer to contend with the
view that France might find herself drawn into war over matters
alien to her true interests, but with the fear that in a matter affecting
the position and prestige of the whole Entente we have been remaining
too passive.[1]

Poincaré felt it necessary to make statements on the foreign
situation on December 5th before the Foreign Affairs Committee of the Chamber of Deputies and on December 21st
both in the Chamber and in the Senate. All these declarations
were virtually identical. He announced in advance that he
would make no reply to questions or interpellations. Speaking
of the crisis and its origins, he sedulously concealed the part
played by Russia since the beginning of 1912 and the naval
convention, with the result that matters appeared to the
Deputies, who were ignorant of the fundamental facts, in a
very different light to the true one. Poincaré said:

---

[1] *Livre Noir*, I, pp. 368–372. Millerand had said to Ignatyev, the Russian
military attaché in Paris: "We are prepared, and that fact must be borne in
mind." Russian military archives, Nos. 130, 328.

From the beginning of the present year it had been easy to observe in Macedonia a sort of latent *malaise* and fever. We had immediately consulted Russia on the situation, which threatened to become worse. We had agreed in our outlook on all possible eventualities, and had studied the means of averting, if possible, a conflict. . . . In April we were informed that Bulgaria and Serbia had joined forces by treaty, that Bulgaria and Greece had begun negotiations, and that these two were also preparing a convention. The statesmen who had conceived or at least renewed and rejuvenated this great and fecund idea of the Balkan Alliance, had succeeded in keeping secret the essential clauses in these agreements, the provisions of which, indeed, have largely been put out of date by subsequent events. But we learned enough during the summer to be apprehensive of an early conflict. . . . We did not hesitate to do at once all that lay in our power to avert a conflict. . . . The strength of an alliance such as that which united us with Russia does not depend only on conventions; it depends above all on the confidence and the intimacy which preside over our daily intercourse. . . . M. Kokovtsov said this week in the Duma that Russia was sure of us.[1] She can, indeed, have no doubt of our support, any more than we have of hers.

He proceeded to pay homage to the allies:

A fine thing is this union of the Balkan peoples for the achievement of national independence; this idea has entered into the soul of the peoples and has moved them to swift action in the name of justice and freedom. . . . Any happening in the world around us (he added) which may modify the international equilibrium directly affects a nation like ours, which is aware of the necessities of the future and is concerned for the safeguarding of its permanent interests.

In September and October, Poincaré had, apparently, been making the greatest efforts to maintain the *status quo* and to prevent any possibility of the belligerents securing territorial gains. In December he was rejoicing at the passing of the Balkans into the hands of the Balkan peoples, and was thus congratulating them on having rejected his advice and ignored his recommendations. It is well known how little the allied leaders had troubled about justice and freedom.[2]

[1] Cf. speech of Kokovtsov in the Duma, December 18th.

[2] Little attention was being paid at the time to Russia's oppression of the Poles. During the World War it was even proposed to turn over to Tsarist Russia the Poles of Galicia, who enjoyed infinitely more freedom than those of Russia.

Poincaré declares that the Chamber was fully informed. "Not a single objection", he writes, "was raised against the policy which we had been following. . . . There was only one interruption, from M. Jaurès; it was brief and eloquent—'Très bien' (Hear! hear!)." Need it be remarked that as the Chamber and Senate were unaware of the part which Russia had played in preparing the war, of the assurances which her Government had been given of French support, and of the conception of the Alliance in the minds of the men in power, they were in reality ignorant of the very essence of the situation? How much, for instance, did they know of the strange delay of the French and Russian Governments in communicating to Britain the secret Serb-Bulgar treaty? Francis de Pressensé had every right to deplore the absence in this great crisis of any real Parliamentary control of the policy of the Government. He points out that the deputies had "to content themselves with official statements which were mere tissues of commonplaces, repeating *ad nauseam* various conventional and hackneyed formulae about our alliances and friendships, but saying not a word about the vital issues involved".[1]

Three speakers in the Chamber, however, made interesting statements. François Deloncle pointed out that the Prime Minister had abandoned the traditional caution with which France had acted since 1870 in connection with Near Eastern questions, and had replaced it by a peace policy which involved active interference. He pointed out that all direct conversations with Austria seemed to have been avoided, though since Algeciras Austria had deserved more consideration than that from France. He demanded that the nation should have freedom to speak openly on all subjects with other countries, whether Austria, Italy, or even Germany:

It is not for us to play Don Quixote in Europe, to go to war for one or another of the Near Eastern countries; our first concern should

---

[1] *Courrier Européen*, January 17, 1914.

Q

be for the maintenance of peace, and I do not see why we should hold aloof from any Power.

As one acquainted with Albania and her language, he expressed his satisfaction at her creation as an autonomous country; she was in truth a nation, and one to whom the Balkan States had done less than justice. Finally, he recalled France's important interests in Turkey, and denounced "any diplomat who is prepared to deal very shortly with the affairs of Turkey in Europe, while preparing surreptitiously and by back-stairs methods for complications across the Bosphorus". Was it not Isvolsky to whom he referred? Vaillant followed, declaring amid Socialist applause:

> The French nation passionately wants peace, and is not prepared to hear any talk of obligations of whatever sort which might drag it in whatever circumstances into war. Republican France has entered into no treaty entailing such obligations. Secret treaties and the obligations which they are alleged to involve have no existence for the nation when even its representatives have not been consulted.

Finally, Jaurès, who had no knowledge whatever of the part played by Russia or, above all, the engagements entered into towards her, appreciated the efforts which the Foreign Minister had made, but still had reservations to make. He declared that Europe had had a considerable share of the responsibility for the conflict, and exhorted workers and democrats to be on the alert and to remain constantly in readiness to defend peace.

It was at this stage that, as Poincaré admits, Russia, without informing France, and disregarding the formal promises made by Sazonov and Isvolsky, "once more embarked on one of those maladroit *démarches* with which the Government of the Republic had several times previously found fault, but which her shifty diplomacy seems unwilling to give up". Russia declared to Turkey on December 23rd that if her resistance to the demands of the Balkan States resulted in the peace negotiations being broken off or even merely suspended, there could be no further guarantee of Russian neutrality. Isvolsky

concealed from the French Government the actual tenor of
the Russian declaration. The Prime Minister showed his
annoyance at the action taken, and insisted once more that
there should be prior agreement—to no purpose whatever, as
will be seen.

It is easy to understand that when the Presidential election
became imminent the Russian ambassador felt that if Poincaré
were beaten it would be a disaster for the Russian Government.
Poincaré was scarcely elected before he declared to Isvolsky
that it would be perfectly possible for him (Poincaré) directly
to influence France's foreign policy, and that the Government
ought to have the opportunity of preparing public opinion in
advance for participation in any war which might break out
over the Balkan question. Isvolsky wrote that

he thoroughly understands the arguments, and shows real solicitude
for our historic patrimony. The French Government is firmly resolved
to fulfil all its obligations towards us as our ally, and recognizes quite
coolly, and with its eyes open, that it is possible that the ultimate
issue of the present complications may involve it in the necessity of
taking part, resolutely and unhesitatingly, in a general war. It is making
no attempt to rob Russia of her freedom of action or to throw doubt
on her moral obligations toward the Balkan States.[1]

The man who could report such remarks baselessly, if he did,
must have revealed in conversation and in his whole manner
of living what he was capable of. Poincaré, for that matter,
knew his defects; the Russian Prime Minister had not scrupled
to give a very poor account of him. Why, then, with what
intention, was he retained in Paris although Georges Louis
was superseded in St. Petersburg? That is the whole scandal.
The more Isvolsky was lying and misrepresenting the opinions
of the French statesmen, the stranger it seems that they kept
among them an individual of this stamp, so surrounded with
evil report, and above all that they admitted him into their
confidence. Poincaré had had proof in November of the

[1] *Livre Jaune*, II, Nos. 33, 37, 40, 45. *Livre Noir*, II, Nos. 9, 15, 18, 21.
Poincaré, II, pp. 416–417.

tendentious nature of his reports, since he had considered it necessary to send a telegraphic correction to St. Petersburg. Why did he not demand Isvolsky's recall then?

After the Turkish *coup d'état*, Jonnart, who had succeeded Poincaré as Foreign Minister, asked Georges Louis, on January 24, 1913, to urge Sazonov once more not to let the Russian Government take any step capable of involving France under the Alliance without first consulting her representatives. Sazonov agreed, but scarcely more than a few hours later he rushed into another move without consulting France. He expressed to the German Government his anxiety about events in Constantinople, adding that in the event of the resumption of hostilities "the Russian Government might be placed in the most serious situation, finding itself clearly faced with an inevitable change in public opinion in Russia in the event of the results of the war being jeopardized". Jonnart protested in a telegram to Georges Louis, who saw Sazonov, but obtained only "a very evasive reply". Forty-eight hours later, as though in mockery of France, Russia repeated her offence. She sent to Bucharest on January 30th a memorandum containing, in Poincaré's words, "the most deplorably tactless expressions", telling Roumania, *inter alia*, that any occupation of territory forming part of Bulgaria would provoke among the Russian public such an explosion of sympathy for Bulgaria that it would be impossible for the Government to remain indifferent to it.

Jonnart made no secret of his annoyance. He wrote to Louis on January 31st:

The step which the Russian Government has just taken seems to me of exceptional gravity. . . . It is a plain threat of armed intervention, on which agreement should first have been secured between the allied Governments. . . . The action disclosed by the note runs the risk of bringing in its train the gravest consequences from the point of view of European peace. There seems, indeed, no doubt that if Russia proceeds to coercive action against Roumania, Austria-Hungary will simultaneously proceed to armed intervention. On that day the danger of a general conflagration would be imminent, for Germany would probably be led to take sides with her ally without waiting to examine the question of the side from which aggression came. The Government of the Republic can take no responsibility for the consequences of the action taken by the Russian Minister in Bucarest.[1]

Had such language been used with St. Petersburg for a year past, it is probable that events would have followed a different course. It was too late now to stem the current which was carrying Russia and Europe towards war. Jonnart's note, in any case, was barren of result. Delcassé replaced Louis in St. Petersburg, the tone of the letters from the French ambassador began to change, and Russia was more certain than ever that she would be supported in any step she might take. France now asked her to build strategic railway lines to speed up the process of concentration on her Western frontier, and also to increase the effective strength of her army, offering to supply all the financial assistance needed. Poincaré entered office as President on February 20th, and issued a manifesto to the country in which he declared that it was impossible for a free people to be effectively pacific without being always ready for war.

On the 25th, Isvolsky handed to the new President of the Republic, by the Tsar's command, the Order of St. Andrew as a mark of the Emperor's personal esteem and friendship for him. Nicholas had sent to Poincaré at the same time by the hand of Baron Schilling a particularly affectionate letter, in the course of which he wrote that "the Alliance which emanates from the very heart of the two nations" formed the basis of his foreign policy. "If it is to bear all the fruits of which it is capable, constant collaboration and permanent contact between the two Cabinets" seemed to him indispensable. Finally, he congratulated Poincaré on having made the use which he had done of his power, and expressed special thanks to him for it. The President replied that he would give careful

[1] *Livre Jaune*, II, Nos. 78, 82, 84, 91, 93, 94. Poincaré, III, pp. 76–81.

attention during his tenure of the presidency to the "maintaining and drawing closer of the Alliance of the two countries".[1]

Delcassé left for St. Petersburg. He would, wrote Poincaré to the Tsar,

be better able than anyone to make arrangements with M. Sazonov to secure common action between the diplomatic staffs of the two countries, the French military effort (the Three Years Military Service Act) making particularly urgent the correlative measures which M. Delcassé will discuss with him.

It was at this time that Count Benckendorff, the Russian ambassador in England, wired to his Government, in terms strangely corroborating Isvolsky's assurances:

When I recall the substance of all M. Cambon's conversations with me, and compare them with M. Poincaré's attitude, I get the feeling, almost the conviction, that of all the Powers France is the only one which, not to say wants war, at all events would see it without regret. In any case, nothing showed me that France is actively contributing to work in the direction of a compromise. Well—compromise is peace; to shut out compromise is war.[2]

Through all the blackness of this winter, while the men in power, with cold resolution, were deciding the destiny of France, under the terms of a treaty of Alliance of the existence of which he had not the slightest knowledge, Jaurès, like a lighthouse amid the storm, stood on watch. But, with no knowledge of the treaty or of the conception of it held by the men in power, with no knowledge of those conversations in which the head of the French Government was declaring to a man of Isvolsky's quality the desires and duties of France towards a régime already completely rotted, what could Jaurès do? In the dense obscurity that prevailed, he had no opportunity to denounce to France and the whole world all this occult diplomacy, or to condemn and checkmate the bellicose and reactionary moves of these politicians who were providing France, under the cover of a nationalist movement comparable

[1] *Livre Noir*, II, pp. 403, 439, 442. Poincaré, III, 132–133.
[2] *Livre Noir*, pp. 303–306.

with Boulangism, with the worst of caricatures of democracy. At best the Alliance seemed to Jaurès more and more a monstrous fraud, and, dimly perceiving all the dark intriguing in progress, he wanted the French people to rid itself of a secret treaty with this Oriental despotism which might involve it in the most disastrous of adventures. He felt that as soon as the crisis was over France ought to deal with this grave question. The Entente with Britain was showing itself more efficacious and less dangerous than the Russian Alliance. The very form of the Entente seemed to him more elastic, with more life in it, and more respect for the conscience of peoples. "Alliances", he wrote,

may at certain moments, through the most unexpected and momentous repercussions, drag a country into complications into which neither its heart nor its reason would bid it enter. . . . The time is coming when it will have to be asked whether France should not revise her too rigid diplomatic system and transform into a broader and broader *entente* an alliance system of which the perils are growing worse and the guarantees provided growing less.

He was anxious not to see France drawn into a general war arising out of the Balkan war:

Nothing would be more humiliating than to regard ourselves as bound to enter into the game of the diplomats and militarists. If the fatal interplay of the powers that be were to end in war, our duty as Frenchmen would be to hold aloof from it and to contract with free England an alliance of peace to put a term to the folly of men. If war were to break out, men would fall, and when they asked themselves, "Why are we cutting one another's throats? What is the idea that we are serving? Why are we killing and being killed?" they would be unable to answer. The Austrian diplomat will try to wash his hands of it all; the British diplomat will say that he had already said "It is insanity." M. Poincaré will say, "I denounced the war as a defiance of humanity." No one will be able to say why men have been at one another's throats. But it may well happen that these men in whose hands the mad folly of rulers has placed weapons to serve their criminal ends may end by turning their weapons against the crime.

Two days later Jaurès put the issue bluntly: "If it came to a struggle, it would be that of Austrian reaction against Tsarist reaction. Republican France has no concern whatever with it."[1]

Meanwhile Francis de Pressensé had been discussing and passing judgment on the Franco-Russian Alliance. He recalled that it had been tainted from the outset by being misdescribed as an instrument for the recovery of Alsace-Lorraine. The loans to Russia had not served her material progress, but had been made the sinews of war against revolution. The Entente Cordiale itself had been diverted from its original purpose to be exploited in connection with the mutual exasperation between Germany and Britain. The politicians had made of the Entente and the Alliance a sort of handy tool for every Tsarist scheme. "France", he concluded, "must free herself from the bonds of this fatal subordination", or she would learn to her cost that "the principles which are the foundation of a régime and should inspire both its home and its foreign policy cannot be outraged with impunity".[2]

Jaurès denounced the Poincaré policy as one of gross chauvinism and retrograde militarism, dangerous alike for France and for democracy, and asked: "Are we destined, then, to be the slaves of reaction at home, and abroad the slaves of Russia?"[3]

---

[1] *Dépêche de Toulouse*, December 7th. Speech on December 11th. *Humanité*, December 13th.     [2] *Tribune Russe*, November 1912.

[3] *Humanité*, January 12. *Revue de l'enseignement primaire*, March 2, 1913. At the beginning of April, when an arrangement was arrived at between Russia and Austria on the subject of Scutari, the Russian Government showing prudence and moderation, the *Temps* supported the Pan-Slavists, denounced the Russian attitude, and described as a gross error the unjustified complaisance of the Russian Government towards Austria, condemning it as a "mad adventure of credulity and weakness", a "humiliating policy, entirely unpopular in France". It was against allowing the London Conference the "liberty of action which it has so regrettably abused", and went so far as to describe the Conference as a body of abdicationists whose services could well be dispensed with without loss to the self-respect of the Triple Alliance. Jaurès denounced "the dark and sinister workings" of this organ in fanning the fires of Pan-Slavism, attempting to discredit and break the European unity, and so making it more difficult for Russia to follow a moderate policy, while inciting French diplomacy to break with British and with those in Russia who wanted to preserve peace. *Temps*, April 3rd, 4th, 5th, 6th, 7th. *Humanité*, April 13th.

The peace negotiations, which had been suspended since the beginning of February, were resumed in March. Austria's proposal of the creation of an Albanian State removed for the time the danger of European war. René Pinon wrote:

Surprising as it may be to find the argument of the right of small nationalities to self-determination wielded by Austrian diplomacy, the right was in this instance irrefutable, for the Albanian race has never tolerated a yoke which disregarded its privileges and its traditional particularism. It was legitimate that the rights of this resourceful race should be safeguarded and that Europe should assume the guardianship over them.[1]

It is none the less true that Austria-Hungary, in agreement with Italy and in disregard of the rights of Serbia, had been mainly concerned to prevent Serbia from gaining access to the Adriatic. That is where the responsibility of the Vienna Government lies. It must in justice be admitted, however, that Aehrenthal had earlier shown himself in favour of the plan suggested by the French ambassador, M. Crozier, for the establishment of a free port served by a railway line unhampered by any restrictions. M. Crozier has related how the Serb extremists wrecked this plan, for fear of its jeopardizing the attainment of their wider ambitions.[2]

In Vienna, the Archduke Francis Ferdinand, and still more the Chief of Staff, Conrad von Hötzendorf, regarded war with Serbia as a necessity. But Germany was resolutely against this.[3] Serbia abandoned her idea of a port on the Adriatic for the moment, since Russia was not yet ready to face a European war. Montenegro, for the same reason, evacuated Scutari.

At the beginning of May, Sazonov told the Serbian Minister at St. Petersburg that the Serbs must "work for the future, for they will get a great deal of territory from Austria". He wrote to Hartwig on May 6th:

---

[1] *Revue des Deux Mondes*, June 15, 1913. On the subject of Albania, see J. Godard, *L'Albanie en 1921*.          [2] *Revue de France*, May 15, 1921.
[3] Cf. *Die Grosse Politik*, Vols. XXXIV–XXXVI, and the Memoirs of Conrad von Hötzendorf.

Serbia's promised land lies in Austrian territory and not in the direction in which she is striving at present and meeting with Bulgarian resistance. It is to Serbia's interest to achieve by dogged and patient work the degree of preparation necessary for the inevitable coming struggle. Time is on her side and against her enemies, who are already showing patent signs of disintegration. . . . A breach between Bulgaria and Serbia would be a triumph for Austria. It would delay her dissolution for years.[1]

Serbia, however, still kept her eyes on Macedonia and Salonica, from which she could not afford to be cut off; she came to an agreement with Greece, directed against Bulgaria, who also coveted Salonica. On May 30, 1913, the Treaty of London was signed.

A financial conference met in Paris. The *Temps* maintained that Russia, as advocate of the cause of the Balkan States, was entitled to count absolutely on French support, for "*in Near Eastern questions it is Russia who is playing the cards of the Alliance* and has the right to state her view first". This claim, Gauvain remarked, was the more disquieting since what the *Temps* had written was expressly stated to be "in entire conformity with the views of the Government". The Alliance must not imply the abandonment of French interests in the Near East nor their subordination to those of Russia. In economic and financial questions, on the contrary, France must count on Russian support. The editor of the *Journal des Débats* recalled rather cruelly that the *Temps* had been "passionately Austrophile during the crisis of 1908–1909"; now, in 1912–1913, it had been "more pro-Balkan than the St. Petersburg Cabinet, and is bitterly fighting in the present crisis arrangements which Russia has accepted".[2] What Gauvain called the "successive conversions" of the *Temps* was perfectly explicable. The *Temps* had throughout represented the views of the Quai d'Orsay. In 1908–1909 the French Foreign Office had rejected the idea of war on Serbia's behalf; in 1912–1913

---

[1] See German White Book and Bogitshevich, *Causes of the War.*
[2] *Temps*, June 2, 1913. *Journal des Débats*, June 3rd, 5th, 7th.

it had seriously considered it. The attitude of the *Temps*
reflected the change in French foreign policy.

The Bulgars, however, held to the terms concerning partition laid down in the treaty of March 1912, refused to accept
the arrangement which it was sought to impose on them, and,
in spite of the Tsar's veto, threw themselves against the Serbs
at the end of June. The "little Slav brothers", allies for a
moment only, had quickly come to blows. Up to 1912 they
had been constantly at one another's throats. Their alliance
had been anything but an expression of the true popular
sentiments; it had been mainly the work of the Tsarist Government and the Balkan statesmen, aiming at aiding one another
in their various ambitions. It had been evident since November
1912 that the alliance would be of short duration. The entry
of the Greeks into Salonica, which the Bulgars coveted since
Russia denied them Constantinople, the refusal of the Serbs
to recognize the Bulgarian claim to Monastir, and the Greek
designs on Seres and Kavala, were bound inevitably to bring
war. "The truth is", wrote Francis Delaisi,

that the allies had constantly in their mind not race nor religion, but
railways. . . . Racial hatreds, religious passion, played an important
part, but these were merely the considerations which divided the
peoples; their Governments were fighting not over principles but
interests. Religion, mother country, faith, honour are the powerful
levers with the aid of which statesmen move the masses, turning
peaceful citizens into fierce combatants. But the levers are brought
into operation by the men of business, who excite or allay these
sentiments and make use of them as suits their schemes for investment
or trade.[1]

Bulgaria was at grips simultaneously with Serbia, Greece, and
Roumania, and soon had to lay down her arms. To soothe her
bitterness and attach her to Russia, Isvolsky tried to get
Adrianople ceded to her. He warned Pichon of the absolute
necessity of measures of compulsion to induce Turkey to
evacuate the town. He went so far as to tell the French Govern-

[1] *Grande Revue*, July 10, 1913.

ment that if Russia was not given adequate support in this question, which affected her dignity and her historic traditions, the results might be most unfortunate for the Franco-Russian Alliance. Pichon, though apprehensive of resistance from French public opinion, replied that Russia might count in the Adrianople question on the entire support of France, even if Russia were obliged to take separate action against Turkey. In the end, however, Adrianople remained Turkish.[1]

The Treaty of Bucarest registered the defeat of Bulgaria, whose one thought thereafter was of vengeance against her former allies, the more since she knew that her road to Constantinople was barred for all time.[2] The upshot had been that neither of the two groups had succeeded. Turkey had been dismembered and thrown back towards Asia; Austria had been finally cut off from Salonica; but Russia had failed in her plans to gain the Straits, and France had spoilt her relations with Turkey, Bulgaria, and Austria for Russia's sake. Finally, German influence in Constantinople and Sofia was even greater at the end of 1913 than it had been in the past.

Thus for Russia the peace of Bucarest was no more than the overture to the play. She now held out to the Serbs the dazzling prospect of certain revenge against Austria and the occupation of Bosnia; for herself she foresaw the final fall of the Ottoman Empire and the partition of Turkey in Asia. But she was convinced that she could only realize her ambitions in the Straits under the cover of a European war. She was sure of French support, especially in the event of German intervention. When General Liman von Sanders was nominated to the command of a Turkish army corps in Constantinople, France advised Russia to despatch a warship to lie off Con-

---

[1] *Livre Noir*, II, pp. 91, 114, 125, 126.

[2] *Ibid.*, II, pp. 169–170. In November 1913 Isvolsky said to Gennadiev, the Bulgarian Foreign Minister, that the Straits and Constantinople were Russia's preserves in future, and that if Bulgaria attempted to try to cross her path the result would be disastrous for Bulgaria.

stantinople until the terms of the German contract had been modified.[1]

Isvolsky was delighted with the action of the French Foreign Ministry. Russia, feeling that she had support at her back, went ahead in the matter so near to her heart. In a report to the Tsar on November 23, 1913, Sazonov wrote:

Russia cannot remain indifferent to the solution of the question of the Straits. We cannot be sure that this question will not arise in the near future. Political foresight demands, therefore, that we should make careful preparation for such action as may become necessary. . . . The question of the Straits can hardly be advanced a step except through some European complication, which would find us in alliance with France.

A special conference met on February 8/21, 1914, and Sazonov then declared that "it could not be assumed that our operations against the Straits could take place except in a general European war". The Chief of Staff, General Zhilinsky, agreed in this view, and Vasily, a Deputy Director in the Ministry of Foreign Affairs, read a memorandum which ended as follows:

Our historic problem in regard to the Straits consists in obtaining possession of them . . . our domination must extend to both of the Straits, in order to assure our passage into the Mediterranean. It is highly improbable that we shall solve this problem otherwise than in the course of a European war. The possibility of seizing the Straits depends on a favourable conjuncture. To create this is the guiding purpose of the Ministry of Foreign Affairs.

The Tsar entirely approved these conclusions.

Thus, in 1914, the Russian Government continued to regard as the principal aim of its policy an objective which it recognized that it could only attain through a European war. It will be seen later that in August 1914 Turkey made a proposal to enter the war on the side of the Entente, and that Russia succeeded in cold-shouldering her into the camp of the Central Powers. It suited the calculations of the Russian Government —to "create a favourable conjuncture"—to work for the entry

---

[1] *Livre Noir*, II, p. 223. *Die Grosse Politik*, Vol. XXXVIII, pp. 191 sqq.

of Turkey into the war as an enemy of the Allies; otherwise Russia would have lost all excuse for occupying the Straits. The attitude of de Giers, the Russian ambassador in Constantinople, goes to confirm this, as do the documents published by the Soviet Government.[1]

If such projects could be entertained and such conferences held in Russia, it is reasonable to suppose that the Tsarist Government had received in 1913 all the assurances which it needed from the French Government. Léon Bourgeois bears witness that Delcassé, while ambassador in St. Petersburg, had promised Constantinople to Russia. Apart from this, dispatches discovered in the archives of the Russian Foreign Office, which had been sent to Sazonov by Isvolsky from Bordeaux in October 1914, seem to show plainly that negotiations took place in 1913 between Delcassé and Sazonov concerning the aims and objectives of Russian and French foreign policy, and that on the Russian side an especial objective was the conquest of the Straits and Constantinople.[2]

Meanwhile there was being pursued in France a nationalist policy reminiscent of the worst days of Boulangism and past nationalism. Jaurès wrote:

The agitation for the Three Years' Military Service Act is arousing the vilest of passions in nationalist souls. Anyone who does not agree unreservedly with this ominous measure is denounced as a traitor in enemy pay. Calumny and mud-slinging are being indulged in in the name of patriotism. . . . If (he added prophetically) a conflict were to come out of these manœuvres, if chauvinists of France and Germany were to succeed in hurling the two countries at one another, the war would everywhere be marked by a savage violence which would embitter men's memories and views for generations. It would stir up all the dregs of the human spirit, and a sanguinary venom would fill hearts and minds. It is our duty to the working class, menaced by this most formidable of reactionary manœuvres, to dissipate all misunderstandings.

---

[1] *Livre Noir*, II, pp. 369–372. E. Laloy, *Documents secrets des Archives du Ministère des Affaires Etrangères de Russie, publiés par les Bolchéviks*, pp. 74 sqq.

[2] Tel. 497, 498. *Carnets de Georges Louis*, II, pp. 245–246.

He wrote that the mediocrity, the feebleness in action, and the lack of conviction of the Radical party had delivered over a whole section of the nation to the wild spirits who were trying to destroy every advance that the country had made. The perils in the Near East had been averted for a moment, but he saw clearly that they might return and fill the whole horizon. Europe had what she deserved; this was the humiliating penalty for all the policies of baseness, violence, lying and intrigue which everywhere, from Morocco to Bosnia-Herzegovina and Tripoli, from Adrianople to Persia, had set at nought every guiding principle of law, of international fair-dealing, of humanity and justice.[1]

The *Correspondant* added its voice to Jaurès', deploring a state of diplomatic morality in which the violation of treaties could be considered the most natural of things:

Which of the Powers at the present moment would consider itself bound by its signature where its interests were affected? There is (the *Correspondant* went on, with justifiable severity towards the men in power) something comic, for all its danger, in the spectacle of all these sovereigns, these heads of States, these Ministers and diplomats of the Great Powers speaking of nothing but peace, of the maintenance of equilibrium, and at the same time doing their best to upset this equilibrium by every imaginable means and to throw the small nations at one another's throats, those small nations which are the pawns with which the Powers play against one another until, whether they like it or not, they have themselves to employ against one another the arms which they never willingly use except against the weak and defenceless.[2]

It was becoming clear that the European war had only been postponed, that the crisis remained as grave as ever, and that on the morrow, on the first pretext, the Austro-Russian duel would be resumed, with all its consequences.

It has been seen how Russia had for a long time been working for war in the Balkans. The documents in the "Yellow

[1] *Humanité*, June 12, 1913. *Revue de l'Enseignement primaire*, March 16th, April 13th, July 13th.
[2] *Correspondant*, October 10, 1911; July 25 and September 10, 1913.

Book", and certain telegrams from Georges Louis which are conspicuously absent from it, show not only how the Tsarist Government engineered the first Balkan war in order at last to lay hands on the Straits, but also how on many occasions, in spite of the most pressing inquiries from France, it kept her in ignorance of its principal actions, and how it took steps likely to bring in their train the most serious consequences.

Through the secret Serb-Bulgar treaty, which, in Poincaré's own words, contained the seeds of war against Turkey and against Austria, the Tsarist Government "started the motor". It was at pains to conceal from France the precise wording of this treaty until August 1912, and represented it as essentially pacific. Sazonov encouraged and afterwards warmly approved Italy's forcing of the Dardanelles, which precipitated events; with Isvolsky he recommended to Paris a Bulgarian loan which provided the sinews of war; he opposed the meeting of a conference to bring the Italo-Turkish war to an end, so as not to tie his hands in face of the grave events which he foresaw. In August he rejected that part of the suggestion put forward by Berchtold which had reference to diplomatic pressure to dissuade the Balkan States from going to war. He raised objections to collective action by the Powers to maintain the *status quo*, and made no use whatever of the power which Russia had under the secret treaty to veto the Balkan mobilization. He was opposed to mediation, and only agreed to mediate with Austria when it was too late. Finally, he allowed the King of Montenegro, a pensioner of the Tsar, to set the Balkans aflame.

After the opening of hostilities, the Russian Government declared that it would intervene if Austria did not remain passive. Isvolsky refused to convey to Sazonov Poincaré's request that the Serb-Bulgar treaty should be communicated to Britain, who remained ignorant of its terms until November 3rd, a fortnight after hostilities had begun, Turkey being then already crushed. Sazonov refused to agree to any sort

of mediation before the taking of Adrianople; then, at the end
of October, he suddenly insisted on a formula of disinterestedness directed against Austria and on mediation of which the
purpose was to prevent the Bulgars from reaching Constantinople; failing mediation, he threatened to send the Black
Sea Fleet to Constantinople.

The Russian Government went yet further. As far back as
the beginning of 1912 it had agreed to the principle of concerted action and had given its promise to the French Government to consult it before doing anything. Yet, in spite of
repeated reminders from Poincaré, it shamelessly broke its
promise again and again. After having refused to communicate
the Serb-Bulgar treaty to its ally until the last moment, it took
two successive steps at a critical stage in the war without
France's knowledge, threatening Turkey with intervention if
she failed quickly to sign a peace in accordance with its views,
and then intervening in Berlin for the same purpose and in
Bucarest, in "the most regrettable" terms, in favour of Bulgaria. To crown all, Sazonov, more or less under the influence
of Isvolsky, refused to give any explanations to the French
ambassador, Georges Louis, who saw clearly through his
game; he decoded Louis' letters; and finally, after "an un-
savoury intrigue", he demanded Louis' supersession.

After all this, Poincaré, who had realized that Russia had
"started the motor" of the war, still persisted against all
evidence in believing in the pacific desires and the good
intentions of the Russian Government. He deplored Sazonov's
"shifting and dispersed activities", his "daily inconsistencies,"
his "indifference to France's desires and advice"; but he did
not harbour the slightest suspicion of his "profoundly pacific"
intentions, and he sacrificed Georges Louis to him. He admitted
the instinctive distrust with which Isvolsky filled him—"a
turbulent diplomat who has succeeded in antagonizing everyone"—and he complained of Isvolsky having taken action
without informing France; yet he stood warrant for the

R

sincerity and the pacific intentions of the man of Buchlau. He went so far as to declare that "clearly" neither Sazonov nor Isvolsky "thought that the *rapprochement* between the Serbs and Bulgars would have the immediate effect of bringing about the mobilization provided for under the convention". Finally, he maintained that the Russian Government, which had "somewhat unwisely taken a hand in the drafting of the Balkan agreements", was obviously still in favour of the policy of peace and the *status quo*, seeing that it had, from the beginning of September, lavished injunctions and reprimands on the Balkan States. Yet it is clear that by then the preparations of the allies were complete and pacific advice was too belated to be of the slightest effect—as the Balkan Governments themselves observed. After July, when the Serb-Bulgar treaty had begun to produce its fated effects, gestures of peace were nothing less than humbug, to throw dust in the eyes of the world.

What explanation, finally, can be conceived of Poincaré's concealment from Britain until the opening of hostilities of the secret Serb-Bulgar treaty which he himself considered to be an instrument of war?

Poincaré had not even any suspicion of double-dealing on the part of Sazonov and Isvolsky, although Jules Cambon confessed to Beyens "how difficult it is to rely on the brilliant and versatile politicians who rule the empire which is France's ally; for they play a double game even with her".[1] Neither Sazonov nor Isvolsky ceased talking of the maintenance of the *status quo*, though for four years, at Buchlau, at Racconigi, in Sofia, they had been working incessantly to end it. Poincaré seems to have had no suspicion that the declarations of the Russian statesmen were frequently at variance with their actions. Five days after Sazonov's interview with Grey at Balmoral and the announcement that the Russian troops were withdrawing from Persia, nine Russian battalions penetrated

---

[1] Letter from Beyens to Davignon, March 18, 1913.

into Persia. Had not Russia done just the same in Manchuria, in spite of all her promises of evacuation and her pacific declarations? Finally, in 1911–1913, in the Charykov affair with Turkey and in her relations with France, in connection with the Serb-Bulgar treaty and her own repeated independent action, was not Russia continually showing the same flat contradiction between her statements and her actions?

Poincaré seemed unwilling to realize that in Russia, as under absolutism was bound to be the case, several policies were being pursued at the same time, giving to her diplomacy a strangely incoherent aspect which explained the "shifting and dispersed activities and daily inconsistencies" which aroused his wonder. Not only did Tsarism turn now towards Asia, now towards Europe, approach now Germany and Austria, now France and Britain, but, above all, in her semblance of power and her actual exhaustion after the disasters in the Far East, she sought any diversion abroad to parry the revolutionary danger at home, and followed a foreign policy of conquest and adventure out of all relation to her strength. Incapable of any settled policy, she was condemned to continual shiftings and perpetual incoherence.

It must also be said that Poincaré had a different Balkan policy from that of his predecessors, and, above all, an entirely new conception of the Franco-Russian Alliance.[1] In his conviction, in the teeth of the evidence, of the pacific intentions of the Russian Government, he was naturally led to give it to understand that France would always stand at its back in the event of a grave conflict breaking out. When the consequences of the secret Serb-Bulgar treaty were implacably unfolding, the question of provocation never came into his mind. In his view, the moment Austria intervened with German support in a purely Balkan affair in which the responsibility for trouble

---

[1] Philippe Crozier wrote that in 1912 a Franco-European policy gave place to a Franco-Balkan policy at the Quai d'Orsay. Cf. *Revue de France*, April 15, May 15, June 1, 1921. *Eclair*, June 13, 1921.

lay with Russia, France was obliged to give her ally the fullest support, or she would be unfaithful to the Alliance. In the same way he would not admit that Russia could do anything but give France her support, even to the length of going to war over colonial questions.

Thus, the moment France came face to face with Germany at any point on the globe, whether by her own fault or that of her partner, the Alliance came perforce into play. This conception of the Franco-Russian treaty, which extended its scope to the whole world, was contrary to the intention of its signatories, who had continually been preoccupied with the prevention of any sort of provocation. Under this Poincarist system, the risk of war could only have been definitely averted by Germany favouring Russia's schemes of conquest in the Balkans, even at Austria's expense.

It must, however, be recognized that this conception fitted well enough both with the spirit and the letter of the modification introduced by Delcassé in 1899 (his presence in the Government in 1912 and his appointment to St. Petersburg in 1913 were no mere coincidence), and especially with the intention of the men in power to inaugurate an active phase of the Alliance and to "feed it on Austro-Russian rivalries". The mistake made by the French statesmen lay in believing that the Russian Empire had had time to recover and that there was any real striking power behind its expansionist policy. Their duty should have been energetically to restrain Russia, holding over her the fear of finding herself alone at the critical moment. Far from this, Isvolsky was satisfied, as he shows in his correspondence, that whatever happened Russia would have France's support; whatever dangerous steps she might take, she would run the risk of French reproaches, even French ill-humour, but never of French abandonment in the hour of danger.

In Poincaré's view, to fail to support Russia in the Balkans was equivalent to a breach of the Alliance; and all this time "the Russian diplomats, soaked in the poison of imperialism, dreaming of a super-State of their own that would reach from the Japan Sea to the Aegean, careless of whether the military organization of the country was adequate to the range of their ambitions, were obstinately preparing for seizing possession of the Straits".[1] In the fear of destroying the Alliance, the country was condemned to lend its support to Russia's schemes of conquest in regions where neither she nor France had any vital interest. It is here that the vicious effect shows itself of this false conception of the alliance with a gangrenous régime which, once entangled in the Balkans, was plunged irrevocably into the course which could only end in a world war.

This conception was particularly indefensible in a country with universal suffrage like France. Even if it were admitted that secret engagements could bind a democracy, it was so much the more indefensible to extend the scope of such engagements and to strain their interpretation in the direction of war when the country had neither agreed to them nor even heard of them.

[1] Gauvain, *L'Europe au jour le jour*, Preface to Vol. IV.

# CHAPTER XIII

# TOWARDS THE WORLD WAR

EUROPE was now approaching a general war. The Governments were preparing for it. The Franco-Russian Alliance was drawn daily more and more into its active phase. France was relying on Russia's strength; her General Staff, her diplomats, her Government, were satisfied of its reality. The semi-official press followed the men in power in continually advertising the might of France's imperial ally.

Only a few months before the war, however, on December 25, 1913, there appeared in the *Correspondant* a grave warning which invalidated all the official statements as to Russia's condition. The article was headed: "Suppose war came to-morrow? 'We have the Alliance.' The true situation." In the view of the anonymous writer, the policy followed for twenty years past had lulled France into a completely false security. He showed how well France had been able, had she chosen, to give to Russia the advice and warnings she needed; and he added that Russia's financial situation was such that if France did not agree to a big loan for her in the early months of 1914 the Russian Government would be in the throes of internal difficulties of extreme gravity. It would take the Russian army two months to complete mobilization after a declaration of war. And he concluded with the following considerations, which subsequent events proved only too well founded:

In the face of the undying illusions of those who do not know the facts and the wilfully misleading assurances of those who do, it is an urgent duty to declare once for all that there is altogether too wide a gap between the nation's expectations and the real future which faces it. . . . Up to now alliance has been a word standing mainly for a contract of very decidedly too unilateral a nature, in which we have given everything and stand to receive precious little. . . . It is high time that our allies should make their own part of the Alliance a reality.

A year earlier, the *Correspondant* had published a prophetic article only too well confirmed by events. It pointed out that France had been regularly and constantly deceived both as to Russia's foreign policy and as to her condition at home. It recalled how the Alliance had above all else been for Russia and for the big bankers a financial affair: she was constantly in urgent need of money to escape from bankruptcy; and they drew large gains from her needs. It mentioned that in the Duma the *rapporteur* of the Budget Committee had just declared, on February 25, 1912, that for twenty-two years past the Russian budgets had shown an unbroken series of deficits. It then proceeded:

It is incredible how the actual happenings in Russia are kept from the knowledge of Europe, and of France in particular. . . . No one is aware of the fact that the country is in a state of latent revolution, and that order is maintained only by means of appalling measures of repression. The calm is only apparent, and Russia offers the singular spectacle of an immense empire governed purely by a police régime. Administration, education, army, navy, everything is in the hands of the police. . . .[1] In the army there are frequent outbreaks of sedition. It is undeniable that there is latent revolution in Russia, and war would bring, and, it is to be feared, in a very much graver form, repetitions of such events as the mutinies on the *Potemkin* and the *Pobiedonostsev*, the riots in Warsaw, Kiev, St. Petersburg, revolts of reservists, and so on. This deplorable régime would certainly be unable to withstand another serious shock, and the French public is deceived when Russia is represented to it as prospering in every respect.[2]

No more terrible indictment could be drawn up against the state of mind of the men in power in France with regard to

[1] "The number of persons arrested grew from 77,255 in 1897 to 96,005 in 1903, 111,403 in 1906, 138,500 in 1907, 166,064 in 1908, 181,241 in 1909, and over 200,000 in 1910. The death penalty is inflicted with a rigour beyond all precedent."

[2] September 25, 1912. The *Soleil* wrote on August 22, 1912: "The whole financial economy of Russia is vicious and anti-social. . . . Alcoholism and famine are the two main sources of revenue. Revolution is latent. . . . French capital has no more than a precarious guarantee, whether from a political, economic, or financial standpoint. . . . Russia's alliance and friendship are costing us more in fifteen years than a century of wars and enmities."

Russian affairs in 1912–1914. It might have been supposed that these articles, published by a Conservative organ, free from any suspicion of revolutionary sympathies, would at least have put political, diplomatic, and military leaders on their guard. They failed entirely to do so. Not only did this clarion call fall on deaf ears, and fail entirely to secure any attention from the French governing class, but even at the beginning of 1914 Stéphane Lauzanne published in the *Matin* a series of articles which attracted considerable attention, in which he sang the praises of the ambitions and the enormous power of France's ally.[1] According to Stéphane Lauzanne, the Russian army, "an admirably trained, organized, and equipped force", had "solved the problem of heavy artillery". Russia was the land of gold, the chief banker of the world. The Alliance had never been more popular. "Russia is a Colossus which could shatter this terrestrial globe with its fist. . . . The supreme hour is approaching. . . . Russia has as yet done nothing at Constantinople, but she will act to-morrow, or the next day, or in a month's time. . . . In Russia there is an urge in all directions . . . let us be prepared to assist the Russian statesmen." It was with such a tissue of ineptitudes that the French public was instructed on the eve of the war. Need it be added that the *Matin* energetically supported the French Government's policy at this period?

Stéphane Lauzanne persisted in his educative mission. On his return from Russia he gave a lecture, organized by the *Foyer*, with Admiral Fournier in the chair, and served up his principal arguments again in the presence of Delcassé and a number of French ambassadors and generals. He spoke of the nuptials of the French Republic and the Russian Empire:

She (France) brought the dowry, he (Russia) the strength. . . . To-day, as though by enchantment, the Russian Empire has become prodigiously rich, immeasurably rich. This wealth I have studied on the spot, dazed but observant. . . . At the 1913 manœuvres

---

[1] January 2, 4, 6, 8, 10, 1914.

General Joffre had the impression of an army of centaurs. . . . I can still hear the voice of General Sukhomlinov, the War Minister, as he said to me: "We want France to realize that our army also is a fine one. . . ." An ally is like a kindly star whose steadfast glow irradiates the night.[1]

Two years before this, the correspondent in Russia of the *Echo de Paris*, G. Dru, wrote in the introduction to a book by Poleyayev:[2] "The Russian army is well trained and excellently equipped." In the *Economiste Européen* of January 1914, Edmond Théry praised "the immense effort being made by the Russian State to educate the people". Yet in 1916 Paléologue could write of "the deep ignorance in which the mass of the Russian people was vegetating".[3] Such was the way in which the French public was served with information on Russia.[4]

[1] *Revue du Foyer*, May 15, 1914. In his book *La Russie dans la Guerre Mondiale*, General Danilov, formerly Quartermaster-General of the Russian armies, has pointed out that in 1914 the Russian army was virtually without either an aviation branch or a wireless organization, and had an inadequate number of guns and an appallingly low stock of ammunition. He also drew attention to the inadequate technical knowledge of the army leaders.

[2] *La Russie de 1906 à 1912.*           [3] Paléologue, III, p. 26.

[4] There came striking evidence of the way in which the public was kept in ignorance. On January 27, 1914, the *Echo de Paris* announced that the great Russian armament firm of Putilov had nearly concluded negotiations for the purchase of their works by Krupps. The news created a sensation in France. These works, which were controlled by Creusot, possessed full details of the secret processes of French gun construction, which were thus in danger of falling into German hands. Astonishment was expressed that the Russian Government had had no knowledge of the deal, and that the French Government had not been informed of it either by Isvolsky, or, above all, by Delcassé, who proved to have known nothing of it. The Russian Government issued a *démenti* saying that there was no truth in the rumour; the Paris press at once calmed down and appeared to be reassured. Tardieu wrote in the *Temps* of January 30th: "Nowadays manufacturing secrets are somewhat blown upon anyhow; to give only one instance, the gun now being made for the Italian army was designed in France." The question was brought up in the Chamber of Deputies by Albert Thomas on March 19th. Doumergue, the Prime Minister, replied that through the intervention of the French Government the matter had been settled in a way that was very favourable to French industry, and declared that the Alliance gave France a strong weapon for the defence of all her interests, and was at the same time a precious guarantee of peace. "I see proof of it", he said, "every day; I am absolutely convinced on this point."

To say the least, the whole affair was very nebulous. The truth about it was exposed by Francis Delaisi in a remarkable study published by *La Paix*

The truth about Russia was altogether lamentable. The *Correspondant* had lifted a corner of the veil. There was also the evidence of the Russians themselves. In April and May 1914, Jean Pélissier undertook a wide survey of the state of Europe. He published his results in the *Dépêche de Toulouse*, in a series of interviews of the utmost interest with the leading politicians of the various countries. The following are the most characteristic passages in the statements made to him by very prominent Russians. These statements, each more sombre than the last, describe the state of Russia as it was revealed later in the course of the World War. They clearly foresaw the coming disaster with all its consequences.

Jean Pélissier noted from the outset that foreign optimism about Russia was belied by a large number of Russians of all classes and of every shade of opinion. "We are", they said,

an unhappy country, doomed to misery and despair. Popular discontent is universal. . . . There is simmering in the soul of the

---

*par le Droit*. (February to May 1914.) For several years the Putilov works, which were under the controlling influence of Creusot, had been manufacturing both field guns of a French type with the assistance of French fitters and foremen, and big guns of a German type for which Krupps had furnished the technical staff. Of twenty-two directors, twenty-one were German, and 60 per cent of the foremen were Germans. These works also built warships under the supervision of the Hamburg firm of Blohm und Voss. Thus, French and German technicians made use together in the Putilov works of the manufacturing secrets of the French and German ordnance departments. This association of Schneider (Creusot) and Krupp was financed by the French Banque de l'Union Parisienne. Another group, formed by the British firm of Vickers and the Société d'Homécourt, and supported by the Société Générale, was installed at Nicolaiev and St. Petersburg, and the two groups competed for Russian armament contracts. The news published by the *Echo de Paris* was only an incident in this struggle. "All that was intended," wrote Delaisi, "was to put pressure on a group of French banks to induce them to finance a scheme in which Creusot was interested. As the banks were somewhat intractable, the Government had to be made to force their hands. And what better way was there to do this than by rousing the public by persuading it that National Defence was likely to be imperilled for the lack of a few millions of roubles?" Was it not with justice that Jaurès said at the time: "The public is aware that the manœuvres of the International of guns and shell may be carried to the length of treason against it. . . . When will the world be rid of these brigands who work together, even when they are fighting one another?" (January 31st.)

people a resentment of which foreigners are unwilling to take note. They are all much impressed by the façade; but behind it there is nothing but decomposition and rottenness. . . . Let another unjust war like that against Japan break out, or let reaction throw off the mask and cynically show its hand, and at the first shock the structure will collapse.

Pélissier showed the incalculability and the disconcerting possibilities offered always by Russia. Brianchaninov, one of the best informed people in the country, husband of Princess Gorchakov, the daughter of the celebrated diplomat, declared:

I am afraid that in their blind reliance on the boundless submissiveness of the Russian people and on the enormous power of repression in the hands of the Government, the French are inviting disillusionment. In time of peace all goes passably well. But once it receives a shock, who knows whether the edifice will stand? This is the question which everyone is asking.

Every manifestation of public opinion was forbidden, and it was consequently impossible to know what was germinating in "the subsoil of the Russian soul", or what was the real spirit of the people. Russia had, in fact, reverted to the pre-1905 situation; the Duma was no more than a screen for a dread police régime. No one knew how the enormous sums voted were expended. Thoughtful people of all parties, even Conservatives, found the existing state of things intolerable. Rodichev, leader of the Cadet party, was particularly outspoken:

You want my opinion of Russia's foreign policy? It is run by France. . . . The situation is well summed up in a cartoon representing an enormous Cossack with his mouth wide open; Marianne at his side, drawing gold pieces from a sack and putting them in his mouth; from the other side, as from an automatic machine, there issue soldiers. France, to me, is like a Jewish money-lender. . . . No one among the mass of the people wants war, whether in Russia or in Germany. . . . If we are to have peace in Europe the Governments must be democratized. Our own needs this more than any other. It seems to take a malicious pleasure in being a source of exasperation to all the citizens of the empire.

Rodichev ended with a denunciation of "the barbarity and narrow-mindedness of the men in power". Pélissier had a very interesting interview with Nisselovich, who had been a member of the third Duma and chairman of the Budget Committee; but he felt it wiser not to publish it in his book on its publication in 1916. So it was that history was written during the war. This interview ran counter to the ideas in favour in the official world in France, and showed to what lengths the misleading of French opinion on Russia had gone. Nisselovich did not mince his words:

The world outside knows nothing about us, and the worst of it is that journalists come here to investigate, see the country's wretched state, and dare not write about it. Our nationalists have forgotten nothing and learned nothing. They declare once more as before 1905 that our soldiers will "not be short of as much as a legging button". My own opinion is that we are not prepared and are heading for a fresh disaster. . . . It makes one redden with shame to think of the type of Ministers who govern us here. We are living under an Asiatic régime of favourites. The most influential man in the empire is a Siberian peasant, virtually illiterate, who forces through his own suggestions on all the questions of high policy, and who seems to be nothing less than a dangerous rogue.

Nisselovich added that at Kiev all the officials stood in awe of a simple student named Golyubev, who had assumed a kind of dictatorship on the pretext that he was leader of a monarchist organization in high favour with the most exalted spheres. "Is not this an unmistakable sign of mental deficiency in our régime, a sort of pure dementia? Is it possible to think without terror of the future of a country so lamentably ruled?"

Pélissier frequently heard similar language from the Liberals. Events were to show how well-founded were these men's views.

Prince Mestchersky, who published the *Graidanin*, denounced the dangerous character of the nationalists and Pan-Slavs, and proclaimed the Russian people's love of peace. "They were capable of enthusiasm for the cause of the liberty of the South Slavs around 1876, but now they are completely indifferent to it." He assured Pélissier that there was no more reality in the much-vaunted Slav fraternity than in the fraternity of the Latin races.

A few reassuring declarations were made to Pélissier, such as that of Rodzianko, whose official character as President of the Duma, however, deprived him of the needed freedom of judgment. He declared that the state of the Russian finances was excellent, enabling the country to face a year of war without a loan. "We have the money, the guns, and the men. If the Germans drive us to war, we shall wage it with the utmost energy, and it will certainly not end indecisively."

Bobrinsky, leader of the Nationalist party, representing, it is true, only a tiny minority, declared that Russia would never permit Austria or Germany to impose their hegemony upon the Serbs and Bulgars. He advocated one single tongue for all branches of the great Slav family, and openly admitted Russia's intentions in regard to Constantinople. Efrimov, leader of the Centrists in the Duma, also admitted that Constantinople was the aim of Russian hopes and aspirations.

On the Polish question, Shebeko, a member of the Imperial Council, protested against Russian oppression. "All the western Slavs", he said, "demand that Russia, before she can dream of placing herself at the head of the Pan-Slav movement, must at last adopt a Slav policy towards the Poles, whom she is exterminating." Shebeko here underlined the hypocrisy of Russia's policy as "protectress of the Slavs". All the Poles whom Pélissier interviewed declared that the reawakening of Russian nationalism had coincided with the resumption of the policy of russification in Poland.

A member of the Right, Count Dimitri Olsonfiero, declared that the Russian people was disillusioned with the sentimental policy pursued in regard to the "brother" Balkan peoples. He added that Pan-Slavism was a chimerical policy, for a long time to come at all events, for the Slavs were brothers at war with one another; there was a profound antagonism between the Catholic and the Orthodox Slavs. He added, however, that "Constantinople is in our blood". He admitted that in the economic sphere, in regard to roads and railways and telegraphs, the Russian Government was doing nothing. This, he said, was "a grave danger for the empire, with the army of the discontented growing daily".

Pélissier was present at a meeting of the Imperial Council. The views expressed by the men of the Right parties made him "shudder"; they made plain to him the tragic situation of modern Russia, whose aspirations towards the light were hopelessly blocked by the obstinacy and ferocity of the representatives of the forces of reaction.

He was brought at the conclusion of his inquiry to the fear that in France there were too many illusions concerning the value of the support which could be counted on from Russia in the event of war with Germany. "To persist in this error", he wrote on May 17, 1914, "would be fatally dangerous for France." Finally, in July, he pointed out the extraordinary power of Rasputin, who had become the adviser of the Tsarina and passed from her private suite to that of the Tsar, where he had established the right to enter at any hour unannounced and to advise the Tsar on all the crucial questions of home and foreign policy. Nicholas II and his entourage seemed to be the victims of a sort of unholy fascination at the hands of an individual who was reckoned no friend to France.

Such was the régime on which the French Government was relying. "Up to the last moment", writes Ludovic Naudeau,

we refused to bow to the evidence. In all that concerned Russia an irrational optimism reigned in France in 1914, but in my own case this optimism was changing to horror. . . . What aberration had engendered in us this blind confidence? . . . Anyone who had attentively observed the successive phases of the war with Japan and given thought to the history of Russia for a century past, might have prognosticated in 1914 with almost complete certainty our ally's defeat, collapse, and disintegration.[1]

---

[1] *Les dessous du chaos russe*, pp. 5, 14.

Yet the Comte de Mun, in his book *L'Heure sombre*, looked forward with enthusiasm to the overwhelming of Teuton by Slav, threatening Germany with the invasion of Russian forces on a colossal scale; and André Mévil, in the *Echo de Paris*, declared that the Russian army was "in a perfect condition of preparedness" and would "play a preponderating part in the next war". He found that the Russian budget totalled 1,500,000,000 francs against the German 1,060,000,000, and declared that the French and Russian armies were in a position to face a struggle against an Austro-German coalition with every prospect of success. Thanks to Poincaré and Delcassé, the Alliance had recovered its full efficacity, and Mévil recommended "a policy of systematic resistance to Germany", since "the anti-German rôle of the Alliance" was "its sole reason of existence".[1]

[1] *La Paix est malade*, pp. 112 sqq.

# CHAPTER XIV

## PALÉOLOGUE'S VISIT TO PARIS (JUNE 1914)

IT was at this moment, when Tsarism already appeared in the eyes of the well-informed as "rotten to the core", when the Russian élite were proclaiming the coming disintegration of a régime which was leading Russia to disaster and the abyss, that there occurred an event of exceptional gravity, and one which shows strikingly the use which France's rulers were making of the Franco-Russian Alliance in defiance of the will of the country, and the extent to which Republican usages had in their hands become nothing more or less than a miserable farce.

On June 5, 1914, three weeks after the general election in which the French people had roundly condemned the policy followed since the beginning of 1912, Paléologue, the French ambassador in St. Petersburg, appointed thanks to his friendship with the President of the Republic, arrived at the Gare du Nord, called on Briand, and asked him to convey to Viviani, who was forming the new Ministry, his resignation if the new Cabinet failed to continue the Three Years' Military Service Act, against which the country had just pronounced so emphatically.

On the next day the news was learnt from the *Paris-Midi*, which vouched for the authenticity of the following statements made to Viviani by Paléologue:

I have exact knowledge of the state of mind of the Court and Government circles in Russia, and must tell you that they are following with close attention the controversies aroused in France over the Three Years Act. If the scheme of military service is modified in the slightest I must also tell you that I shall find myself forced to send in to you my immediate resignation, as I should be unable in such conditions to return to the post entrusted to me.[1]

---

[1] *Paris-Midi*, June 6th. Three days later the *Paris-Midi* published a sort of revised version which explained Paléologue's step by putting into his mouth some such words as these: "The Russian Government would be

On the very day of Paléologue's arrival the *Matin* published a news paragraph from St. Petersburg which contained the following remarks:

In the view of the immense majority of Russian politicians the Three Years Act is absolutely indispensable not only for the maintenance of the Balance of Power in Europe, but for the proper functioning of the Alliance. . . . For France to revert to a two years' military service period would be considered all over Russia as a very heavy blow against the Alliance. . . . There is the greatest confidence at St. Petersburg that M. Poincaré will not allow any such injury to the Alliance. (*Matin*, June 5th.)

This was virtually the same language which Paléologue used in his interview with Viviani. The same evening the *Temps* gave extracts from certain Russian newspapers (*Novoye Vremya*, *St. Petersburgskaya Vyedomosti*, and so on), with the following commentary:

It is only natural if the Russian papers are crying "Take care!" and warning us with the authority given by friendship and treaties against the certain dangers to which the friends of MM. Jaurès and Caillaux are bent on exposing our frontiers and *our self-respect as a nation*. . . . Feeling is growing hourly tenser in Russia, where those who are associated with us by virtue of treaties are anxiously wondering whether the representatives of the French people can possibly commit this sorry act of self-stultification.

The *Temps* and the *Matin* must apparently have known all about the representations which the ambassador had come to make. Paléologue's account of the affair should be read in the *Revue des Deux Mondes* of January 15, 1921. He decided, evidently on the strength of friendly advice, not to include it

greatly astonished if it found France altering her military organization and method of recruitment, seeing that Russia has modified her own mobilization plans at the insistent request of France. The Court would certainly take exception to measures of that kind being adopted without its knowledge, in view of the attitude taken up by successive French Ministries regarding the Russian frontier defence troops and garrisons on the Western frontier. One of my predecessors, indeed, was perpetually at issue with various Russian officials over this question. He was incessantly making representations to the Russian Government about the standards that were being maintained either in *matériel* or in *personnel*."

S

in his three-volume memoirs, though it might well have served as an introduction to them. The perusal of his article is extremely suggestive, revealing, as it does, the type of mind on which the destinies of peoples depend, under a supposedly democratic régime, at critical moments in their history. Briand, according to Paléologue, told him that the Socialists and the Unified Radicals were "in a fair way to ruin France". Paléologue declared—more than three weeks, be it observed, before the assassination of Archduke Francis Ferdinand—that war was now "inevitable and imminent".

The crisis was prolonged, for the President of the Republic was intent on maintaining the Three Years Act. After Viviani had failed to form a Government, the Ribot Cabinet, constituted without regard to the views of the majority of the Chamber, was defeated on the very day it took office (June 12th). Viviani then succeeded in forming a Ministry which secured a vote of confidence, but at the cost of offering a prospect of "easing the military burdens". On June 18th Viviani sent for Paléologue, and a memorable interview took place. Paléologue said once more that war was threatening to break out at any moment. In the light of all that we have since learned of the responsibilities for the World War, this assertion is extremely significant.[1] Viviani asked how soon the storm would burst. Paléologue replied: "It is impossible for me to fix any date. But I should be surprised if the state of electrical tension now prevailing in Europe were not soon to end in a catastrophe." Paléologue describes how the French Premier received this strange declaration:

---

[1] On July 31st, when Paléologue received a visit from a mobilized French officer in St. Petersburg, he appeared certain that war was coming, and "almost rejoiced at the prospect, since he considered the situation was the most favourable that could have been hoped for: 'At no time', he said, 'have we been so well supported or so well prepared'." (*Correspondant*, September 10, 1914.) Paléologue's mentality may be further studied in his letter to the *Temps* of March 15, 1922, in which he charges Rouvier with having sacrificed Delcassé to Germany, and in the replies of Thomson and Bienvenu-Martin on March 18th.

Suddenly he was transfigured; his face lit up with a mystical illu-
mination. "Well," he said, drawing himself up to his full height,
"if it has to come to that, we shall do our duty, our whole duty. France
will be once more as she has always been—capable of every heroism
and every sacrifice. We shall see again the great days of 1792!"

Paléologue then put this question:

You are determined, then, to prevent any tampering with the Military
Service Act? I may assure the Emperor Nicholas of this?

Thus it was as the messenger of a Tsar under the thumb of
a Rasputin that Paléologue had come to demand from the
French Government, in defiance of the will of the people, the
maintenance of the Three Years Act, a measure based on two
errors of the first importance—the myth of the "lightning
attack" and the underrating of the reserves—which were both
to be exposed by the war in their full ineptitude. It might
have been supposed that a Prime Minister at all acquainted
with Russian affairs, at all cognizant of the evidences and
warnings which had been multiplying for twenty years past,
would have resented a French ambassador's making himself
the mouthpiece of demands of such audacity at a time when
the French Government would have been justified in presenting
claims of its own against an already rotting Tsarism. But was
the Tsar really the moving spirit behind these representations?
Had the head of the Government been determined to get to
the bottom of the matter, he would immediately have communicated it not only to the Cabinet and the President of the
Republic, but to the Chamber and Senate Foreign Affairs Committees. It would certainly have been well for France if she had
had at the end of July 1914 a different representative in Russia.
But Paléologue knew before he left St. Petersburg the kind of
man he would have to deal with. Viviani's attitude shows us into
what hands the guidance of France had fallen at one of the
gravest moments of her destiny, and explains many things which
have remained obscure. He simply replied to the ambassador:

Yes, you may assure him (the Tsar) that the Three Years system will be maintained without restriction and that I shall allow nothing to be done which might enfeeble or relax our alliance with Russia.

Paléologue then asked Viviani to dissuade one of his friends from meeting the Kaiser, who would give him the impression of one of the most peaceful of sovereigns, while German diplomacy would continue its intransigent and vexatious proceedings. Viviani, who had indeed found his master, undertook to advise his friend not to go to Kiel—a most striking instance of contempt for the will of the country. Clemenceau, when he heard of Paléologue's action, said with justice: "I know of no other country in Europe in which so scandalous a manœuvre could be carried on with impunity." It was the clear duty of the Premier to recall the ambassador. . . . It was impossible to allow a wildly prejudiced official "to attempt to impose his will on the constituted organs of sovereign authority—a step that would lead straight to the utter disorganization of society".[1] Baron Guillaume, the Belgian Minister in Paris, considered that the action Paléologue had taken was of ill omen for the future of France. He wondered whether Russia's attitude were based on a conviction that the crisis was at hand in which it would be possible to make use of the tool which she wanted to see in the hands of her ally.

It is clear what must have happened. In calling upon Russia to increase her army and her strategic railways, the French Government must have pointed out what a heavy burden France herself was undertaking in the Three Years Act. It was to be feared that, if France repealed the Act, Russia would soon relax the efforts which had been asked of her.

Sukhomlinov, the Russian Minister of War—the same man who was found guilty of treason in 1917—supported Paléologue in his intrigue on behalf of the Three Years Act. After the fall of the Ribot Government, the Russian Cabinet, at a special meeting, decided to send instructions to Isvolsky to use his influence against any modification in the Act.

[1] *L'Homme Libre*, June 10, 1914.

It would be interesting to unravel all the threads of this intrigue; St. Petersburg was involved, but the principal centre of its shrewd spinning was apparently Paris. Paléologue's intervention shows that in French and Russian official quarters war was regarded as inevitable and action was taken accordingly, even before the assassination of the Austrian Archduke. Jaurès had every right to ask, "Is France still her own mistress? Is she still a republic? Is she still a free nation? Or is she perhaps in bondage? And to whom?" (June 8th.) And what, at this moment, were the driving-wheels of the Russian governmental machine? "Germans, traitors, above and beneath. Ministers without responsibility. Rasputin was the keystone of this crumbling edifice."[1] There could be no severer condemnation of this intrigue of Paléologue or of the attitude of the men in power at the time in France.

Under the whip of reaction, however, opposition was raising its head in Russia. In May, Goremykin took away even from the tame Duma its right of interpellation and of putting questions to Ministers, and reduced its right of initiative. Deputies were prosecuted for speeches which were considered to contain attacks on the régime. Sixteen Socialist deputies were expelled. On May 23rd Milyukov had drawn the attention of the Foreign Minister to the growth of the spirit of chauvinism, which threatened a fresh catastrophe, and pointed out the danger involved in the control exercised by French finance over Russian policy. In June, several deputies, even among the Octobrists, criticized the promotions of certain inefficient generals, the corruption and waste in the army, its deplorable health record, the amazing ignorance of the officers, and the harsh treatment of the soldiers, whose hatred of their officers was becoming a danger to the defence of the country.[2]

---

[1] Ch. Rivet, *Le dernier Romanov*, pp. 128, 144.
[2] The Tsar and the King of Roumania met in the course of June at Constanza. Sazonov asked Bratianu what would be Roumania's attitude in the event of an armed conflict between Russia and Austria-Hungary if Russia were compelled by the course of events to take the initiative in the

Vandervelde, on his return from a visit to Russia in the middle of June, said that he had gained the impression of a régime of crushing severity, which weighed heavily upon all speech or political activity. It was a situation analogous to the White Terror of the French restoration. "But", he added, "it will not last. I brought away with me the vision of a proletariat superbly steeled in the struggle."[1]

For Paléologue, for France's rulers and governing class, the trouble was not in Russia but in France, in the attitude of the Socialists and the Radicals. The enemy was not Rasputin but Jaurès.

On June 28th came the Serajevo outrage, out of which arose the World War.[2]

resort to arms. He had great difficulty in soothing Bratianu's fears by assuring him that the only case in which Russia could not remain indifferent would be that of aggression against Serbia.—R. Martel, *L'Orient et la guerre d'après les archives diplomatiques russes*, in the *Monde Slave* for October 1926.                    [1] *Humanité*, June 21, 1914.

[2] On the subject of responsibility for this crime the *Correspondant* wrote as early as July 10, 1914: "Some have affected to believe that this double crime was the work of isolated anarchists. . . . It is obvious that to get such crimes committed it is not always possible to rely on official agents; in this case, indeed, that would have been too compromising. But *is fecit cui prodest*. There is not a Foreign Minister or ambassador of any Great Power—in London, Rome, Vienna, or Berlin—who is not perfectly well aware where the responsibility must be sought on that principle, and I have no doubt that the same may be said of the Quai d'Orsay. The crime bears the stamp of the same hand which had King Alexander and Queen Draga struck down, which had Stambulov killed in Sofia, which had Michael Obrenovich assassinated—to mention only a few of its atrocities.

"It is difficult to share the opinion of those who think that this event will avoid having consequences of the utmost gravity."

# CHAPTER XV

# RUSSIA AND THE WORLD WAR

POINCARÉ decided that he must go once more to Russia. Jaurès, almost as though he had a foreboding of the evil happenings that must follow, made an eloquent protest in the Chamber of Deputies on the vote of credit, going at length into the original intention of the Franco-Russian Alliance and the way it had been manipulated in recent years. He alleged that illegitimate use was made of such journeys as Poincaré's in entering into obligations in the name of France of which France had no cognizance, obligations which weighed even on her home policy. The allusion to the Three Years Act was clear. He refused more energetically than ever to countenance the practice and policy of secret treaties which, in virtue of clauses unrevealed, might be called into play in connection with Balkan affairs. "In our view", he said, "it is inexcusable to make France liable to be involved in mad schemes arising out of the tangled problems of the Near East, under treaties of which she knows neither the text nor even the purport, neither the limits nor the scope." He added that the more the Duma, under the working of the Russian counter-revolution, lost important rights and functions and powers of control, the more surely France on her side would be losing one of the guarantees that the treaty would at least be applied with prudence and wisdom, and not for schemes and intrigues in the Near East, the scope and repercussions of which might well be incalculable.

Viviani, the Prime Minister, declared that the history of the past twenty years had shown plainly that the Alliance was in accordance with the desires of the two countries and with their true interests:

Never has its efficacity been more clearly demonstrated than in the past two years. Thanks to it, the two countries have been able to maintain a close intimacy of thought and aims, with the object primarily of preventing conflicts, and secondarily of endeavouring to set a limit to them. It is a bulwark for the maintenance of peace, which is the best of all things provided that the two countries preserve it in independence and with dignity. I appeal to you to bear witness to your firm adherence to an inviolate Alliance.

The *Temps* regarded Jaurès' protest as part of a Socialist campaign for the upsetting of the existing alliances. But no patriotic Frenchman, it declared, could agree to a political *entente* with Germany. (July 9th.) Outside the Alliance with Russia there was "nothing but dangers and hazards for Democracy and for our country". (July 21st.)

The details of Poincaré's visit to Russia are well known. Paléologue has told the story with touching naïveté: the stout affirmations of the President of the Republic, particularly to Count Szápáry, the Austrian ambassador, and to Nicholas II; the characteristic toasts at Peterhof and Kronstadt; the vicarious warrior spirit of the Grand Duchesses Anastasia and Militza; and the state of mind of Paléologue himself.[1] "This story", wrote Denys Cochin, "troubles me and leaves me perplexed. . . . I know that those days in St. Petersburg were not the actual cause of the catastrophe, and that the awful mine was already laid; but these official receptions and conversations were part of the trail of powder that set it off."[2] What is less well known is the nature of the reception which the President of the Republic had from the Russian people. His arrival was marked by a revolutionary outbreak among the workers, who rose to the number of a quarter of a million

---

[1] For an account of the last days of July and the mobilization, see Paléologue's article in the *Revue des Deux Mondes* and his book *La Russie des Tsars pendant la Grande Guerre*. There are numerous discrepancies between the text of the article and that of the book; the latter introducing a number of important modifications and additions, mainly aimed at demonstrating the pacific intentions of the men in power in France, which were apparently not brought out sufficiently clearly in the first version. In the book certain phrases expressing exaggerated flattery of Poincaré or depreciation of Delcassé have been removed.

[2] *Figaro*, January 18, 1921.

in exasperation against Tsarist oppression. Jaurès greeted this move towards freedom with joy. "The task", he wrote, "is to fill the visitor with shame for his complaisance and his adulation of a régime which has filled the prisons and the convict settlements with countless martyrs."[1]

In the toasts Poincaré sang the praises of the Alliance as a powerful mainstay of European equilibrium; he spoke of the ideal of "peace with power, honour, and dignity". At the moment when he was telling the nobility and gentry of St. Petersburg that all classes in Russia had given their sincere assent to the *rapprochement* between the two countries, and assuring them that the diplomatic agreements had been ratified by public opinion, the movement among the working classes was becoming a real revolution. The general strike had begun, barricades sprang up, a hundred and fifty trams were destroyed, there were sanguinary collisions between workers and troops, and attempts were even made to set fire to the barracks. The position of the Government was becoming extremely insecure, and its fall, according to Alexinsky, seemed imminent.[2] But fortunately war, that effective diverter of men's minds, came just in time to save the situation for a little longer.

We do not propose to deal in detail with the diplomatic and military events which came hot on the heels of one another at the end of July 1914; to do this would carry us beyond the scope of this study. One thing only we would point out—that France came into the conflict in observance of the terms of the Alliance which bound her to Russia.

Before the ultimatum to Serbia, Poincaré had said to Viviani, in St. Petersburg: "Sazonov must stand firm, and we must support him." The French Government was already determined to fulfil in the Serbian affair all the obligations of the Alliance. Sazonov knew the attitude which Poincaré had taken up for two years past on this subject. Immediately after the delivery of the Austrian ultimatum, Sazonov stated to the

[1] *Humanité*, July 24th.　　　　[2] *Russie et la Guerre*.

British ambassador that if Russia felt she could rely on French support, she would contemplate the risks of war with equanimity. On July 27th, when Sazonov had definitely deprecated any offer of moderating counsel in St. Petersburg, declaring that the position he had taken up could not be modified in any respect, he received a telegram from Isvolsky saying that he (Isvolsky) had been struck by the calm and steadfast bearing of the French Ministers in their determination to accord to Russia the most entire support and to avoid the slightest sign of any divergence of view between the two countries. On the 28th, acting on instructions received from his Government, the French ambassador called on the Russian Foreign Minister to assure him that France was entirely ready to fulfil her obligations under the Alliance if the need should arise. On the 29th, Viviani reiterated to Isvolsky that the French Government was fully determined to act in agreement with Russia, and instructed Paléologue to tell Sazonov that Russia "may count entirely on the support of her ally France". On the 30th, at the moment when the Tsar, under pressure from Sazonov and Sukhomlinov, was issuing orders for a general mobilization "in order not to let the allies down", Viviani telegraphed to St. Petersburg that "France is determined to fulfil all the obligations which arise from the Alliance with Russia". Sazonov replied: "I knew I could rely on France." Finally, on July 31st, on learning of the German declaration of war on Russia, Poincaré declared to Isvolsky that he had no doubt as to the French Government's being prepared to demand from Parliament "the fulfilment of the obligations of the Alliance".

In short, the French Government had given the Russian Cabinet assurances of unlimited assistance even before the German mobilization began.[1]

[1] Paléologue, I, Chapter 1. British Blue Book, Nos. 6, 17. *Livre Noir*, II, pp. 280–282. Russian "Orange Book", Nos. 55–58. Stieve, *Isvolsky and the World War*, pp. 214–215. Day-book of the Russian Foreign Ministry. Buchanan, *My Mission to Russia*, pp. 196 sqq. Paléologue quotes a tele-

On August 3, 1914, Sir Edward Grey told the House of Commons that

The Government and the country of France . . . are involved in [the war] because of their obligation of honour under a definite Alliance with Russia.

The Tsar hastened to express his gratitude to France, who, he said, "in showing herself so faithful an ally, has given the world an unforgettable example of patriotism and loyalty". Paléologue commented that the French Government had earned these thanks "by the promptitude and determination with which it has fulfilled its duties as an ally".[1]

Yet Poincaré, who had stated on August 1st that he would rather see the initiative in the declaration of war taken by Germany, so as to avoid "a public debate on the application of the Treaty of Alliance",[2] claims that "*our Alliance had not been required to come into play*".[3] It is true that in this tragic crisis none of the representatives of the French people, either deputies or senators, displayed the slightest desire to ascertain the facts about the Franco-Russian military convention. On August 4th Viviani took the text of this convention to the Chamber of Deputies in case any member should ask for it to be laid on the table, but not a single deputy even put any question to him on the subject. The French Prime Minister in his narrative of events, and the French President in his message, alike ignored the Alliance and its obligations altogether; France's entry into the war was attributed to one sole cause—the "sudden, hateful, unheard-of" aggression of Germany, which forced upon France a war which she had not desired. "In face of Germany's aggression", wrote Poincaré in 1921, "everyone realized that the wanton attack of which we were victims robbed of all practical interest any examination

gram sent by the Tsar to the Kaiser on August 1st which began with the words: "I quite understand that you are obliged to mobilize".
[1] Paléologue, I, pp. 53–54.
[2] Isvolsky, telegram No. 222. *Livre Noir*, II, pp. 297–298.
[3] Lecture, February 16, 1921, on the origins of the war.

of the agreements come to twenty-two years before between France and Russia."

Yet it would have been interesting to learn what occurrence had led to Germany's declaration of war against Russia, and to know that the Russian general mobilization, ordered at 4 p.m. on July 30, was the first of the general mobilizations. Viviani's silence and Poincaré's statements are all the more peculiar when it is remembered that from 1917 onward the men in power in France were incessantly reminding Russia that France only entered the war in loyalty to the Alliance. Paléologue himself, who knew what he was talking about, said to Count Witte on September 12, 1914: "The world is in a welter of blood to-day for a cause which is primarily Russia's, a cause essentially Slav, a cause of no concern to France or to Britain." Again, on April 9, 1917, he said to Milyukov: "This frightful war broke out over a question of Slav politics. France hastened to your rescue without a moment's bargaining over the extent of her aid."[1]

One man alone would have been able to put questions in the Chamber and demand the needed explanations. But on August 4th he was no longer living. For two years Jaurès had in vain been sounding the alarm. In his speech at Vaise on July 25th he had shown up the responsibility of the various Governments in the issue. He had denounced "France's colonial policy, Russia's shifty tactics, and Austria's brutal obstinacy" as contributing "to create this horrible state of things", adding:

Citizens! If the storm were to burst, all of us Socialists would be concerned to extricate ourselves as quickly as possible from the effects of the crime which the rulers had committed; meanwhile, if we have still a few hours left, we shall redouble our efforts to prevent the catastrophe.[2]

On the 29th, at Brussels, he had declared that the duty of the

[1] Paléologue, I, pp. 119–120; III, p. 297.
[2] See Rappoport, *Jean Jaurès*, pp. 83, 87, and the Lyons *Avenir Socialiste*, No. 384, August 1–7, 1914.

Socialist party was to urge the French Government to speak strongly to Russia to induce her to abstain from the resort to force, and, if Russia took no notice, then

when we are reminded of the secret treaty with Russia we shall appeal to the public treaty which we have with humanity.[1]

In the hours that followed Jaurès made no secret of his alarm; he went about repeating his warnings, and imploring the advisers of the Government to insist that it should not give way to panic or surrender to the intriguings of Russian diplomacy. In the Chamber of Deputies, in the Salle des Quatre Colonnes, surrounded by deputies and journalists, he declared that: "This is Isvolsky revenging himself on Aehrenthal. Are we to allow war to break out because he is furious at being cheated of his commission in the Bosnia-Herzegovina affair?" As Malvy passed, he shouted to him: "Well, M. le Ministre, are you going to permit this—the France of the Revolution being dragged by *muzhiks* against Reformist Germany?" To some journalists he exclaimed: "What! Have we refrained for forty-four years from war for France, for Alsace-Lorraine, to go to war now for Serbia, for Russia?"[2]

On the afternoon of the 31st, finding no opportunity to meet Viviani, he made to the Under-Secretary of State for Foreign Affairs, Abel Ferry, a protest against the passivity of the French Government. Haunted by the fear that the Quai d'Orsay and the Elysée were acting as tools in the hands of Tsarist wirepullers, he reproached the Government with failing to speak with the needed firmness to Russia. Jean Longuet was present at this interview. "You are failing in your duty", Jaurès told Ferry. "Very well! I swear to you that if under such conditions you lead us into war, we shall rise against you, shout the truth to the people . . . even if you have to get us shot at the first street-corner."[3]

[1] *Humanité*, July 30, and Rappoport, *Causes occasionnels et permanentes de guerre.*     [2] E. Buré, in *Eclair*, July 31, 1921; Rappoport, pp. 30–33.
[3] Longuet in *Progrès Civique*, July 29, 1922.

That evening, when he was on his way to write for *Humanité* a long article in the vein of Zola's *J'Accuse*, in which he would have shown clearly where the whole responsibility lay, denouncing the Russian intrigue, its origins and its consequences, he was assassinated at a prearranged spot, in order to rid Isvolsky of an accuser and the Government of an opponent who, with his insight, his courage, his conscientiousness, no less than his influence over the working class of all Europe, would have been singularly troublesome.[1]

One has only to recall Jaurès' actions and to read his principal articles and speeches to be quite sure what he would have said and done. It is safe to assume that the rotting and bloodstained régime of Tsarism, which he had been denouncing all his life, as he had been denouncing the Alliance itself ever since 1904, would not suddenly have seemed to him to be transfigured, to be a rampart of Civilization, of Law and Order, of Freedom and Justice. These are impostures which he would not have been content merely to reject in horror.

For all the events of July and August 1914 we can only refer our readers to the works of Fabre-Luce, Demartial, Renouvin, Montgelas, Barnes, Morhardt, Gouttenoire de Toury, Pevet, and the rest. We do not share all the ideas and conclusions of certain of these writers. Nor do they claim to have written definitive history. They have contributed, however, their particular contention, their stone to the edifice

---

[1] The statement was made to E. Renauld that Jaurès intended to bring against Isvolsky, in a speech in the Chamber, grave charges in connection with Isvolsky's personal vendetta against Austria. (*Histoire populaire de la guerre*, I, p. 141.) Princess Paley has told of a luncheon-party at which Isvolsky was present on the morrow of the Austrian ultimatum to Serbia. "Isvolsky was unable to forget his defeat on the occasion of the annexation of Bosnia and Herzegovina, when Baron von Aehrenthal got the better of him, and was anything but displeased at the tension between Austria and Russia." (*Revue de Paris*, December 1, 1923.) J. Mesnil has related on good authority that Maître Labori, who was chosen as Public Prosecutor in the Villain case, declared in 1915 to several persons that he had proof that Jaurès was assassinated by the Russian police at the instigation of Isvolsky. The Russian police had, he said, merely made a tool of Villain.

which the historian of the future, far from the struggle and
its repercussions, will be able to construct at leisure, writing
with full knowledge of the documents in the archives of the
Ministry of Foreign Affairs, which are still inaccessible in
France, and setting down the truth with unclouded composure.
To have done as much as that is no small service; but they
have done more. At a time when those whose mission should
have been to search for truth[1] were silent or made themselves
the advocates of the official doctrine, these men said without
faltering what their conscience dictated. They may sometimes
have exaggerated, but, none the less, they represented at that
critical moment the greatest thing in the world—independence
of thought. When all were vacillating they did not waver, and
in spite of abuse their names will stand at the outset of any
impartial inquiry into this great problem.

As for the rest, who had not even the moral courage to
denounce the overwhelming responsibility of Tsarism in the
Balkan war, which led to the World War, and its equal
responsibility in July 1914—and whose silence or utterance,
whose reticences, quibbles, equivocations, excuses, and heavy-
witted irony only went, after all, to support official statements
which are becoming every day recognizably further divorced
from truth—may the burden of conscience rest lightly on
them![2]

This war, which France's rulers and her great newspapers
represented as desired by all Russia in the defence of the little
Slav brothers, was, as the *Correspondant* admitted, not expected
and still less desired by the Russian peasant; "if the whole
truth is to be told, he had not the slightest comprehension of

---

[1] As defined by Gaston Paris in his inaugural address at the Collège de
France during the war of 1870.

[2] Some, who affect to be admirers of Jaurès, but are very little interested
in the investigation of war guilt, may be reminded that in his *Histoire de la
guerre de 1870* Jaurès devoted 14 pages out of 241 to the description
of the military operations and 227 to the study of the question: "Who was
responsible for the war?"

what it was about". What cared he for the imperialist or Pan-Slav dreams of the townsmen? What meaning had those high-sounding names Constantinople and St. Sophia for him? What did he care for the little brothers? "He had scarcely heard of Germany, and if he had, it had generally been in friendly terms. Many of the peasants scarcely knew of the existence of France. The war, for them, was thus both unexpected and inexplicable." (July 10, 1916.)

Ludovic Naudeau also reports that in 1914 the Russian peasant was almost a complete stranger to patriotic feeling. It was, he adds, of much less importance for most of the Russians to win victories over neighbour peoples, "with regard to whom they had in reality no feeling of hatred whatever", than to hasten the downfall of the tyranny which was brutalizing them within their own frontiers. "And it was precisely to this state of feeling that political France obstinately refused to open its eyes at any price."[1]

Did not this, with the bankruptcy of the Alliance, completely dispose of the reasons for which France had entered the war? The fact did not prevent Raphael-Georges Lévy, a member of the *Institut*, from writing in the *Revue des Deux Mondes* (November 1, 1914):

The inhabitants of the Empire are marching with unanimous enthusiasm against the Germanic tyranny. Nothing resembling the revolutionary movements which accompanied and followed the struggle with Japan is to be feared. . . . The Russian budget has for a long time been in a satisfactory condition. . . . We may face the financial future on the banks of the Neva with as much confidence as the military future. The economic equipment of our allies is in no respect inferior to that of their troops.

Everyone knows what the war meant on the Russian side. It was not only a diversion seized on by a tottering Government, but an opportunity for the pitiless pursuit of its adversaries,

---

[1] *Les Dessous du Chaos Russe*, pp. 8, 12, 25. "The average Russian", wrote Ch. Rivet, "understood but little of the war, in which he had taken part only under the Tsar's orders." (*Le Dernier Romanof*, p. 326.)

Liberals, Socialists, Jews.[1] The Duma, which had been elected in accordance with the expressed policy of the Government, and which took an important share in the organization of industrial mobilization, lived amid perpetual threats to its existence. Paléologue's interviews with Ministers—Sheglovitov, Krishovein, Kulomzin—in 1915 revealed the madness of those in whose hands Russia was. The maintenance of autocracy and orthodox religion were dogmas which no one was allowed to challenge. Between rulers and ruled there opened a constantly deepening chasm.

The military and civil organization revealed from the first unmistakable symptoms of inevitable collapse. Paléologue notes that by December 1914 the artillery had already run out of ammunition and the infantry of rifles. Within the War Ministry itself a whole band of traitors were busy. Colonel Myassoyedov, formerly one of the most valued instruments of Tsarist reaction, was in personal touch with the German Emperor during the war; in the end he was arrested and executed. General Sukhomlinov, Minister of War from 1909 to 1915, himself sabotaged the manufacture of guns, ammunition, and rifles, was in touch with German agents, received enormous bribes from contractors, and refused to allow munitions to be sent into the country from France. General Yanushkevich declared in the course of the Sukhomlinov trial that hundreds of thousands of soldiers had been sent into battle with one rifle to every five or six men.[2]

An army commander wrote to the Chief of Staff in 1915: "Our army to-day, with its artillery and infantry reduced to silence, is being drowned in blood." The lives lost amounted to 350,000 to 450,000 men every month. On August 13, 1915, an ex-officer of the Guards said to Paléologue: "The army no

---

[1] Jews were forbidden to go for treatment to the urban first aid centres, and officers were forbidden to report cases of Jewish heroism at the front. —Ch. Rivet, *Le Dernier Romanof*, p. 155.

[2] See extracts from Sukhomlinov's diary, published in the *Matin*, December 2, 1922; Paléologue, I, p. 231.

T

longer has any belief in victory; it knows that it is sentenced to death as surely as a flock led to the slaughter-house. The day will come, perhaps soon, when there will be universal despair; the men will fight no longer, put up no more resistance." The Octobrist Guchkov declared to him: "Russia is lost, there is no more hope for her."

It was madness to suppose that in such conditions Russia would be able to carry on a prolonged war. Nothing but the amazing blindness of the men in power in France, all infatuated with their vision of complete victory, could make the idea credible. In October 1915 Lord Kitchener wrote to Millerand, who was then Minister of War: "The state of Russia is most alarming . . . there is treachery everywhere . . . the situation from the munitions point of view is dreadful and almost irremediable."[1]

Treachery even established itself at the head of the Government. Nicholas II made Sturmer Prime Minister. Sturmer delayed the dispatch of reinforcements to Roumania, and hence allowed her to be crushed. He was even prepared to agree to a partition of her territory if a separate peace could be made with the Central Empires. He was followed by Protopopov, a victim of general paralysis. The Tsar was reduced to a puppet in Rasputin's hands.[2]

During all this the French press went on concealing the truth from the public. Ch. Rivet was reduced to sending his articles to Swiss newspapers in order to make public some little of the truth about Russia. Yet Paléologue persisted in believing that the Russian people was resolutely determined to pursue the war until complete victory was attained. There was another thing yet more amazing. The more Tsarism advanced towards decomposition, with an army on the point of falling to pieces, the more illimitable became its plans of

---

[1] *Matin*, April 29, 1920. (Re-translated.)

[2] See the record of the Interrogation of Ministers, Councillors, Generals, etc., on the Extraordinary Commission of the Provisional Government of 1917.

conquest. The French Government, instead of restraining and advising moderation, encouraged the Russians in their folly.

It is only fair to observe that this Tsarist imperialism was the principal cause of the prolongation of the war. It is known now that at the beginning of August 1914 Turkey offered Russia a military alliance in consideration of the cession of part of Thrace and some of the Aegean islands. This would probably have changed the face of things and hastened the defeat of the Central Empires, but it would have meant putting off the day of the realization of the Russian dream of possession of the Straits and Constantinople. Sazonov accordingly gave a non-committal reply, without informing the French Government. The Russian Commander-in-Chief was also opposed to the suggested alliance. Not until August 15th and 16th, when it was too late, did Sazonov make up his mind to inform France and Britain of the matter. Isvolsky confined himself to mentioning it to Delcassé, who was not then a Minister; Delcassé remarked that the pourparlers with Turkey could not "carry us far". The proposal came to nothing because Russia imagined herself already mistress of the Straits and would not listen to it.[1] In such conditions it was very difficult for the Turks to believe in the sincerity of the Russian Government when, at the end of August 1914, it signed with Britain and France a declaration (limited to the duration of the war) guaranteeing the inviolability of Turkish territory.

Up to the time of Turkey's entry into the war, Russia, to avoid differences with Britain, contented herself with claiming the freedom of the Straits *with sufficient guarantees*, having the assurance of energetic support from France, who could be relied upon to "use her influence with England in the right

[1] See Aulard's article in the *Oeuvre*, March 3, 1927. Professor Shatzky makes no mention of these documents in his essay on "The question of Constantinople and the Straits, based on documents published by the Soviets", in the *Revue de l'Histoire de la Guerre Mondiale* for October 1926 and January 1927, nor of the result of the conference of February 1914, which showed clearly that the Tsarist Government's alleged "fervent desire" to avoid war with Turkey was non-existent.

direction". But the closing of the Straits and the Turkish attack made it possible for her to put forward more definite claims. At the beginning of November, Grey agreed, apparently in order to keep Russia among the combatants, that if Germany were crushed the fate of the Straits and Constantinople should undoubtedly be determined in accordance with Russia's interests, and King George said to Benckendorff: "It is clear that Constantinople should belong to you." On November 14th Buchanan, the British ambassador, said to Sazonov that the British Government had come round to the view that the questions of the Straits and of Constantinople ought to be determined in conformity with Russia's wishes. The Russian Government considered this statement insufficiently precise, and asked for a promise in more definite terms. This, however, it did not get; for an opportunity soon came of making peace with Turkey. Mehemet Ali, Commandant of the 1st Turkish Army Corps in Constantinople, offered to carry through a *coup d'état* and to break with Germany if the Allies would guarantee the integrity of Turkey. The British Government was inclined to agree to this, but Sazonov intimated that Russian claims in regard to the Straits had been considerably stiffened.[1]

On February 26, 1915, Sazonov telegraphed to Isvolsky a statement of the considerations which made for Russian annexation of the Straits, and defined the frontiers of the hinterland needed for their protection. On March 1st he demanded the annexation of Constantinople, and on the 3rd

---

[1] B. Shatzky, "La question de Constantinople et des Détroits", in the *Revue d'Histoire de la Guerre Mondiale* for October 1926 and January 1927: a study based on documents published by the Soviet Government. Paléologue I, pp. 192, 199 sqq. Buchanan, *My Mission to Russia*, I, pp. 224–25. The attack on the Dardanelles by the British and French forces made Russia somewhat uneasy. On February 26, 1915, Prince Trubetzkoy, Russian Minister to Serbia, telegraphed to Sazonov: "In my view the war against Germany and Austria and the alliance with France and Britain are but means to the attainment of this national end. The conquest of the Straits without us would be disastrous, and in this event Constantinople would become the gravestone of our existing alliance."

the Tsar declared to Paléologue: "I should give a radical solution to the problem of Constantinople and the Straits: the city of Constantinople and Southern Thrace must be incorporated in my Empire. . . . I agree to all that your Government may desire. Take the left bank of the Rhine, take Mainz, take Coblentz, go farther still if you think fit."

On the following day Sazonov sent to the British and French ambassadors a memorandum expressing the desire to add to Russia as a result of the war the following territories: Constantinople, the western shore of the Bosphorus, the Sea of Marmora and the Dardanelles, Southern Thrace up to the Enos-Midia line, the coast of Asia Minor between the Bosphorus and the river Sakaria, with certain points on the Gulf of Ismid, the islands in the Sea of Marmora, and the islands of Imbros and Tenedos. In addition, there were demanded in Asia Minor the provinces of Erzerum, Trebizond, Van, and Tiflis, and the territories of Southern Kurdistan.[1]

Delcassé is understood to have asked from Russia a promise to guarantee the entire freedom of the Straits, through the setting up of a European Control Commission. Sazonov replied that the Russian people would accept no other solution than the undivided sovereignty of Russia over Constantinople and the Straits.[2]

Prince Trubetzkoy, Russian Minister to Serbia, wrote to Sazonov on March 9th:

The Straits should belong to us. If we can obtain them with France and Britain against Germany, so much the better. If not, it will be better to obtain them with Germany against the others. If there were a failure over this question, all Russia would ask us why our brothers' blood has been shed.[3]

Yet France had entered the war in loyalty to the Alliance for

[1] E. Laloy, *Documents secrets publiés par les Bolcheviks*, pp. 107–110.

[2] R. Martel, *L'Orient et la Guerre d'après les Archives diplomatiques russes*, in *Le Monde Slave*, October 1926, pp. 135–136. Letter from Isvolsky, March 6th; from Sazonov, March 7th.

[3] Martel, p. 134. Cf. Rosen, *Forty Years of Diplomacy*, II, pp. 102–103.

the sake of Serbia! Her representatives might have recalled to the memory of the Russian Government the declarations made to Ribot by de Giers in 1891–1892 on the subject of Constantinople and the Straits.

On March 8th Paléologue declared to Sazonov, on the strength of a telegram from Delcassé, that he could count on the good will of the French Government for the settlement of the question of Constantinople and the Straits in conformity with Russia's views. Sazonov thanked him effusively in the following terms: "Your Government has rendered to the Alliance an incalculable service, the full importance of which you perhaps do not suspect." On March 12th Buchanan informed the Tsar of Britain's acquiescence in the memorandum of March 4th. In return, Russia recognized the incorporation of the neutral zone in Persia in the British zone. On the same day Buchanan transmitted the written consent of the British Government to the annexation of Constantinople and the Straits, subject to the condition that the war was brought to a successful termination and that the British and French aims were realized. Among the latter were Mesopotamia for Britain and Syria for France. On April 10th Paléologue transmitted an identical note to the two Powers.[1]

These commitments seemed to be necessary to prevent Russia from making a separate peace. Sir Francis Bertie wrote in his *Diary*:

> The Russians, who are in want of rifles, are showing a ravenous appetite and nobody says them nay.[2]

Soon, however, in face of the Russian reverses, the folly of the dream of Constantinople began to be realized even in

---

[1] Paléologue, I, pp. 312 sqq. Buchanan, *My Mission to Russia*, I, pp. 224 sqq. "Give Russia all she wants", was the watchword. "We know", wrote Gauvain, "that such independent publicists as ventured to criticize, in private conversation, the work of Russian diplomacy, had a reception which made further conversation difficult". (*Journal des Débats*, September 28, 1918.)    [2] Vol. I. p. 131.

Russia. General Alexeyev, with the assistance of Prince Kubashev, the head of the Imperial chancellery, began to advocate a separate peace with Turkey, in order to set free the Caucasus army for service against Germany, the principal adversary, whom it was of prime importance to defeat. "Any other aim is a mirage; it is more important to recover Courland than to seize the Straits." This was only possible if the dreams of Constantinople and the Straits were abandoned, at least for the time. It might have meant salvation. But the Tsar and Sazonov would not hear of it.[1]

Meanwhile "public opinion" in Russia was veering round. In June 1916 Paléologue observed in political circles in St. Petersburg a strange tendency to dismiss the idea of annexing Constantinople and the Straits. It was argued, with good reason, that annexation, far from solving the Near East question, would postpone a solution indefinitely, for neither Germany nor Austria nor the Danube States would ever resign themselves to leaving the keys to the Black Sea in Russia's hands. The essential thing for Russia was to assure herself freedom of passage through the Straits by the creation of a neutral State guaranteed by the Powers. Accordingly, when, on December 2nd, Trepov declared in the Duma that "the agreement made in 1915 with Britain and France definitely established Russia's right to the Straits and Constantinople", and that "the Russian people must know why it was shedding its blood", the phrases were received in dead silence, "a silence born of indifference and surprise". The public was equally unresponsive: "There was the same effect of indifference and astonishment", notes Paléologue, "as if Trepov had exhumed an old utopia, once cherished, but long since forgotten." Shortly afterwards he remarked that the Russian people had "long since renounced the Byzantine dream".[2]

The Russian people was thinking of peace, and knew that

---

[1] See B. Shatzky, January 1927.
[2] Paléologue, II, 293–294; III, 105–107.

this dream could only postpone it. In Paris, Trepov's declaration produced the opposite impression, a very favourable one. It was just this moment, on the eve of the Russian revolution, that the French Government chose for securing from the Tsar the express promise to have inserted in the treaty of peace a clause giving France full liberty to determine the fate of the territory on the left bank of the Rhine, in return for the recognition of Russian claims to Constantinople and the Straits. It was felt to be necessary to bind the Russian Government by a written and detailed agreement. To this end Doumergue set off for Russia, accompanied by General de Castelnau, Lord Milner, and Scialoja. On February 15, 1917, Doumergue was received by the Tsar. He referred to the various aspects of the question of the left bank of the Rhine, political, military, economic, and, quoting the engagements entered into on November 21, 1914, and March 13, 1916, he announced that the French Government had determined to include among the conditions of peace to be imposed on Germany the following stipulations:

(1) Alsace-Lorraine to return to France. (2) Its frontiers to extend at least to the limits of the former Duchy of Lorraine, so as to incorporate the Saar basin in French territory. (3) The remaining territory on the left bank of the Rhine to be entirely detached from Germany politically and economically. (4) The territory not incorporated in France to form an autonomous and neutralized State, occupied by French troops until the guarantees demanded by the Allies had been brought into effect.

The Rhine was, in fact, in future to constitute a strong strategic frontier. Doumergue expressed the hope that the Russian Government would not refuse to give its formal consent to these proposals. The Tsar gave them his unqualified approval.[1]

[1] For the Doumergue Mission, see E. Cordonnier, *Autour d'une Mission Française en Russie pendant la Grande Guerre* (1917), which appeared in part in the *Revue* for August 1917.

In return, Russia's claim to Constantinople and the Straits was formally recognized. Paléologue subsequently sent to Pokrovsky a letter containing the French conditions of peace, and asked the support of the Russian Government towards their realization. Pokrovsky replied that France might count on the Imperial Government's support. In informing Isvolsky of this interview, Pokrovsky took occasion to recall to his memory the view expressed by the Russian Government on February 26, 1916, that complete liberty should be allowed to Britain, France, and Russia in determining their respective frontiers with Germany and Austria. "It would be well", he added, "to take the opportunity to ask the French Government to reiterate its consent to Russia's freedom of action in fixing her future western frontiers." Sazonov demanded in addition that the Polish question should be excluded from international settlement. On March 11, 1917, Isvolsky reported the French Government's agreement, in the following terms:[1]

The Government of the Republic, desiring to emphasize the significance and importance of the treaties concluded in 1915 with the Russian Government with the object of settling the question of Constantinople and the Straits, at the end of the present war, in conformity with the Russians' aspirations, and desiring also to furnish its ally with all the guarantees, both military and industrial, which are desirable for the security and economic development of the Empire, recognizes Russia's entire liberty in the determination of her western frontiers.[2]

Ribot has disclosed that Doumergue "did not feel authorized"

[1] M. Briand was then Prime Minister.
[2] Secret telegrams Nos. 507 and 168. Paléologue, III, pp. 176 sqq. R. Martel, in *Monde Slave* for October 1926, pp. 139–140. Kerensky stated in a lecture in Paris on March 11, 1920, that this reply, intended for the Tsar, was received by the Russian Provisional Government.
On February 21st Pokrovsky proposed in a long report to the Tsar that an expedition 250,000 strong should be dispatched in October 1917 to take possession of the Straits in anticipation of the conclusion of peace, as, if the British and French were to gain successes on the western front which secured results satisfactory to them, there was very little likelihood of getting them to continue the war for the sake of Constantinople and the Straits.

to admit Lord Milner to the secret of the mission which he had to fulfil with the Tsar. Consequently the letters exchanged at St. Petersburg remained unknown to Lord Milner and were not communicated to the British Government, which was able to declare to the House of Commons that it had known nothing of the secret agreements between France and Russia and had not approved them.[1]

The *Correspondant* wrote in July 1918: "The war has become a war of conquest. The publication of the secret treaties has provided irrefutable proof of this. It is puerile to attempt to deny it."[2]

Yet the *Temps* expressed its gratification on March 5, 1917, at the important political and military results that had been obtained from the Petrograd conference. There had, it said, been an important advance towards unity of views and action; the Allies were progressively perfecting the concerted utilization of their resources and means of action. And this at the very moment when, on Paléologue's own admission, revolution was threatening, the Russian people was refusing to take further interest in the war, and the spirit of anarchy was spreading in all classes! It was impossible to rely on the army to deal with a rising. Already, on October 31, 1916, two regiments brought up to intimidate the strikers had fired on the police. "My conclusion", said Paléologue to Doumergue, as the latter was leaving Petrograd, "is that time is not on our side, at all events in Russia; from now onwards we must reckon with the probability of the defection of our ally, and base our whole programme on the recognition of this."[3]

---

[1] A. Ribot, *Lettres à un ami*, pp. 223–224.

[2] July 10, 1918. Mr. Austin Harrison wrote in the *English Review* of April 1918: "The louder we talk of 'crushing militarism,' the greater the power of militarism reveals itself. The fiercer men denounce imperialism, the more intense it shows its Hydra reality."

The *Correspondant* had written on August 25, 1917, that for two centuries Tsarist Russia had been "the chief disturbing factor in Europe".

[3] Paléologue, III, p. 198.

On his return from this mission to Russia, Doumergue told the *Petit Parisien*, with delightful optimism (March 6th):

Agreement has been complete. How could it have been otherwise? We all had the impression of being gathered in a family circle. The Entente is more intimate than ever. Russian collaboration has never changed and will not change.

He was still more explicit in an interview with a representative of the *Matin*:

I have brought back an excellent impression from my journey. . . . It is clear from all the conversations that I had and all that I saw that Russia is filled with a unanimous will to pursue the war to a complete victory.

The *Matin* emphasized the "tone of absolute conviction" in which Doumergue had spoken. This was on March 12th. Next day France learned of the collapse of Tsarism in face of a revolution aimed against the war.

# CHAPTER XVI

## THE ALLIANCE AND THE RUSSIAN REVOLUTION

THIS book is not concerned with the details of the Russian
Revolution or with its historical significance. Some light has,
however, been shed on its causes in the ·preceding chapters.
Just as the 1905 Revolution arose out of the Russo-Japanese
War, so the Revolution of 1917 was a direct result of the
Great War. Its immediate author was the Workers' and
Soldiers' Soviet of Petrograd, which was an embodiment of
the will of the common man—artisan, peasant, private. The
Duma, the product of a corrupt electoral system, which had
forfeited all prestige by its subservience to the Administration,
followed the popular movement, but only half-heartedly and
after having attempted to salvage the monarchical principle
by offering the throne, from which Nicholas II had abdicated,
to the Grand Duke Michael. In Maklakov's words, "the
victory was won, not by the Duma, but by the revolutionary
rank and file".[1] This was the exact opposite of the views
generally held in France at the time.

The Soviet, which was the true representative of the masses,
was bound to take the lead in face of the impotence and lack
of authority of the Duma. What is more, the first Provisional
Government would have been quite incapable of directing the
movement and would have collapsed within an hour if the
Soviet had not supported it. The latter could have brushed it
aside and seized the reins of government itself had not the
leaders thought it necessary to stand in with the Cadets.

The essential objects of the Revolution were, first, to bring
an end as speedily as possible to the war foisted upon the
people by the old régime, and, second, to inaugurate radical
measures of social reform. Paléologue reports that, as early as
March 14th, the main slogan and battle-cry of the Soviet was

[1] *Revue de Paris*, October 1, 1924.

"Peace and Social Revolution".[1] And a few months later the *Correspondant* stated clearly that "all our speculations about Russia must start from the basic fact that the Petrograd rising of March 1917 was a mass movement directed against the war".[2] As Ludovic Naudeau has written, "the *muzhiks* were tired of fighting without weapons for war aims which to them were meaningless".[3] But the French Republic was once more misled, and on this occasion more grossly perhaps than ever before. Russia's violent demonstration of protest against the war was interpreted by the French Government, the French press, and even the French Socialist leaders, as an outburst of outraged patriotism, and all France's mentors laboured to convince her that the Russian people had revolted with the object of insisting on a more resolute prosecution of the war against Germany. Notwithstanding the fact that all the Russian Socialist groups, under the chairmanship of Kerensky, had issued a unanimous statement as far back as the end of 1915 to the effect that the nation was "heartily sick of the war" and out of sympathy both with the motives of those who had brought it about and the aims they were pursuing, and that "the time was not far distant when Russia would be compelled to repudiate her treaty obligations and make a separate peace",[4] the French Socialist Ministers, Guesde, Sembat, and Thomas, welcomed the Revolution by sending Kerensky a telegram containing the following phrases:

Let us now join hands to prosecute the war to the bitter end, until Prussian militarism is finally crushed. France hails with joyful confidence the redoubled efforts of the Russian people, now wholeheartedly bent on carrying the struggle to a successful conclusion. Victory will soon reward our zeal and restore peace to the nations of the world, with permanent guarantees for their welfare and their liberty.

---

[1] Paléologue, III, p. 230. Cf. Buchanan, *Memoirs*, pp. 177 sqq.

[2] October 10, 1917. The same journal had written prophetically on July 10, 1916, that, "with the restless instability of the Russian temperament, there is always a danger of over-confidence in success changing suddenly, after a number of setbacks, into exaggerated despair, followed by an uncontrollable desire to put an end to the struggle".

[3] *Illustration*, April 12, 1924.     [4] Paléologue, II, p. 148.

Not to be outdone, Renaudel, the editor of *Humanité*, also sent a message by telegram:

We are relying on the Russian proletariat, after dealing with disloyalty at home, to renew the national effort to crush the forces of darkness abroad.[1]

---

[1] The French *Ligue des Droits de l'Homme* organized a big public meeting on April 1st in honour of the Russian Revolution, which was attended by more than six thousand people. Vandervelde was one of the speakers, but when he asserted that "we are more determined than ever to carry on the war against those who provoked it, and we are justified in saying to the Russian people that their task is not yet finished"—his voice was drowned in protests, and he was obliged to sit down. Neither Jouhaux nor Renaudel could make himself heard, but Séverine restored quiet by expressing the real feelings of the audience, speaking of peace and good will, and of the longing for that freedom which the Russian people had now won, but of which the French nation had been deprived for the past three years. (*Journal du Peuple*, April 3, 1917.) Earlier in the meeting, pro-war homilies had been delivered by Victor Bérard, Victor Basch, and Aulard under a running fire of interruptions. The speeches should be read in full in the *Bulletin* of the League (July 1–15, 1917). Aulard declared that the Russian patriot felt as keenly as the French of the Revolutionary era had done, that the first duty of the Revolution was to expel the foreign invader. Basch was especially positive:

"We are profoundly convinced, in fact we are certain, that both the Provisional Government and the popular bodies in Russia, fortified by the unshakable will of the nation as a whole, will now march forward to victory with renewed energy, grimmer determination, clearer vision, cooler judgment, sounder organization; that we shall see no more of that pro-German vacillation; that the entire nation, elated with the new wine of independence, will now rise as one man against the aggressor."

Séverine commented shortly afterwards on the twofold mistake made by the League in a remarkable article in the *Journal du Peuple*:

"The League has no idea how widespread certain views have become. There are some among its members who could enlighten it if they would, but they mislead it because, in their hostility to those views, they shut their eyes to their obvious and undeniable growth. The university intelligentsia who control the League did emerge from their ivory tower to deal with the Dreyfus case, but since then the shades of the study have closed about them almost entirely. From their exalted observatory they may command extensive vistas, but the immediate foreground is obscured."

They had been ill-advised to attempt to hold an open meeting.

"The demonstration of feeling was an entirely spontaneous outburst. These 'drunken helots cowering in their dens' have come forth, walking upright, with clear eyes and cool brains, and they simply refuse to listen henceforward to certain men, refuse even to look at them. That is the whole truth." (*Journal du Peuple*, April 12, 1917.)

Paléologue had no difficulty in persuading Milyukov, the Russian Foreign Minister, of the genuine warmth, determination, and will to victory expressed in these appeals.[1]

As a result of this complete lack of understanding of Russia's real character, opinion in France clung to certain entirely fictitious notions suggested by self-interest and ambition, and, what is more, tried to foist them on the Russians themselves. They were France's allies, whose function was to hold up half the total number of enemy divisions on the Eastern front; they were simply not recognized in any other rôle. But those allies were men worn out, body and soul, by repeated defeat and base betrayal; a human mass quivering from three years' continuous butchery, but still full of proliferating life; a nation that had been hurled against its will into a war it did not understand, but which had now had its revolution. French egoism would fain have shut its eyes to these facts, have cried halt to the march of events at the point at which they threatened to neglect French interests, have enforced the claim that the requirements of the war were paramount, demanding the last sacrifice from everyone. But reality was more complex than that. As far back as 1897, Anatole Leroy-Beaulieu had prophesied that the transition from absolutism to responsible government could not take place without a violent upheaval, and had emphasized that "a revolution in Russia would be characterized by entirely novel and original features unlike anything to be expected from other continental nations. . . . Since it would almost inevitably tend to develop into a kind of agrarian Socialism, it could not fail to differ from anything of the sort previously experienced elsewhere."[2] Yet the statesmen and the governing classes in France were blind to the meaning of the Revolution when it came. Politicians and professors alike persisted in maintaining that it was following in all respects the precedents of the French Revolution.

[1] Paléologue, III, p. 257.
[2] *L'Empire des Tsars et les Russes*, II, pp. 622–625.

Actually, as already mentioned, not only the Soviet, but also the majority of the Provisional Government, in harmony with the deepest aspirations of the Russian people, turned their minds from the outset towards securing peace—not a separate peace, but a general peace. In the words of the Soviet manifesto of March 28th, "the democracy of Russia urges all the nations of the world to make a combined effort to set on foot negotiations for universal peace", and, as a first step, it proposed to convene an international conference. Three-fourths of the Soviet, as Ribot admitted, were opposed to the continuation of the war. On April 10th, in a solemn proclamation, the Provisional Government announced that:

Russia, having attained her freedom, now aims, not at dominating other nations or robbing them of their national heritage or taking possession of foreign territory, but at establishing permanent peace in the world on the basis of the right of every people to determine their own fate. . . . The Russian nation does not desire to enslave or humiliate anyone.

This pronouncement was by no means to the taste of the French ambassador, who went to Milyukov in indignation: "What! no mention of the determination to carry on the struggle to the bitter end, until complete victory is attained! No mention of Germany! No mention of our war aims!"[1] Milyukov consequently felt constrained to send out the proclamation accompanied by a commentary of his own which seriously weakened its effect: the will of the nation to carry the war to a successful conclusion was more resolute than ever; the Provisional Government would adhere scrupulously to all the agreements concluded with the Allies, and would insist on guarantees and "sanctions" for a lasting peace.[2] But the Soviet promptly sent a memorandum to the Government

[1] Ribot, p. 228. Paléologue, III, pp. 256–257. Cf. Chernov on "The Petrograd Soviet", in the *Revue de Paris*, August 1, 1917.

[2] In Milyukov's view, the Dardanelles should have been taken over as an integral part of the Russian Empire and kept strictly closed to warships of all other countries. (*Vide* his article in the *Journal*, December 12, 1916.)

protesting against any attempt to solve present problems by methods smacking of the Tsarist régime and demanding the opening up of peace negotiations on the basis of "no annexations and no indemnities". A storm broke over Milyukov's head, and on May 16th he was obliged to resign. In any case, by its declaration of April 10th, the Government had placed the Allies in the position of being forced to define their war aims, and from thenceforward France and Russia began to drift steadily apart.[1] Some idea of the gulf which opened up between the new Russian democracy and the French ruling class can be gained from a survey of the chief organs of the French press which reflected official opinion.

It will be remembered that, right up to the Revolution, it had been regarded as a kind of point of honour in France not to interfere in the domestic affairs of Russia, even when Sturmer, by his betrayal of Roumania, showed obvious signs of engineering a separate peace with Germany, and when Rasputin had become the real ruler in Russia. Prior to 1914, indeed, whenever any member of the Chamber of Deputies raised his voice against the orgy of execution by rope and bullet which was raging in Russia, against the prevailing corruption which contained the seeds of disaster, or against the massacres of Jews organized by the Russian Government, authoritative speakers among the parties of the Centre and the Right, supported by the Radical Ministers Delcassé and Pichon, silenced the protest by declaring that those were matters of Russian domestic policy which France had no right to criticize. But no sooner had the Revolution broken out than the French press—subject all the time, be it remembered, to Government censorship—took up a very different standpoint, adopting one

[1] When Cachin, Moutet, and Lafont visited Russia, they were asked, together with the English Socialist visitors, to explain how it was that the French and British Socialists were so much concerned with regard to nationalities oppressed by other countries than their own and so little with those under the yoke of Great Britain and France. The catechism grew so warm that Cachin quite anticipated that the visitors would have to take their departure. (Ribot, p. 231. Paléologue, III, p. 303.)

U

after the other arguments such as these: France welcomes the Russian Revolution only in so far as it connotes an intensification of the conduct of the war and of the pursuit of the war aims already agreed upon between the Allies; a political revolution is all very well, so long as it is "nationalist" and bellicose, but no social revolution is acceptable—and attempts were at once made to fix the limits which the Revolution must not presume to overstep on pain of becoming a "Boche manœuvre" and hence beyond the pale. From the earliest days, moreover, the Paris press and the leading politicians maintained an attitude of surly suspicion, characterized by incessant reproofs, attacks, even insults, *vis-à-vis* the Workers' and Soldiers' Council, which was the real protagonist of the Revolution, though French statesmen persisted in attributing this rôle to the Duma.

And then, embroidering on these themes, the whole doctrine of Counter-Revolution gradually took shape as events progressed—a doctrine which was definitely anti-democratic, not to say imperialist, and harmonized very closely with those principles of reactionary authoritarianism, of dictatorship, against which the French nation had always protested at every election for half a century past and which had been represented as the chief enemy it was engaged in fighting. Under cover of the war, those elements which had always been compelled to take refuge in obscurity, which had always been defeated at the polls, had obtained a firm footing in the real government of the country, and were now propagating their views in every department of public life—views which were essentially at variance with the true aspirations of the people. For instance, while the press still went on repeating that the nation was fighting for the right of self-determination for all peoples, the semi-official journalists, led by Joseph Reinach, raised violent protests against the abandonment by the new régime in Russia of the Tsarist designs on Constantinople.

Tereshchenko, the new Russian Foreign Minister, was bent

on securing the earliest possible conclusion of peace between all the belligerents, without annexations or indemnities, on the basis of the proclamation issued on April 10th. Expressing the deepest instincts of the Russian people, he announced that the new Democracy was "afraid of being a cat's-paw in annexationist aims of no interest to itself if it remained bound by the old treaties, and that this fear was disturbing its self-confidence and sapping its energies". To make the agreements public without more ado would be equivalent to breaking with the Allies, and this would lead to a separate peace. Accordingly, Kerensky and Tereshchenko, chiefly concerned with the agreements negotiated by Doumergue in February 1917, suggested to the Allies that negotiations should be commenced with a view to reaching a mutual understanding and revising the Allied war aims.[1]

It would seem as though such a proposal, showing that Russia had abandoned designs which were calculated to prolong the conflict and stiffen the resistance of the Central Powers, ought to have met with a favourable reception from the Government of the Republic, especially as the British Government replied on May 9th that they were "quite ready to review the agreements".[2] But Clemenceau and his Cabinet, together with all the semi-official press, refused point-blank to consider any revision of war aims and replied that France required "pledges" and "guarantees", vague terms open to the widest interpretation and evidently synonymous in the French view with the

---

[1] Detailing his views, Tereshchenko explained that he visualized "a just peace, which would leave no traces after the war of hatred or estrangement, such as always subsist where one nation emerges from the struggle enriched at the expense of others, or where one nation is overwhelmed and forced to sign a humiliating peace. Wanton injury and injustice are never forgotten. Violence breeds hatred. . . ." (*Temps*, May 22nd.) Cf. his statement to Albert Thomas on June 16th: "Russia aims at establishing peace throughout the world on a basis which will preclude any measures of violence from any quarter, and also any imperialist designs however disguised. The Russian people are desirous of realizing their ideals of equality and justice, not only in their own internal affairs, but also in international relationships."

[2] Ribot, *Lettres d un ami*, pp. 236–237.

left bank of the Rhine. At the same time Paléologue wrote that France must insist with the utmost firmness on the maintenance of the agreements with Russia and reaffirm her determination to pursue the war to a definitely victorious conclusion.[1] This policy was regarded as very shrewd, but it undoubtedly resulted both in alienating the sympathy of Russia and in increasing Germany's resolution. Further, the French Government denounced with savage vigour as a Boche manœuvre the idea of a Conference at Stockholm, to which Branting had invited the Socialists of all the belligerent Powers, and, whereas Lloyd George was disposed to allow the British Socialists to attend,[2] the French were refused passports and abused as German hirelings. The Government went still further, and made it appear as though Kerensky were hostile to the Conference, whereas he had specially announced his support of it.

During all this period, and right up to the time of the Bolshevik Revolution, the leading statesmen of France were constantly calling upon Kerensky to take his stand against the Soviet, the prime mover of the Revolution, and to dissolve it by force. Finally, despairing of accomplishing this, they gave open support to Kornilov's military conspiracy against the Provisional Government itself, hoping that, if Kornilov succeeded in becoming dictator, he would be able to compel his countrymen to continue the war to the bitter end. This attitude, combined with the sanguinary defeat of the Galicia offensive undertaken at the behest of the Allies, and the shelving of the land question—which, as Prince Lvov admitted, was the only real concern of the Russian people besides the conclusion of peace—is enough to explain the triumph of the Bolsheviks. The foolish obstinacy of the French rulers played straight into the hands of the apostles of violence. And this campaign synchronized with the Malvy and Caillaux cases in home politics. These, again, sprang from the

---

[1] Paléologue, III, pp. 315-316.    [2] Ribot, pp. 257-358.

same causes, displayed the same mentality, produced the same effects.

Let us cast a rapid glance at the chief organs of the French press and the statements of the leading politicians during the period from March to October 1917. From these we shall obtain a good idea of the attitude of officialdom in France towards the Russian Revolution. We will take first the *Action Française*, which was fated to exercise such a decisive influence on the French Government in that year. On the eve of the Revolution, Bainville, in an article entitled "No Humbug!", asserted that he did not believe in the likelihood of a Revolution, as there were no real revolutionaries in Russia. All reliable information available as to the state of opinion there went to support the general impressions gleaned by Doumergue. The Revolution broke out on the following day, but Bainville, unabashed, maintained that it was a mere repetition of 1830, a pseudo-revolution. "The present crisis is unique in that it has been precipitated by purely patriotic motives."(March 17th.) It was a nationalist revolt. (This idea was developed in a long article in the *Revue des Deux Mondes* for April 15th.) Léon Daudet, piqued at his colleague's success as a prophet, asserted that all intelligent observers must have been struck by the obviously nationalist and anti-German character of the Russian Revolution. (March 19th.) Bainville went on to deplore Russia's renunciation of her designs on Constantinople. "A Russian Revolution without Constantinople would be like France's Revolution without expansion to her natural boundaries." He confessed that it would be preferable to avoid reducing the issues of the war to questions of principle, for fear it might not last very long. Go on being shot at for the sake of Justice and International Morality? A poor prospect, according to him. He had enough vision to see that the average Frenchman had been disturbed in his mind by the Revolution in Russia. "France is an essentially Conservative country. Formerly, revolution in other lands had no terrors for her. The word seemed as natural as the thing itself." (April 20th.)

Gradually Bainville's eyes were opened. He realized that Russia had no real fear of the German peril. He criticized his fellow-countrymen for their self-deception in regard to the Russian Alliance. The *muzhik* had much less veneration for the Tsar than a French peasant had. France was still clinging to the effete conceptions of a past age. "The fact is that we contracted an Alliance with a Russia in decay, whose prestige was already crumbling, to all eyes but our own. A more accurate estimate of her real situation would have helped us to strike the right note in the framing and management of the Alliance." These were words of wisdom, but came, alas! five years, ten years too late. "In 1917, as in 1892, we have to deal, and come to a working agreement, with Russia as she is, not as we should like her to be." (September 14th.) This was sound advice, but, alas! was not followed. If only the Radical Ministers of the Republic had taken warning from this counsel from a Royalist regarding revolutionary Russia!

The *Liberté* regarded the Revolution as complete as soon as the events of March 17th had taken place. "Russia has now experienced her 1789, or rather, perhaps, her 1830. We sincerely trust that her imitation of France will not extend to a repetition of 1793."

Hervé wrote that the internment of the Tsar had "somewhat taken us aback" in France. From April 8th onwards he advised the Provisional Government to "perform a surgical operation" on the Workers' and Soldiers' Council. Later on, he deplored the fact that Constantinople was not "in Russia's pocket" (July 29th), and condemned the Soviet for having raised the land question instead of postponing it until after victory had been won. (August 6th.) He advised Kerensky to suppress any paper and court-martial any writers that dared to talk of peace, and to suspend the right of public meeting. (September 6th.) Finally, he wished Kornilov luck in his military adventure.

Lysis, in Hervé's journal, denounced the "pacifist Utopia embodied in the amazing humbug of a League of Nations". (July 7th.)

In the *Echo de Paris*, Jean Herbette wrote that "the Petrograd peace-mongers must be amply provided with funds from Germany." (March 31st.) Russia's destiny demanded that she should occupy Constantinople, and any hesitation or drawing back would constitute a danger and a complication. (April 29th.) Shortly afterwards, Pertinax, incensed at Kerensky's weakness, called for a Government which would concentrate on the prosecution of the war (September 11th), and lamented Kornilov's failure. In the *Revue des Deux Mondes* (April 1st), Charles Benoist regretted that the Russian Revolution had not been checked at an earlier stage. "We shall assess its power for good by the degree of improvement it brings to the military resources of the Allies." He referred appreciatively to "the Tsar's scrupulous loyalty", and denounced the Soviet as a "parasitic organ". Gauvain, in the *Journal des Débats*, maintained that the Revolution was directed against Germany. Later, he advised the press of the Allied countries to decline to accept the assertions of the Workers' and Soldiers' Council as representing the will of the people, and deplored the abandonment of the claim to Constantinople. (March 20th, May 9th, and May 18th.)

To turn over the files of the *Temps* is to discover the secret thoughts at the time of the Quai d'Orsay and of the French ruling class, then firmly in the saddle. The entire Russian nation, stanchly maintaining a magnificent social *union sacrée*, was determined to fight on to victory. (March 6th–15th.) A Constituent Assembly was all very well, but a Tsar was a necessity. But soon the very idea of a Constituent Assembly became a bogy, and the Russians were urged to concentrate on "avenging the wrongs of the last fifty years". (March 20th and 21st.) Later on, the almost daily theme was abuse of the Soviet as self-elected, unrepresentative "fanatics". When the

Russian Government called for a revision of war aims, the official attitude was to decline to enter into any discussions of the subject, since that would entail the grave disadvantage of either setting limits to legitimate ambitions in the event of victory in the war, or else disclosing aims which could hardly be reconciled with the right of self-determination. Accordingly, the *Temps* took the line that it was idle to discuss peace terms until one was in a position to impose them on the enemy. (May 28th.) For instance, "the liberation of Alsace-Lorraine, and the *determination, at our own discretion, of the guarantees* that it will be necessary to secure *against German aggression in the future*—these are claims which no spokesman of France could ever allow even to be discussed".

Ribot, the Prime Minister, bowing to the keen desire for peace of the majority in the parties of the Left, did accept on May 24th, in the Chamber of Deputies, a motion limiting French war aims to the recovery of Alsace-Lorraine and a demand for reparations.[1] But a great many people did not intend to let it rest at that. The insidious ideas of "pledges" and "guarantees" to prevent German aggression in future were put into circulation. By playing on the nation's fears, it was hoped to open the door to more far-reaching ambitions. "The more formidable the dangers", wrote the *Temps* in explanation,

the greater the need for guarantees. . . . We have a right to insist on measures being adopted which will prevent a repetition of this crime. The Allies' war aims are what German barbarism has made them. It is the duty of the civilized nations of the world, not only to punish the outrage that has been committed against Law and Order, but also to obtain guarantees for the future. (June 9th.)

---

[1] In his speech on this occasion, Ribot said: "We have followed the progress of the Russian Revolution with sympathy, occasionally mingled with a certain degree of uneasiness. . . . Our uneasiness has been caused by the way in which the Government has been surrounded by outside influences which have hampered its actions and conduced to a sort of anarchy which, if it developed, would swallow up the Revolution itself. . . . And now, to arms again!"

Ribot's action was violently attacked by Clemenceau, and, like a reed in the wind, after a stormy meeting of the Senate,[1] he refused the Socialists their passports for Stockholm and replied to Tereshchenko in terms which suggest Clemenceau's own style. The wording of the note, coming immediately after the defeat of the offensive of April 16th, is illuminating:

> France cannot contemplate any other conclusion to the war than the triumph of Right and Justice. As to her own part, she intends to recover her faithful provinces of Alsace-Lorraine. . . . In company with her allies, she will fight on until victory is attained, and with it the complete restoration of their territorial integrity and of their political and *economic independence*, together with due *indemnification* for all the wanton and inhuman destruction committed, and *indispensable guarantees* against the recurrence of the evils caused by our enemies' incessant provocation.

This is the precise antithesis of Tereshchenko's declaration. What country in all the world can possibly lay claim to economic independence, seeing that, in the very nature of things, all are closely interdependent one on another? This marks the first emergence of a new theory, that of reparations in kind, distributed at the discretion of the victors. The *Temps* took upon itself to disclose this masterly conception of the men in power:

> The Allies will need above all to divide among themselves the raw materials in their possession. After the war, Germany intends to flood our markets. Was not industrial overproduction in Germany one of the causes of the war? And is it imagined that this danger will be warded off by merely removing a few territorial boundaries? (September 21st.)

It would have been difficult to go to greater lengths to snub the Russians in their hour of prostration.

Henry Bérenger, member of the Senate for Guadeloupe, who at that time had a good deal of influence with Clemenceau, defined the Government's views on political and economic

---

[1] Under pressure from Clemenceau, a meeting of representatives of the various groups in the Senate had eliminated from the motion a paragraph dealing with the League of Nations. (Ribot, p. 246.)

guarantees still more clearly in articles in *Paris-Midi* and the *Matin*. He reproached the Russians for their "defeatism" and demanded all possible *permanent guarantees* against the free economic development of the German people.

It would be intolerable if the Germans, Kaiser or no Kaiser, were allowed to resume after the war those methods of commercial trickery, industrial blackmail, and economic espionage which, favoured by the Kartell system and the Delbruck Act, have been the curse of European trade for the past thirty years.[1]

Joseph Reinach ("Polybe" of the *Figaro*) admitted that Tsarism "was rotten to the core", but deplored the abandonment of the claim to Constantinople, which was the object of Russia's agelong policy, "the symbol of her loyalty to the past, to her very self". "Was not the aim of the Revolution in France to extend her boundaries to their natural limit, the Rhine—that is to say, as soon as the Revolution had got rid of the naïve pacifico-humanitarian fancies of the Constituent Assembly of 1789?" (April 13th.) Sorel has demonstrated, however, how the conquest of the left bank of the Rhine involved the Republic in endless wars and was the cause of its downfall.

At the same time Reinach attacked the Soviet as a collection of riff-raff "led by fanatics and rogues and vagabonds in the pay of the enemy", and called upon the Provisional Government to dissolve it. "The new Russia must be patriotic or it will cease to exist", he asserted dogmatically. (May 10th, May 14th.) In face of Tereshchenko's announcement, he had the temerity to deny that there had ever been any secret

---

[1] Writing in the early days of the Revolution, Bérenger said that "in this abrupt transition from one régime to another, the thing to safeguard is the only feature they have in common: hatred of the Boches". (*Paris-Midi*, March 17th.) The *Matin* wrote: "When the criminal aggressors have been forced back into their lair, ramparts must be erected between them and the civilized world." (June 4th.) Senator Flandin, who had taken a prominent part in the Malvy case, asserted that "the Boches must be confined within frontiers that will separate them from civilized nations by obstacles difficult to surmount. . . . In addition to material punishments, they deserve moral chastisement in the shape of ostracism." (*Petit Journal*, June 9th.)

diplomacy in the history of the Third Republic. (June 10th.) Finally, he lost all patience with the Revolution. Poisoned by Germany, it had degenerated into anarchy. "The beast which dwells in the depths of human nature has been unleashed. It should have been seized at once, muzzled, and chained." (July 27th.) Lenin was nothing but a German spy. History would reveal the dealings of the German banks with him and his accomplices. (July 30th.)

Last of all, Clemenceau. Let the reader read, mark, and inwardly digest the substance and tone of his writings, for they were typical both of the mood of the time and of the man who was soon to become the head of the Government. He began by reaffirming that the Russian people had overthrown autocracy with the object of ensuring victory in the war; he hailed the Duma as the sovereign author of the Revolution and denounced the members of the Soviet as "disloyal to the Duma, to which they owe their very existence". (May 13th, May 17th.) This was, of course, the exact opposite of the truth.[1] He admitted that he judged the Russian Revolution solely from the standpoint of its effect on the "crushing of Boche barbarism". Tereshchenko's note naturally annoyed him, for "we are at war in support of Russia against German aggression". He prophesied that, after the war, the "Boches" would have no use for humanitarian gestures of amity. Their whole minds would be filled with the idea of revenge, for "*that is the law of human nature*". He criticized Ribot severely for having, in his speech in the Chamber of Deputies, limited France's claims to Alsace-Lorraine plus reparations, and for having overlooked the

primary need of the Allies, *and even the neutrals*, for pledges and guarantees. This most regrettable oversight brings the Prime Minister within hailing distance of the views of certain revolutionary elements

---

[1] His friend Pichon also, in the *Petit Journal*, after praising the Tsar's "splendid loyalty", denounced the Soviet as the cause of all the trouble. (March 15th, March 17th.)

in Russia, of which Tereshchenko has constituted himself the mouthpiece, but it places a gulf between him and the necessary conditions of peace to which we are entitled. (May 23rd, May 25th.)

As Chairman of the Foreign Affairs Committee and of the Army Committee of the Senate, Clemenceau was able to force Ribot to adopt the formula of "pledges and guarantees", which had the natural result of increasing the estrangement between France and Russia. It goes without saying that he took up an attitude of definite opposition to the Russian Minister's proposals for negotiations to revise the war aims. "Russian democracy is new-born! It must win its spurs before having the right to theorize." He congratulated the French Socialists on having refused to fall into the "German trap" of the Stockholm Conference (repudiated, according to him, by Kerensky) *at the very moment when all the conditions of victory are assured*. (May 26th and 31st.) "First show your mettle in battle against the common enemy, and then you can talk", was his advice to the Russians. Only the war, the whole war, and nothing but the war, could bring about a peace consonant with the self-respect of humanity. Russia, moreover, had no right to ask France what her war aims were. He added, with perfect composure, that, since the French nation "had acquired organs of popular control which secured the great advantage of government *coram populo*", it had consistently demanded a restoration of equilibrium in Europe based on justice. (June 24th.) "Let us be perfectly frank", he said to the Russians, who were then engaged in the tragic Galician offensive, "a wholehearted effort is necessary." (July 4th.) The Soviet representatives who came to Paris to expound Russia's new aspirations got on his nerves. "We Frenchmen alone have the duty and privilege of determining the course of French history." (July 31st.)

After this the tone grew sharper. He urged Kerensky to take action against the Soviet, that "chosen soil for German propaganda. . . . It is high time it was swept away. Two rival

Governments are impossible!" He went so far as to write: "If the Russian people had not been in the habit for generations past of submitting to conditions of utter slavery, they would have shown by now some signs of organizing their elements of sanity and cohesion", and he charged them with having "failed in their duty to themselves at a time when it would have been comparatively simple to set on foot some ordered evolution". (August 7th to 10th.) Clemenceau had a conveniently short memory. He had written the exact contrary in 1901–1905. He forgot that the Russian people had been making incessant and superhuman efforts for twenty years past to attain some proper measure of parliamentary control, and that their efforts had been constantly frustrated by French loans. He forgot, too, that he himself, when Prime Minister in 1906, had sanctioned the loan that saved Tsardom from immediate disaster, and had hastily read the decree of prorogation in the Chamber of Deputies to prevent it from sending its congratulations to the Duma, which was dissolved a week later.

Disregarding the failure of the offensive in Galicia, Clemenceau continued to assert that Russia could only be saved by military action. Lenin and the Bolshevik party were in the pay of Germany. A separate peace was unthinkable. Kornilov's rebellion was neither more nor less culpable than that of the Provisional Government in March. (September–October.) In his last article, he wrote that the Soviet was merely a

gang of scoundrels in the pay of the German Secret Service, a band of German Jews with a more or less plausible Russian veneer, repeating what they have been taught to say in Berlin. . . . In the name of that "working class" so self-sacrificingly cherished by our friend Malvy, on behalf of that "democracy" to which M. Caillaux is so devoted, the Hebraico-Teuton Soviet, in the pay of the Kaiser, obediently prepares and carries on its subsidized intervention.

With his record, Clemenceau was admirably qualified to hurl an insult of this description at the Bolsheviks! The very next day he was called upon to form a Government.

Meanwhile the Bolsheviks, having successfully intervened to checkmate Kornilov's attempted military *coup d'état*, had gained enormously in prestige, and were regarded by the mass of the people as the saviours of the Revolution. Trotzky was elected chairman of the Petrograd Soviet, and on November 7th Lenin and his associates seized power. "The triumph of the Communist party", as Prince Lvov, the ex-Prime Minister, admitted, "was equivalent in the eyes of the people to the triumph of the Revolution over the forces of reaction."[1] The Provisional Government had only succeeded in irritating the Russian masses by refusing them, under pressure from the Allies, Peace and Land, the only two things that mattered to them, with the result that it had played straight into the hands of its opponents. The Bolsheviks, according to Maklakov, "maintained, with good show of reason, that the Government had never sufficiently emphasized the pacifist programme and had never stood up to the Allies sufficiently firmly. Arguments of this sort gave them an immense advantage in a country which was utterly sick of war".[2] On November 8th, the day after the Bolshevik *coup*, the new Government issued a *pronunciamento* in favour of a general peace without annexations or indemnities. This suggestion eliciting no response, and the Russian army being incapable of continuing the struggle, the Bolsheviks, in the absence of any reliable support, had to make up their minds to conclude a separate peace. (March 1918.) This marked the final and complete rupture of relations with the French Government, which had never shown any comprehension for the sincere aspirations of the Russian people.

Before bringing this chapter to a conclusion, there is one point to which it is important to draw attention. In his book on the "Austrian Peace Offer", Prince Sixtus of Bourbon-Parma has revealed that, in the course of the interview on May 20, 1917, at which he communicated to Ribot the Austrian

[1] *Revue Mondiale*, September 15, 1921.
[2] *Revue de Paris*, November 15, 1924. Cf. *Correspondant*, May 25, 1919.

proposals, he also drew the French Prime Minister's attention to the events then in progress in Russia. The latter replied: "We do not propose to tell Russia about these negotiations until they are practically concluded." As, however, the negotiations fell through, the Austrian offer was not transmitted to the Russian Government in time. "It is true", adds Prince Sixtus,

that even if Baron Sonnino had not taken steps to prevent the acceptance of the peace offer of the Dual Monarchy, M. Ribot would himself have done all in his power to circumvent it, since, in the way it was put forward, it failed to meet with his personal approval, as he did not fail to indicate.[1]

It is hardly necessary to point out that, if Kerensky had been informed of Austria's proposals at the time when the Galician offensive was just being planned, he would certainly have notified Sonnino of the state the Russian army was in and the urgent need of entering into pourparlers with the Dual Monarchy. A separate peace with Austria would have shortened the war considerably, and Germany would probably have capitulated a year sooner than she did. It is noteworthy that this statement by Ribot was made at a time when French statesmen were busy discussing the "pledges" and "guarantees" to be exacted from the enemy. Within a year came the slaughter at Montdidier and Château-Thierry. How, after realizing all this, and knowing the plight of the Russian army in 1917–1918, and the attitude of the Entente Powers towards the Russian people's desire for peace, can one judge with any severity the so-called "treacherous" treaty of Brest-Litovsk?

France's Russian policy subsequent to the Bolsheviks' accession to power really followed as a logical consequence on the line she had adopted up to that time.[2] The outstanding features, in the order of their occurrence, were: the refusal to meet the Russian delegates at Prinkipo, as President Wilson

---

[1] Pp. 199 and 386.
[2] Cf. R. Labry's article in the *Mercure de France*, 1920, and his *Autour du Bolchévisme*.

had proposed; the shelving of the Bullitt Report;[1] the blockade of Russia; the Noulens mission. There were statements by successive Foreign Ministers, which seemed to have been modelled on Pitt's references to the National Convention;[2] diatribes by leading politicians, even by the *Ligue des Droits de l'Homme*,[3] culminating in Clemenceau's proposal to surround Russia with a barbed-wire fence. Then began an organized crusade against the Soviets, a policy of armed intervention in Russia—a country with which France was not at war—with a plan for an expedition to Georgia. In November 1918 the French Government went so far as to contemplate the dispatch to South Russia of an army corps of 60,000 men, and the Admiralty actually chartered the necessary troop-ships, but owing to defective organization and liaison between the two Services the evolutions were carried out, according to Henry Chéron, "in a way which was open to serious criticism from the point of view of the Treasury".[4] This was followed by a regular policy of support to adventurers of the worst type, such as Kolchak, Yudenich, and Denikin, who were represented as knights-errant and protectors of widows and orphans—a policy capped by Millerand's official recognition of Wrangel.[5]

The French press, taking its lead from the Government, constantly accused the Bolshevik Revolution of being the sole cause of the disintegration of the Russian army,[6] and announced

[1] Cf. Temperley's *History of the Peace Conference*, VI, pp. 311 sqq.

[2] Cf. my paper on "Jacobinism in the Debates of the British Parliament in 1793–4" (*Annales historiques de la révolution française*, July 1925).

[3] Cf. this League's strange "Inquiry into Bolshevism". (*Bulletin officiel*, March 1–15, 1919.)

[4] *Vide* Chéron's Report to the Senate. (July 1921, No. 537.)

[5] For the period 1917–1918, see Sadoul's letters to Albert Thomas in his *Notes sur la révolution bolchévique*; A. Pierre's *De Kerensky à Lénine* and lecture (May 9, 1920) on the "Causes of the Bolsheviks' rise to power"; also Ossip-Lourié's *La Révolution Russe*.

[6] General Danilov, in his *La Russie dans la guerre mondiale*, 1914–1915; J. Legras, in his *Mémoires de Russie*, and Paléologue show that this disintegration dated from the very earliest stages of the war. Cf. *Le Monde Slave*, January 1927.

each day that the next would see the downfall of the Soviet Republic. When the great famine came, the leading French newspapers attributed the whole responsibility to the Bolsheviks (whereas even before the war famine had been an endemic scourge in the Tsarist Empire), and advised the public not to contribute to the relief funds, seeing in the disaster only a means of overthrowing Bolshevism.[1] Thus, from start to finish, France's whole policy with regard to Russia is seen to have been one long series of blunders.

[1] The *Temps* (September 11, September 17 and October 1, 1921) and the *Journal des Débats* (August 5 and 17, September 2, 10 and 26, 1921, articles by Bernus and Gauvain) were particularly prominent in the chorus of hatred. Cf. Mermeix' article in the *Figaro* (July 21, 1921), Binet-Valmer's letter to Gorky (*Figaro*, July 22, 1921), and Boulenger's article in the *Comoedia* of August 23, 1921, which are very significant.

X

# CHAPTER XVII

# THE CAUSES OF FRANCE'S BLINDNESS

FRANCE knew nothing of Russia: nothing of her real nature, nothing of what was happening there. The opinions current in France in regard to her ally were utterly at variance with the facts. The truth is that the facts were systematically concealed from the French public. What were its sources of information? On the one hand, a press in the pay of Tsarism, and, on the other, diplomatic representatives in Russia, most of whom, knowing nothing of the language and steeped in the traditions of the past, took no interest in anything but the Court, the Ministers, and the aristocracy, between whom and the people lay a great gulf. They did not mix with the cultured classes of the intelligentsia, and *a fortiori* were entirely ignorant of the aspirations of the masses, of the living realities of Russian life, of the Liberal and Socialist circles, of the big popular movements, of all the revolutionary ferment. They made no attempt to plumb the depths of the Slav soul, but merely transmitted their own false impressions: a Tsar adored by his people, an aristocracy of the highest quality, and below these a swarming peasantry full of unquestioning patriotism —in other words, a picture of reality inaccurate in every particular. They were not even capable of warning their Government when the régime reached the stage of putrefaction in which a Rasputin was supreme. Even the *Temps* admitted (March 27, 1917) that "the diplomatic representatives of the Republic have seldom remembered that they were speaking in the name of a democracy, and when they have remembered this, it has generally been in an apologetic spirit". How, given these conditions, could they be expected to show any comprehension of the Socialist movement and the Russian Revolution?

The French bourgeoisie, true to their traditions, took a

snobbish delight in the after-dinner speeches of the Tsar and the French Presidents and in the mutual official compliments that passed, handed over their money, and took no further interest in the proceedings. Raoul Labry, a former member of the Institut Français of St. Petersburg, said bluntly that "our knowledge of Russia was not even a surface knowledge",[1] and Charles Rivet, the *Temps* correspondent, wrote that "the French people have taken as a portrait of Russia what was only a bad caricature".[2] As for the press, which ought to have published the true facts, confidential reports from Arthur Raffalovich, a secret agent of the Russian Finance Minister, to his headquarters in St. Petersburg, which were published in 1923–1924[3] and the authenticity of which has never been challenged, have disclosed the astounding degree of venality of the leading French journals, which for many years received subsidies from the Russian Government. As the *Correspondant* of September 25, 1912, put it:

The Russian Government takes the necessary steps to ensure that public opinion in France only knows what it is meant to know. In 1910, and there is no reason to doubt that the same state of things exists to-day, the Russian Embassy in Paris had at its disposal the sum of 1,200,000 francs per annum for use in this way, not counting the cost of financial advertisements.

In February 1905 the organization representing the members of the Paris Bourse intimated to Raffalovich that they would not quote or deal in the new Russian loan unless the Russian Government placed at the disposal of the French press a monthly subvention of 200,000 francs during the whole of the duration of the Russo-Japanese War, in addition to what was spent on financial announcements. This manna fell on all the leading papers as well as on some publications of very limited circulation. In 1912, at the time of the Balkan crisis,

[1] *Mercure de France*, March 15, 1920, and his *Autour du Bolchévisme*.
[2] *Le dernier Romanof*, p. 317.
[3] *Humanité*, December 1923 and January 1924.

Isvolsky took a special interest in these operations and repeatedly urged upon his Government the "necessity of providing ample material means for influencing the French press". Poincaré was aware of these transactions, and the sums were actually distributed according to suggestions made by Klotz, the Finance Minister. The chief object at that time was to suppress the campaign against a war arising out of events in the Balkans. This was how the truth was sedulously concealed from the French nation, how confidence was maintained in Russia's credit and her loyalty to the Alliance![1]

But the venality of the press and the poor quality of the French diplomatic personnel would not be entirely sufficient explanation of French ignorance of the truth about Russia. The attitude of the leading French journals has not changed since the fall of their imperial paymaster. They were after all, from 1891 to 1917, merely expressing and reflecting fairly faithfully the sentiments of the French bourgeoisie, and in the mentality of the latter lies the root cause of France's blindness in regard to Russian affairs. It was not that it was impossible to get at the truth. There were intimations and warnings of all sorts. One had only to listen carefully. A very little critical acumen would have seen through the clumsy lies of the French press.

In the first place, there were the Russian thinkers and men of letters, from Gogol and Dostoyevsky to Tolstoy and Gorky, who might have enabled the nation to penetrate to the depths of the Russian soul and Russian life, which were a closed book to France. Secondly, there were men of irreproachable probity like Anatole Leroy-Beaulieu, a moderate-minded observer, who, over a period of twenty years, was constantly issuing warnings, a Conservative review like the *Correspondant*, investigations by *La Revue* and *L'Information*, articles by Lysis, Jaurès, and Francis de Pressensé—all these revealed

[1] Cf. Félicien Challayé's article on "The Venality of the French Press" in the *Cahiers des Droits de l'Homme*, March 1924.

different aspects of the truth. Finally, there was the teaching of history. Later generations will surely marvel that Russia's deplorable defeats in Manchuria, the pogroms, the 1905 Revolution, and Tsardom's world-wide reputation for corruption did not open the eyes of the French ruling classes and occasionally, at least, suggest some presentiment of the coming financial and military breakdown. The fact is that the governing classes of France, from which her diplomats, her staff officers, and her business men were recruited, did not attempt to find out the truth, did not in fact wish to know it, because the critical sense, the instinct to investigate, to inquire, to verify, was not in accordance with their habits of mind, and particularly because the Russian people's aspirations were totally at variance with their political and social ideals. They read very little Russian literature, having no particular taste for it, and learned nothing from it. Leroy-Beaulieu was reduced to writing for an obscure weekly, the *Courrier Européen*. As for Jaurès, he inspired such a thorough distrust in bourgeois circles that they always adopted on principle the opposite course from that which he recommended, without bothering to note whether his advice was borne out by subsequent events. Historical facts left them cold. It was their established practice to stick to their prejudices in the teeth of evidence, to regard as dangerous those men who issued warnings, and to charge them, when the time came, with responsibility for the disasters they had foretold. They merely applied to the Franco-Russian Alliance the same criteria as they did to the Dreyfus Case and to the Caillaux Case. Ludovic Naudeau went so far as to assert that:

If anyone had taken it into his head to publish accurate revelations concerning the great Russian Empire, he would have made a host of very influential enemies. He would very likely have been accused of attempted blackmail, of being a contemptible hack in search of hush-money, and it is by no means certain that patriotic citizens would not have called him a pro-German without more ado.[1]

---

[1] *Les dessous du chaos russe*, p. 134.

Astonishment has been expressed, reasonably enough, that official France never approached the Tsar to advise him to listen to the voice of his people. But how could the French ruling classes have done this, or even dreamed of doing it, seeing that their constant attitude at home to any movement of the slightest socialistic or democratic tinge was one of surly hostility? They regarded the Russian Alliance, which was their own creation, which they were never tired of praising, and which they forced on the country like a shibboleth, as essentially a counter-weight or drag on democratic advance, and they exploited it as an instrument of reaction.[1] How could they have favoured the establishment in Russia of a parliamentary régime, of universal suffrage, while they were showing their abhorrence of these at home, and doing their utmost to discredit and checkmate them? They were logically bound to applaud the dissolution of Dumy with a socialistic tendency, since at home they had always advocated the limitation of the powers of the legislature and carried on the most violent campaigns against Chambers of Deputies which they suspected of working against their interests. How could they fail to contribute towards the crushing of the 1905 Revolution and to show every hostility to that of 1917, when their primary object at home was to stifle the Socialist movement and to stem the tide of popular democracy, placing all their hope in methods such as those of Fascism? It was a considered stroke of policy for them to assist Tsarism to strangle liberty, to suppress Parliamentary control, and to crush the Revolution, and their subsequent crusade against the Bolsheviks was only the logical outcome of their previous practice in the handling of the Alliance. They affected to be scandalized at the actions of the Democrats, and heaped insults on them, but they had only excuses and charitable sentiments for the vile corruption

[1] "All our Clericalists and Nationalists, in their advocacy of the Franco-Russian Alliance, knew very well that it would tend to the establishment of counter-revolution in France." (Anatole France, February 1, 1905, *Vers les temps meilleurs*, III, p. 17.)

of Tsarism, for that degraded régime, the byword of the whole world, which ended in the mud of Rasputinism.

Yet throughout all these unworthy manœuvres the French bourgeoisie, by preventing Tsardom from developing and marching with the times, only succeeded in depriving it of the very conditions of success in the war, and was therefore working all along for bankruptcy and violent revolution. French gold paved the way for disaster, and France herself would have shared the same fate but for the other Allies.

Amongst the mistaken ideas so complacently held, there was one—the principle of continuity in foreign relations—which we have already examined and found wanting. To hear certain people talk of this principle, one would think that it had some peculiar inherent virtue, as if a policy ill-adapted to the facts could lose its harmfulness and produce beneficial results by the mere effect of its continuity. Of course, any policy, any line of conduct, demands constant revision, constant adjustment, in a world which is never still. Continuity in outworn formulae can only lead to disaster. The Franco-Russian Alliance is the most striking confirmation of this.

The leading representatives of the rich middle class, who were the chief partisans of the Alliance, talk to-day of nothing but the "facts", the "realities of the situation". But what amount of attention did they pay to facts and realities in their attitude to Russia from 1890 to 1917? The army officers, blind to the lessons of the Russo-Japanese War, judged the Russian military machine by a few carefully picked regiments, without troubling to investigate the state of the armaments, the training of the officers, and the military organization in the army as a whole.[1] The wiseacres of the *Institut*, taking no steps to

---

[1] Ludovic Naudeau relates that in July 1914, when he was in St. Petersburg, he met Lieutenant-Colonel Boussé, who confided in him his fears and the alarming facts he had discovered. But he was determined to say nothing about them to his own superior officers, for, as he put it to Naudeau: "If I were to say anything, I should be told to hold my tongue, and I should only end in getting a bad name." (Op. cit., p. 133.)

ascertain the real facts, displayed a childish credulity. One of them invented the myth of the "Russian steam-roller". And the world of Big Business, the proprietors of vast enterprises in Russia, the Schneiders of the Putilov Works, the Homécourt concern, and so many others, those who possessed large undertakings in the Donetz and in Poland, and the bankers of the Union Parisienne and the Société Générale who were their financial backers, all the big technical men who were in such a favourable position to see everything and ascertain the truth—how did these men react to the realities of the Russian situation, to the facts which were staring them in the face? They either saw clearly and said nothing, or they were blind. What is one to think of such people, who have the audacity to come forward to-day and offer to act as our mentors in politics?

What remarkable insight Jaurès displayed when in 1914, just before the war, he drew attention to the selfish inertia of the governing classes, whose sole remaining energy was devoted to resisting progress:

The deplorable feature of this spirit of resistance is that it is not merely selfish, but reveals defects of intelligence, initiative, and decision which react on the whole conduct of the affairs of the State. Our public life is being paralysed by the spirit of petty meanness. Thought and the conscience of the nation are growing stunted. The stubborn attachment now being displayed to forms of taxation which are unjust and obsolete is not only a sign of something sordid in the minds of the governing classes, but is equivalent to an abdication of intelligence and will-power. It is like the Three Years' Military Service Act, a triumph of intellectual laziness, and we cannot continue in these ruts of thought without ultimately arriving at a kind of national stupefaction.[1]

No less heavy is the burden of responsibility which falls on the politicians, who, with the exception of those of the Extreme Left, noticed nothing and did not try to find out the truth. They, too, had warnings enough. But they never had sufficient determination to insist on the necessary explanations or to

[1] *Humanité*, May 6, 1914.

exercise one of the main functions of a Parliament, namely, the control of foreign policy and of the realities of diplomatic action. The heavy fathers of the political stage were as refractory as children under the hard lessons of experience. How contemptible they now sound, those pæans of adulation, those fervid expressions of faith in the Russian giant, uttered periodically by the Mélines, the Ribots, the Poincarés, who at the same time held up all doubters to popular execration. In the blackest hours, when some citizens had committed the crime of showing enthusiasm for abstract ideas which had not been approved by Big Business and the parties of Reaction, one of these oracles would arise, draped in secrecy, to silence the sacrilegious tongues and proclaim, in a voice trembling with emotion, the holiness of the Alliance, the nobility of soul of the Tsar, and the might of the Russian army. It was a spectacle in which the elements of the sinister and the grotesque were equally blended.

What a poor figure, too, the younger generation of politicians cut who had entered the arena at the time of the Dreyfus trial and claimed to be realists. Instead of endeavouring to ascertain the truth about Russia, revealing the facts, proclaiming the dangers, they found nothing to say, and in their anxiety to be regarded as sane, safe, moderate men and so to get preferment, these clever, brilliant fellows behaved in every crisis like the most ignorant of their kind. What they lacked was character, which has been described as the highest form of cleverness.

What are we to say of the "great" Radical party—of those Radical Ministers, like Delcassé and Pichon, who could only reply to Jaurès' prophetic warnings by holding him up to public contempt, accusing him of treason, and thus inciting against him the hand of the assassin? Did not Delcassé himself, by the modification of 1899, completely transform the sense and scope of the Alliance?[1] Far from protesting against the

[1] Delcassé said to Charles Rivet: "Russia, for me, is only a diplomatic and military entity, and the fate of her 180 million *muzhiks* does not interest me." (*Le dernier Romanof*, pp. 321–323.)

secrecy of the treaty and demanding details of France's commitments, the Radicals, by their action in 1893, 1896, and 1897, showed that they regarded the Alliance primarily as an instrument of revenge against Germany. Denys Cochin, although a Conservative, raised a far more energetic protest than they against the extension of the Alliance and against secret diplomacy, and was alone in expressing his amazement at the St. Petersburg conversations of July 1914 when they were revealed by Paléologue.[1] As for Léon Bourgeois and Clemenceau, the attitude they adopted in 1906 in regard to the loan which saved Tsarism and to the proposed address to the Duma is sufficiently indicative.

There is little doubt, then, that the ignorance of the French politicians, fostered by the Quai d'Orsay, the Government, and the ruling class as a whole, was one of the chief causes of the trouble. If they had only had a modicum of faith in the principles they were elected to defend, they would have seen that nothing but a thoroughgoing transformation could restore strength to Russia and stability to her finances, which was the only guarantee for the French holders of Russian bonds, and that, moreover, this transformation could only be effected at the instance of the Russian nation through its elected representatives and by the Russian nation itself. They would have seen, too, that the adoption of an aggressive foreign policy by such an ally would expose France to the utmost peril.

The French Republic had at that time a diplomatic corps which, as Denys Cochin has admitted, was "composed of survivors from former royal Courts and the nominees of aristocratic Governments",[2] and a General Staff in which democratic views were a bar to promotion. The reason for this was that the politicians did not realize that disputes over the word Republic were now *vieux jeu* and that the parties of Reaction no longer found it desirable to advocate a monarchy, the fall

[1] Yet Cochin had been a Cabinet Minister during the war.
[2] *Figaro*, January 18, 1921.

of which would entail their own fall from power, but preferred a régime in which they could pull all the strings, introduce their own ideas with impunity, and keep the Democrats and Socialists in subjection in the name of Republican order. Disregarding, most inexcusably, that antinomy between the label and the reality which gives rise to the constant contradictions from which the nation still suffers, the politicians failed to appreciate the fact that France's foreign policy was that of a monarchy and that her representatives were fawning obsequiously on an autocracy dominated by a Rasputin. They not only raised no objection to secret treaties, but also swallowed the refusal of the Government to afford any information regarding France's commitments abroad. Albert de Mun was justified in saying in 1910: "It is amazing that the very country most notorious for its secret diplomacy should imagine itself to be in constant control of its own destiny."[1]

The men in power in France seem always to have overlooked the fact that Tsarism was not even a proper autocracy, but an Asiatic régime having much more in common with the government of the Shah and the Celestial Empire than with any European State, and that the accepted method of carrying on the Alliance only resulted in postponing and actually preventing the radical reconstruction which alone would have made Tsardom a real power in the world. It would seem, in fact, as though the most Conservative elements in France, by reason of their very desire for a strong Russia, for war and for peace, should have been the ones to feel the greatest aversion for the régime as it existed, which was heading for disaster. The Alliance had the effect of causing democratic France to acquiesce and assist in the expansion and success of an autocracy which was opposed to all the principles for which she stood—a success, moreover, which could, as a rule, only be attained at the expense of France's real influence in the world. Thus the Republic, bound hand and foot to Tsarist ambitions,

[1] Speech in the Chamber of Deputies, December 15, 1910.

was forced to deny her own true instincts and to combat all that had gone to build up her strength and prestige.[1] The history of the Franco-Russian Alliance is really inseparable from France's internal political history. Whenever the forces of reaction were in the ascendant and the traditions of the Republic seemed to be dormant, the Alliance flourished. Whenever democracy seemed to be gaining ground and France reawakened to a sense of her prestige, acquired from the ideals for which she stands in the world, the Alliance wilted, for then it was generally recognized for the incoherent, illogical anachronism that it was. When, however, the forces of mercenary nationalism succeeded in seizing the reins of power by virtue of the catchword of "national unity", reinforced by an aggressive foreign policy and a recrudescence of the struggle against Socialism, then the Alliance stock went up again.

The ultimate condemnation of the Franco-Russian Alliance lies in this—that it drew its strength from the degradation of the two peoples, that it constituted an obstacle to political and social reform for a quarter of a century, that it served to bolster up one of the most abominable régimes known to history, and, finally, that it contributed in large measure to the outbreak of the most awful cataclysm of modern times.

[1] When Francis de Pressensé protested against the ban on the immigration of French Jews into Russia on the score that French citizens ought to receive equally favourable treatment to that shown to Russian subjects in France, Poincaré replied that "French law could not supersede Russian law in Russia. . . . That would be a challenge to Russian sovereignty to which no independent nation could submit. . . . No modification in the Russian social system could be expected to be secured by outside pressure, which would outrage national sentiment." To this Pressensé replied by pointing out that Poincaré, speaking in the name of the Republic, was going beyond anything that had previously been stated by any other régime. (*Bulletin officiel de la Ligue des Droits de l'Homme*, 1912, pp. 1104 and 1180; 1914, p. 181.)

# CONCLUSION

The Russian Alliance forms one of the blackest pages in French history. From whatever point of view it is considered, it was a most lamentable failure. Regarded from the standpoint of France's material interests, the blindness of her statesmen and middle classes beggars description. To have lent million after million without ascertaining whether the debtor was solvent, without inquiring how the loans were to be used, without requiring any guarantees of sound administration! And when the debtor was an autocracy at open war with its subjects, and constantly on the verge of a revolution, the lenders' risk of losing their money was still further enhanced. When, finally, the lenders prevented the debtor's crumbling régime from reforming itself, from carrying out the radical reconstruction by which alone it could have been saved, then they were surely heading straight for disaster.

These would-be realists, having seen Tsardom go to pieces once in a series of crushing defeats, persisted in the same courses as before, imagining that in the space of a few years, with no change in its methods, a régime of that character could recover and regain its strength. Giving a false complexion to the Alliance, contrary to both the spirit and the letter of the original pact, though Delcassé had already done something to reshape it, they even embarked on an active policy, and allowed their ally, then "rotten to the core", to act the part of a Great Power and drag them inevitably into a war. Such deeds are beyond excuse.

The fatal error of the French governing classes, especially after 1912, was to go on believing in Russia's strength and to stake their all upon it, in spite of the most categorical warnings and the most conclusive ocular evidence, instead of persuading Tsarism, then in an advanced stage of decomposition, to take a long rest, to maintain a policy of modest reserve, and to recuperate its strength. On the contrary, instead of restraining Russia's insensate designs on Constantinople, the Straits, and the Balkans, in the pursuit of which she could not fail to run foul of Austria, they gave her the fullest assurances of unconditional support in the event of the intervention of the only enemy she really feared—Germany. They coolly faced the prospects of waging a war arising out of Balkan affairs in company with an ally in Russia's condition. Their attitude towards Tsarism under Rasputin on the eve of a war which, but for the support of her other allies, might have been disastrous for France herself—their utter blindness to reality, in short, is beyond all justification.

The Alliance begins to take on the proportions of a colossal fraud when one sees Russia at Björkö in 1905, at Buchlau, Racconigi, and Potsdam in 1908–1910, entering into secret agreements with the Triple Alliance Powers, especially with Germany, behind France's back and at her expense; while absurdity reaches its height when, after having to put up with a policy like this, we see that France could not even secure any preferential treatment for her traders in the Russian market. The Alliance was concluded after France had recovered without assistance from her defeat in 1870 and reorganized her finances and army, so that it cannot even claim to have assisted her in that task. The "isolation" from which it is alleged to have rescued her was infinitely less dangerous, as subsequent events have proved, than the risks she incurred of being dragged into war for objects alien to her vital interests.

But to material failure on this vast scale there must be added the unprecedented moral bankruptcy, the betrayal of the ideals and the very meaning of democracy. The Alliance was a standing insult to the memory of those who, by the force of their intellect or the sacrifice of their lives, founded the French Republic. It can no longer be doubted that it was France's financial, material, and moral support that saved Tsarism from 1894 onwards, patched up and consolidated the most loathsome autocracy known to history, the object of world-wide contempt, and in consequence perpetuated the oppression of a nation, facilitated the strangling of a beneficial revolution, the repeated dissolution of a national assembly, the rejection of every demand for reform, the most sanguinary repression, and the constant organization of frightful massacres of Jews. This is an indelible disgrace, a degrading betrayal of the very basis of the French people's prestige and self-respect. The verdict of history will be that this régime gained a further lease of life for twenty years solely by the aid of French capital and the support of the Government of the Republic. That is the part France was made to play by the bourgeoisie and its leading politicians.[1]

When the French governing classes in 1917, besides hurling insults at the real authors of the Russian Revolution, maintained that the struggle must be continued, while still declining to restate their war aims and emphasizing their intention to secure "guarantees"—a phrase susceptible of the most imperialistic interpretations—it is not to be wondered at that the Russian people, in their exhaustion and defencelessness, determined to break the vicious circle of the Alliance.

The inner history of the Franco-Russian pact throws a vivid light on the domestic policy of the Third Republic, under which, except for short intervals, the classes hostile to democracy, in their unremitting endeavours to combat the spirit and the achievements of the French Revolution, have succeeded in forcing upon successive Governments their political and social shibboleths. If France is to resume her proper place in the world, she must insist on her representatives taking full control of her foreign relations, and must set her face against and repudiate all secret treaties and all secret clauses of treaties. As Jaurès once said:

[1] "In attacking the Alliance with Russia we are ridding France of a lie and delivering her from a corpse." (Jaurès, in the *Vie Socialiste*, February 5, 1905.)

When a country sees her liberties openly confiscated, she at least knows where she stands, but when her constitution provides for self-government while, under cover of this formula, arbitrary decisions and secret designs continue unchecked, she runs the gravest of risks.[1]

Let France not only take control of her foreign relations; let her shun the whole policy of alliances, which are always liable, in certain hands, to become an instrument of imperialism and war. Let her at last realize the true end of democracy by exercising a constant supervision over her political representatives, her "statesmen", and her press, whose contemptible lies about Russia will be an everlasting stigma upon the present régime. Let her beware above all of drifting into a state of tutelage to High Finance and Big Business, the leaders of which were among the warmest partisans of the Russian Alliance, and which, if they are allowed steadily to increase their hold on the State, will lead the nation once more along the precipitous path of military adventure.

[1] From a speech in the Chamber of Deputies, June 16, 1911.

# INDEX

Adam, Mme, 15, 84
Adam, P., 110
Aehrenthal, von, 178–180, 187, 249
Alexander I, 178
Alexander II, 11, 78
Alexander III, 12, 17, 24, 26, 32, 35 sqq., 44 sqq., 219
Alexeyev, 119, 295
Andrássy, 11
André, 111
Appert, 12
Aubert, 202
Aulard, 302
Azev, 171

Bainville, 309–10
Barbey, 26
Barrès, 136
Barthou, 76, 87
Basch, 302
Baudin, 127
Benckendorff, von, 230, 246, 292
Benoist, 311
Berchtold, 222
Bérenger, 111–12, 213–14
Bertie, 294
Beyens, 226, 258
Beylis, 173
Bezobrazov, 119
Bieberstein, see Marschall
Bismarck, 11, 12
Blum, Léon, 235–6
Bobrinsky, 269
Bogdanovich, 146
Boisdeffre, de, 25, 41 sqq.
Bompard, 143, 144
Bos, 86
Boulanger, 17
Bourbon, Prince Sixtus of, 318–19
Bourdon, 160–1
Bourgeois, Léon, 156, 159, 254
Branting, 171
Bratianu, 277–8
Brianchaninov, 267
Briand, 114, 129, 156, 274
Brisson, Henri, 102
Buchanan, 292, 294
Bullitt, 320

Bülow, 13, 145
Burdeau, 147
Burtzev, 171

Caillaux, 127, 148, 164, 166, 200–1, 308
Cambon, Jules, 217, 258
Cambon, Paul, 215, 217, 229, 236–7, 246
Caprivi, 25
Carnot, 26, 27, 30, 55
Casimir-Périer, 60, 80
Cassagnac, P. de, 71, 84, 113
Charmes, 127
Charykov, 198, 208
Cheradame, 119
Claretie, 110
Clemenceau, 72, 83, 85, 94–5, 110, 113, 120, 138, 150, 156, 159, 160, 276, 307, 313, 315–17, 320
Cochery, 147
Cochin, Denys, 116–17, 122, 187, 280, 305, 330
Combes, 102, 130
Conrad v. Hötzendorf, 249
Constans, 24
Coppée, 85
Cornély, 84
Crozier, 181–2, 184, 187, 249, 259
Cruppi, 194
Cyon, de, 14, 16, 18, 19

Danev, 207
Danilov, 265
Daudet, Ernest, 26
Debidour, 29, 79
Delafosse, 73, 74, 84
Delaisi, 233, 251, 266
Delcassé, 20, 45, 101–7, 111, 113, 116–18, 119 sqq., 136, 137, 138, 163, 191, 202–3, 236, 245–6, 254, 264, 291, 293, 305, 329
Deloncle, 241–2
Demartial, 220
Denikin, 320
Depasse, 71
Déroulède, 15, 94
Descaves, 110

Y

Deschanel, 70
Develle, 58, 59
Deville, 127
Disraeli, 11
Dolgoruki, 155
Dorizon, 121
Doumer, 84
Doumergue, 162, 265, 296–9, 307
Dreyfus, 99, 102
Drumont, 136, 139
Dumaine, 214
Dupuy, Ch., 80, 102
Duruy, G., 71, 73

Edward VII, 177
Ephremov, 269
Eustis, 100
Eydoux, 232

Fabre-Luce, 85
Fallières, 74
Farrère, de, 232
Faure, Félix, 82, 93, 94
Ferry, 285
Finot, 149, 156
Flandin, 314
Fleuriau, 222
Flourens, 13, 16, 73
France, Anatole, 110, 142, 152–3, 326
Francis Ferdinand, 249, 274
Francis Joseph, 58, 178
Frederics, 19
Freycinet, de, 19, 24, 26, 30, 35 sqq., 58

Garnier, 84
Gauvain, 141, 167, 197, 206, 225, 250, 294, 311
Geffroy, 142
Gennadiev, 252
George, Lloyd, 308
Gérald, 165
Ghika, 26
Giers, de, 12, 13, 16, 17, 26 sqq., 37 sqq., 48, 57, 58, 86, 213, 219
Goblet, 99
Goltz, von der, 232
Gorchakov, 11, 12
Goremykin, 153, 277

Gorky, 136, 154, 161
Gouthe-Soulard, 74
Grévy, 22
Grey, Sir Edward (Lord), 180, 211, 231, 237, 283, 292
Guchkov, 290
Guesde, 73, 301
Gueshov, 205, 207, 222, 224
Guiche, de la, 239
Guillaume, 276

Hanotaux, 81, 90, 99, 105, 182, 186
Hansen, 24, 26, 35, 36, 40, 59
Harmand, 120
Harting, 171
Hartwig, 205, 224, 249
Herbette, 311
Hervé, 310–11
Hohenlohe, 83, 84
Hoskier, 13, 18, 19
Hötzendorf, see Conrad
Houx, des, 73

Isvolsky, 119, 120, 144, 176–85, 194, 195, 196, 197–201, 204, 206, 209–12, 215, 216, 217, 223, 230–1, 234 sqq., 245, 251–8, 277, 282, 286, 291, 297

Jaurès, 22, 23, 69, 70, 73, 76, 77, 81, 82, 87, 88, 89, 90, 97, 114, 115, 122–31, 137, 138, 142, 152, 155, 158, 160, 163–5, 168–9, 171–2, 183, 187–8, 222, 226–8, 241, 242, 246–8, 254–5, 277, 279–81, 284–6, 325, 328, 335–6
Jonnart, 244–5
Judet, 97

Katkov, 14, 15, 16
Kaulbars, 213
Kerensky, 297, 301, 307–8, 319
Khomiakov, 170
Kitchener, 290
Klotz, 85, 324
Kokovtsov, 150, 169, 211, 216, 240
Koltchak, 320
Kornilov, 308, 318
Kovalevsky, 170
Kropotkin, 12

Krushevan, 133
Kuropatkin, 119

Laboulaye, de, 13, 25 sqq.
Labry, 166–7, 323
Lacroix, 113–14
Lamarzelle, de, 188
Lamsdorff, 144
Lanessan, 96
Laurent, 128
Lauzanne, 189, 264
Lavisse, 106
Lavrov, 77
Lenin, 318
Leo XIII, 13
Leroy-Beaulieu, 20, 21, 22, 28, 121,
    134, 135, 137, 140, 151–2, 157,
    162, 168, 303, 324–5
Lévy, R. G., 288
Lieven, Prince, 202, 204
Liman v. Sanders, 252
Lobanov, 93
Lockroy, 128
Lombroso, 100
Longuet, 285
Loti, 232
Louis, Georges, 195, 196, 200, 202,
    208–11, 214–15, 238, 244–5, 256–7
Lvov, 308, 318
Lysis, 150–1, 165

Maeterlinck, 110
Maklakov, 155, 300, 318
Malet, 233
Marchand, 121
Margaine, 148
Marschall von Bieberstein, 91
Mathiez, 104
Maurras, 29, 80, 211
Mehemet Ali, 292
Méline, 76, 80, 82, 98, 99, 128, 193
Meslier, 163
Mestchersky, 268
Meunier, 86, 94
Mévil, 191, 193, 271
Michael, Grand Duke, 300
Milhaud, 144, 233
Millerand, 73, 76, 82, 88, 89, 97,
    98, 236, 239, 320
Milner, Lord, 296, 298

Milyukov, 277, 284, 304–5
Mirbeau, 110, 139
Miribel, 40, 45, 59
Mohrenheim, von, 12, 16, 24, 31,
    32, 36, 41, 59, 92
Montebello, 38, 40 sqq.
Mun, de, 271, 331
Muraviev, 93, 104, 203
Myassoyedev, 289

Naudeau, 270, 288, 301, 325, 327
Nekludov, 224
Nelidov, 92
Neratov, 224
Nicholas II, 81, 82, 83, 103–4, 113,
    141, 143, 144, 145, 173, 177, 186,
    195, 207, 270, 277, 283, 293, 296,
    300
Nicholas, King, 225
Nisselovich, 268
Noulens, 320

Obolensky, 24, 36
Obruchev, 26, 47, 50 sqq., 67, 92
Olsonfiero, 269

Paléologue, 5, 161, 236, 265, 272–8,
    280, 283–4, 289–90, 293–4, 295,
    297–8, 300–1, 303–4, 308, 320
Paley, Princess, 286
Panafieu, de, 197–8, 208, 222
Pélissier, 266–70
Peytral, 147
Pichon, 163, 165–6, 170–1, 183–4,
    187–8, 252, 305
Pinon, 182, 249
Piou, 74, 201
Plehve, von, 119, 132
Pobedonostsev, 93
Poincaré, 28, 29, 46, 81, 155–6, 193,
    194–6, 201 sqq., 207, 209, 211,
    215 sqq., 229 sqq., 245–6, 257–60,
    279 sqq., 324, 332
Pokrovsky, 297
Poleyayev, 265
Pressensé, de, 138, 142, 204, 241,
    248, 332
Protopopov, 290

Rachkovsky, 24, 40

Raffalovich, 323
Rambaud, 72
Ranc, 88
Rasputin, 270, 277, 290, 322
Raynal, 76, 87
Recouly, 121
Reinach, 127, 189, 306, 314–15
Renaudel, 302
Renault, 157
Ribot, 26 sqq., 35 sqq., 58, 59, 66, 67, 68, 70, 80, 189, 193, 194, 219, 274, 297, 304, 312, 318–19
Rivet, 290, 323
Rizov, 206
Rochefort, 84
Rodichev, 267–8
Rodzianko, 269
Rothschild, 38, 152
Rouanet, 73, 76, 163, 165–6
Rouvier, 38, 153, 163
Rozhestvensky, 130

Saint-Aulaire, de, 212
Saint-Brice, 136
Sanboeuf, 85
Sanders, Liman v., 252
Savich, 78–9
Say, Léon, 29
Sazonov, 187, 198, 204, 207, 208–12, 214, 216–18, 223, 226, 229–34, 237–8, 244, 249, 253–4, 256–8, 281–2, 291–7
Schnaebelé, 52
Seignobos, 153
Selves, de, 195, 196, 200–1
Sembat, 160, 301
Semenov, 161
Séverine, 110, 143, 302
Shebeko, 269
Sixtus, Prince, see Bourbon
Sonnino, 319
Spuller, 76
Staal, 161
Steeg, 158–9
Stolypin, 167–8, 170–3

Sturmer, 290, 305
Sukhomlinov, 265, 276, 289
Sviatopolk-Mirsky, 133

Tardieu, 113, 120, 188, 192, 194, 199, 265
Tereshchenko, 306–7
Théry, 265
Thomas, Albert, 265, 301, 307
Tittoni, 184, 197
Todorov, 214
Tolstoy, 78, 108–9
Tony-Révillon, 95
Trepov, 140, 295
Trotzky, 318
Trubetzkoy, 292, 293

Vaillant, 170, 242
Vandervelde, 278
Vannovsky, 47 sqq.
Vauvineux, de, 60, 146
Verstraete, 147–8
Vilaine, G. de, 188
Villain, 286
Vishnegradsky, 18
Viviani, 73, 91, 274–6, 279–85
Vogüé, de, 16

Waldeck-Rousseau, 96, 102, 111
Werder, von, 61
Wilhelm I, 17
Wilhelm II, 25, 27, 58, 81, 83, 143, 145, 186
Willm, 163
Wilson, 319–20
Witte, 92, 93, 113, 121, 143, 144, 155
Wrangel, 320

Yanushkevich, 289
Yudenich, 320
Yurussov, 156–7, 208

Zhilinsky, 253
Zola, 110

GEORGE ALLEN & UNWIN LTD
LONDON: 40 MUSEUM STREET, W.C.1
CAPE TOWN: 73 ST. GEORGE'S STREET
SYDNEY, N.S.W.: WYNYARD SQUARE
AUCKLAND, N.Z.: 41 ALBERT STREET
WELLINGTON, N.Z.: 4 WILLIS STREET
TORONTO: 77 WELLINGTON STREET, WEST

# The Little Entente
## By ROBERT MACHRAY

*Demy 8vo.*        *Illustrations and Maps*        12*s.* 6*d.*

This full and authoritative account of the origins, aims, and history of
the Little Entente (the defensive alliance of Czechoslovakia, Yugoslavia,
and Rumania) is the first English work to be published on the subject.
Based on the belief that the New Europe of the Peace Treaties, on which
the Little Entente was founded, is politically and ethically an improvement on the pre-War Europe, it shows how this organization is making
for peace and stability in Central Europe and, therefore, in Europe
generally.

# Self-Determination for Austria
## By FRIEDRICH F. G. KLEINWAECHTER
### TRANSLATED FROM THE GERMAN

*Cr. 8vo.*        *With Maps*        3*s.* 6*d.*

The author pleads for Austria's right of self-determination, which was
one of the Allies' declared war aims. Her people, he urges, are German
in race, culture, and sentiment, and their overwhelming desire is for
union with Germany. Moreover, she cannot develop her high national
culture isolated within the prison walls of her neighbours' tariffs ; but
economic union involves political union as well.

# The Real Situation in Russia
## By LEON TROTSKY

*La. Cr. 8vo.*    TRANSLATED BY MAX EASTMAN    7*s.* 6*d.*

"The book is alive with the violent spirit of the man who perhaps
more than anyone else contributed by his boundless energy to the material
triumph of Bolshevism in 1917. Some of the facts are new and others
are for the first time told in full detail. The sociologist of the future will
find in them much light on the internal decay and gradual decline of a
power which at one time threatened to overrun Europe. What is
particularly interesting is Trotsky's account of the present state of
Russia."—*Times.*

# The Russian Revolution
## By THE LATE PROFESSOR JAMES MAVOR

*Royal 8vo.*        21*s.*

"It was a happy thing that Professor Mavor lived to finish this work.
. . . A scholarly and well-documented history of the internal affairs of
Russia."—*Economist.*

"This book is one of the best that have appeared dealing with the
social and economic effects of the Bolshevik upheaval."—*Daily Mail.*

# Information on the World Court

## By J. WHEELER-BENNETT AND

*Demy 8vo.*    MAURICE FANSHAWE    10s.

A full account of the origin, personnel, and procedure of the Permanent Court of International Justice ; a review of the cases, and of the important work for the peace of the whole world, together with the text of the Statute, Court Rules, and other documents.

# The Ordeal of This Generation

### The War, the League, and the Future

## By GILBERT MURRAY, LL.D., D.Litt.

*La. Cr. 8vo.*    *Halley Stewart Lectures for* 1928    4s. 6d

"Will be widely read by thoughtful men and women. . . . The reader will be dull indeed who does not appreciate the beautiful coherence of the argument."—*Times Literary Supplement.*

"As lucid as it is profound, it is probably the most helpful book for the general reader that has been published on this subject."—*Nation.*

"This is the book of a statesman, a thinker, and a seer. . . . No finer or saner plea for a new world has appeared in our time."—*British Weekly.*

# The Origin, Structure, and Working of the League of Nations

*Royal 8vo.*    By C. HOWARD-ELLIS    21s.

"It is such a mine of useful information that the present reviewer is tempted to recommend it to the exclusion of all others on the subject of international relations."—*New Statesman.*

# Nationality : Its Nature and Problems

## By Dr. BERNARD JOSEPH

*Demy 8vo.*    INTRODUCTION BY G. P. GOOCH    10s. 6d.

This is a critical study of the entire question of nationality. The various attributes of nationality, such as race, language, tradition, religion, culture, national consciousness, etc., are analysed in detail in an effort to establish the importance of each in the formation, development, and preservation of nationality. The principal nationalities of the world and the factors which have contributed to their formation are considered in detail in order to establish the fundamental basis of nationality. The book deals further with the various problems affecting nationality, such as the relationship between nationality and cosmopolitanism, nationality and the State, nationality, patriotism, and war, etc. It indicates the real nature of nationality and its importance in the social order.

*All prices are net.*

---

LONDON : GEORGE ALLEN & UNWIN LTD

Signora Sangasole

Casa Massella

Uggiano

la

Chiesa

Lecce